TIDES OF MIGRATION

IMMIGRANT COMMUNITIES & ETHNIC MINORITIES IN THE UNITED STATES & CANADA: No. 64

ISSN 0749-5951

Series Editor: Robert J. Theodoratus
Department of Anthropology, Colorado State University

TIDES OF MIGRATION

A Study of Migration Decision-Making and
Social Progress in São Miguel, Azores

Francis W. Chapin

AMS Press, Inc.
New York

Library of Congress Cataloging-in-Publication Data

Chapin, Francis W.
  Tides of migration : a study of migration decision-making and
social progress in São Miguel, Azores / by Francis W. Chapin.
    p. cm. — (Immigrant communities & ethnic minorities in the
United States & Canada ; 64)
  Bibliography: p.
  Includes index.
  ISBN 0-404-19474-5
    1. São Miguel Island (Azores)—Emigration and immigration.
2. United States—Emigration and immigration. 3. Immigrants—
United States. 4. Azoreans—United States. I. Title. II. Series:
Immigrant communities & ethnic minorities in the United States &
Canada ; 64.
  JV8269.Z6S263 1989
  325.469'9—dc19   89-6507
                                                                       CIP

All AMS books are printed on acid-free paper that meets
the guidelines for performance and durability of the Committee on Production Guidelines for Book Longevity of the
Council on Library Resources.

AMS PRESS, INC.
56 East 13th Street
New York, N.Y. 10003, U.S.A.

MANUFACTURED IN THE UNITED STATES OF AMERICA

TABLE OF CONTENTS

LIST OF TABLES

vii

LIST OF MAPS

LIST OF FIGURES

ACKNOWLEDGEMENTS

The encouragement and cooperation of many people made this study possible. Funding for the research was provided through a pre-doctoral fellowship from the Social Science Research Council in New York and a Vilas Travel Award from the University of Wisconsin, Madison. Many people at the University of Wisconsin gave generously of their time and among those I am specially grateful to Robert J. Miller, as well as to Arnold Strickon, Aidan Southall, William Elmendorf and Stanley Payne. I am deeply indebted to M. Estellie Smith, who initiated me into the joys and trials of anthropological fieldwork, and to Richard Pollnac, who provided welcome encouragement and ideas while I was in the field. The contributions of various people in Lisbon and at the Instituto dos Açores, whose friendships and cooperation facilitated the study, are greatly appreciated, as are the good humor and encouragement of other friends and my family.

I want to express here my gratitude to the numerous people in São Miguel and Fall River, young and old, in the city and in the countryside, who warmly welcomed me into their homes and lives, sharing countless stories, experiences, and friendships. Their names and stories have been altered in this study to maintain their privacy, but I hope that the richness of their experiences and thoughts has been preserved.

CHAPTER 1
INTRODUCTION

Emerald green islands jutting out of the mid-Atlantic, the Azores were frequently described as 'picturesque' and 'idyllic' by nineteenth century European travelers. In spite of their natural beauty many Azoreans have sought to leave home and the islands have a long history of population mobility. The movement of people from one geographical region to another changes both the lives of the migrants and the lives of those who remain in the homeland. Understanding of how that migration process affects those who remain and the decisions they subsequently make about migration is illuminated by data from São Miguel, one of the nine islands of the Portuguese Azores.

For three centuries islanders have left the Azores to seek their fortunes in other countries, establishing a variable yet persisting pattern of international mobility. The history of migration in the Azores is in some respects comparable to that of other European societies such as those of Ireland, Italy and Greece: migration is characterized by a pattern in which waves of migrants have gone to North America since the early 1800's, escaping the problems of overpopulation and poverty in the homeland and at times causing problems of depopulation resulting from emigration. The situation differs from that of Ireland, Italy and Greece, however, in that there has been very little internal migration from the Azores to other

1

parts of Portugal or labor migration to the industrial centers of Europe. Also, the rate of permanent return is very low. These same characteristics distinguish Azorean migration from that of mainland Portugal.[1] In a surge of Portuguese emigration in the mid-1960's over half of the mainland Portuguese migrants went to France instead of the North American and Brazilian destinations of previous eras. In 1979 83% of Portuguese workers in other countries of Europe were living in France (Hudson and Lewis 1985). By contrast, Azoreans did not engage in permanent or temporary migration to European labor markets, continuing instead to migrate to the U.S. and Canada as permanent residents. The Azorean Archipelago is separated from mainland Portugal by over fourteen hundred kilometers of ocean and a strong sense of cultural autonomy has developed during the five centuries since the unpopulated islands were first discovered by the Portuguese in 1427. This spatial and cultural distance from the mainland has contributed to the development of distinct migration patterns in these islands, which are located on what was once one of the major sailing routes between Europe and the New World.

Recent emigration from the Azores to North America contributed to a dramatic population decline of almost 25% between 1960 and 1975. In 1975 the rate of emigration for the Azores was twenty per thousand inhabitants compared to the rate of two per thousand inhabitants for mainland Portugal (I.N.E. Boletim 1975). The migrant stream is equally represented by males and females, and over half emigrate in family groupings. Almost one quarter of the migrants are under the age of ten. The youthful character of migrants has been primarily responsible for an increased proportion of older people in the home population since 1950, and a declining rate of natural population increase. Emigration is an integral part of the past, and clearly a dynamic force which is still shaping the future of the islands.

In the late 1930's, a period of minimal emigration and high population growth, officials in the Azores suggested that excess population be channeled out to Portuguese colonies in Africa (Leite 1940:449). It was not until the 1950's that substantial numbers of migrants began to leave, bound for America, not Africa. In the early 1980's concern is expressed about the loss of people, mostly unskilled and skilled workers, and some worry what continuing emigration will mean for future development at home. The last thirty years have seen vast improvements in the standard of living and in education, but industrial and commercial developments have been slower.

MIGRATION IN SÃO MIGUEL

My first contact with Azoreans was in 1972 in Provincetown, Massachussetts, where I joined in an investigation of Portuguese ethnicity.[2] Very few of the Azorean fishermen in Provincetown were recent immigrants to America, but I was struck by the extent to which they maintained ties with their homeland.[3] As one local Yankee phrased it, 'they are tied to the end of a string, and the other end is tied to the Azores'. Four years later I embarked on my own research project to examine the nature of that link between migrant and homeland and what effects it has in the homeland.[4] I found that 'the string' consisted of two-way channels through which people, goods, and information flowed and I became interested in the ways in which these flows influenced the nature of subsequent migration. The original data from 1976-78 is presented here in the light of developments in the literature on migration since 1980.

In São Miguel, the process of migration is woven into the lives of individuals throughout the society and into the fabric of the social system.

> The neighbor women who had gathered, embroideries and crocheting in hand, were busily discussing the benefits of retirement in Canada and differences of opinion were becoming more heated....In between statements from the other side of the room that demanded our attention, Maria began to talk to me about emigration. She was propped up in her invalid's bed, as she has been for the last fourteen years;

> They all go. Ask anyone except the sick or the old and they all want to go to America. Soon it will only be those sick and old people that are left here.

* * *

> Coming out of a city shop with cigarettes and the evening paper in hand, Jorge came and stood by his car reading the headlines. Exclaiming critically over the latest political and economic problems, he concluded as always that he still had another option;

> If things get worse....I am ready...we can always leave and go to America. It would be more difficult

for me there, I know that....I just don't know
what will happen, but if things get worse....

He shook his head as he got in the car and I too
shook mine with distress at the prospect of him
trying to work in some New England factory,
wondering what other possibilities a Portuguese
trained office worker would find in America.

* * *

Lourdes spent the afternoon talking to me about
the delights of America.   She says she is fed up
with the constant work, the dirty clothes, the dirt
floors, and no chance to get ahead in S. Miguel.
She has written her sister in Boston about sending
a petition now that she has been there for three
years.   She is hoping that her husband will want to
go when the time comes.

* * *

Seventy year old José laughed as he tied up corn
to dry when I asked him if he had ever wanted to
go away from S. Miguel;

Why should I go?   My older brother went to New
Bedford and all he came back with to show for it
was an accordian!....I never thought of leaving.   I
worked hard and now I have a little.   I have a good
life here.
           (Excerpts from Fieldnotes, São Miguel 1978)

In São Miguel emigration is an opportunity that people in many sectors of society weigh against the situation at home. For some there is no question about the superior benefits of emigration; for others the balance falls in the other direction. Whether or not individuals seriously explore the possibility of leaving, the effects that migration has on the home system touch their lives and their futures. At the most basic level migration is a process which involves individuals making personal choices, choosing strategies which they hope will solve their personal problems. The strategies of migration include moving on a seasonal, temporary or permanent basis from one location to another. The choice of any one of these strategies is constrained by regional, national, and international policies. At the individual level the choice is also affected by the particular personal context. Individual Azoreans who contemplate migration rarely give more than a quick thought to the world economy, the balance of trade, or changes in the labor force. They are concerned with solving their personal problems, issues which revolve around owning a house, making the most money, buying land, and their childrens' futures. The decisions they make may involve an element of risk, as in the choice to migrate, and that decision is based on the information that the individual has about conditions at home and conditions in the potential destination area. Much of the latter information results from the personal networks people have with previous emigrants.

In the Azores I found that the exchange of information in the form of letters, media, visits, gifts, and money, is a crucial factor in the context of migration decision-making, not just for the close kin of emigrants, but for the whole population. As might be expected in a class structured society, the type and extent of contact with migration associated information varies significantly for different social groups within the society. What the upper class knows about options in America is quite different from what a farm laborer in a village might know and interest in knowing about migration varies along with the opportunities it variously affords people. Information also varies over time, as does the situation in which it is received. The context of migration decisions therefore consists of factors at the family, community, regional, national and international levels.[5] At any particular time in history these factors will differ and for any particular individual the specific complex of factors which influence migration decisions will be somewhat different than for any other individual. Thus in situations of ongoing population mobility such as that found in the Azores, previous migration contributes to shaping the context in which subsequent migration occurs.

The Home System in Context

Presentation of the data on São Miguel aims to contribute to the scant ethnographic literature on the consequences of migration on the home society, specifically the consequences for subsequent migration. It also serves to illustrate the value of a regional focus for an area of study using multiple levels of analysis and the utility of a processual approach which takes into account the effects of interactions between migrants and home over time in a situation of ongoing migration. The scope of this study is therefore broad, sacrificing some of the wealth of detail possible in a study of one community. It is not a full ethnography of São Miguel, it is an ethnography of migration in São Miguel.

When I initiated this project in 1976, the vast amount of literature on migration, spanning numerous disciplines, was dominated by research on the adjustments of rural migrants to urban destinations (the earliest tradition of this type of research grew out of anthropological work in Africa, e.g., Wilson (1941)). Considerably less attention was given to the effects of these migrations in the society of origin, the home system. Studies of international migration were largely overshadowed by research on post World War II internal (within one national boundary) population movements, primarily rural to urban, and problems of urbanization (e.g., Southall 1973; Mangin 1970).[6] In the 1980's, after several decades of emphasis on internal migration, a growing awareness has emerged of the significant changes in the scale and character of international migration. Permanent transcontinental migrations such as that of Azoreans have slowed, although significant flows to the U.S., Canada and Australia continue. Interregional and international movements of temporary labor, on the other hand have increased. The dramatic increase in labor migration in Europe and many parts of the developing world since the 1960's has led to a new emphasis on international migration and the effects in both host and sending, or home, societies (Kritz, Keely and Tomasi 1981; Lewis 1986). At the same time, the quest for all encompassing migration theories has been challenged by more particularistic approaches which suggest that migration is a highly variable process, and that subregional models are required (Pryor 1981). Focusing on local conditions to which international migrants are responding is seen to be more fruitful than searching for single relationships between international migration and possible consequences, e.g., uneven regional development (Lewis 1986).

Much of the research on sending societies has concentrated on broad economic consequences and the debate over whether or not migration benefits the sending region through remittances and return of better off migrants, or merely acts as a release valve which maintains the status quo (Hudson and Lewis 1985). Social consequences have received less attention than economic ones, particularly in situations of international migration (Kritz, Keely & Tomasi, 1981). Economic models have tended to focus on wage differentials and rates of employment to explain migration patterns (Todaro 1976). However, there is a growing emphasis in migration studies on essentially non-economic factors (Hugo 1979; Piore 1979). For example, the importance for migration behavior of social ties that link potential migrants in the home system to migrants in the destination areas has been empirically demonstrated in recent research on Mexican migration to the U.S. (Massey and España 1987). The present study assumes that economic factors (widely defined) are important, but focuses on sociocultural constraints and incentives as the factors producing greatest variation and change in migration patterns. The separation of social and economic variables is conceptually useful although it is recognized that in real life they may be inextricably interwoven (Baric 1967:254).

Migration studies which incorporate discussion of the homeland tend to be either very broad in scope or examine only one community or part of a community as the unit of study. Population movement between nations has been examined using aggregate statistics and longitudinal data, but these studies tell little about what is going on at present at community and individual levels (Kennedy 1973; Thomas 1954; Weaver and Downing 1976; Böhning 1975). Anthropological research on the homeland includes studies which look at how migrants in urban areas affect traditional homeland culture (e.g., Read 1942; Schack 1973; Van Velsen 1960) and studies from the perspective of the home community such as that of Isbell (1974) on the role of migration in cultural transformations or Watson (1977) and Friedl (1976) on the importance of the economic support of migrants for individuals in the sending region. A limited number of studies have looked in depth at a specific community, focusing on the social change due to migration amidst the modernization of peasant society (Brandes 1975; Lopreato 1967; Perez-Diaz 1971; Friedl 1976), the problems emigration poses for economic development in the homeland (Baucic 1974), and the adaptive nature of the home community (Gonzalez 1969). Some studies have expanded their focus to two communities, village and city, examining migration phenomena from both sending and receiving ends of the continuum (Kemper 1977; Bradfield 1973; Lewis 1965; Schreiber 1976). The village-city interface has been discussed primarily in relation to how rural patterns affect the urban adaptation of migrants.7

There have been very few attempts to study migration phenomena in a broader context than one community and still retain a concern with individual behavior and social structure in the home society. This type of regional approach to the home and destination areas has been taken by Cronin (1970) in her study of Sicilians in Sicily and Australia and by Karpat (1976) in examining Turkish rural to urban migration as part of social change. Other examples of research that take a regional approach and a cross-sectional view of the home society include Philpott's

(1973) study of the effects of migration on social structure in two dissimilar communities in the West Indies, and Lee's (1985) study of migration intentions in the northwestern Philippines. With the exception of limited examples, however, the home system, although invariably designated as one pole or end of a continuum in the location of migration phenomena, is rarely central to the study of migration.

The Migration Process

In this study of Azorean migration the focus is on local conditions in the context of migration from one specific home region, São Miguel, to a broader receiving region, North America. Using the island as the area of study enables one to go beyond the limitations of one community in observing and analyzing specific social and cultural conditions under which migration occurs and the subsequent effects of migration on those conditions. The use of both historical and contemporary materials from various levels of the migration system (including individual behavior and its context) permits a delineation of the process rather than a static view of migration variables at one point in time.

New and developing approaches to migration, which examine both individual and societal levels, diverge from the previously dominant macro-level approaches. Only ten years ago proponents of the latter view were repeating the call for more generally applicable theories of migration *per se* (Long 1977:559). Macro-studies formulate explanatory and predictive models using aggregate data.

They are frequently limited by the necessity to simplify the range of factors considered and the conditions under which migration takes place (Lee 1966). General trends during one period may not continue to change in the same ways, however, and there is little hope of perceiving potential for change unless individual level variation is taken into account. Macro-models are useful for comparing general past and present patterns in world migration. However, they have proved inadequate for analysis of what is actually going on at the 'ground level' (among recognizable people) and for projection of changing patterns in specific cases of migration.[8] Unlike the widely used models of migration which see migrants as 'pushed' and 'pulled' by forces in the home and destination areas (i.e., Lee 1966), an actor-oriented approach recognizing decision-making shows that migrants are not merely 'reactors' to circumstances beyond their control, but are 'architects of their own destinies' (Douglass 1970:27). Analysis of decision-making necessitates considering a wide range of decisive factors and multiple levels of investigation (DuToit 1975; Schreiber 1976).

Emigrants from São Miguel are conceptualized as responding to perceived circumstances and choosing migration as one alternative adaptive strategy among others. The rationality of this choice is based on their perceptions of options and the need to satisfy a complex nexus of conditions. The individual choice of migration is affected by both short-term and long-term considerations. The cumulative pattern of those individual choices is reflected in changes over time, for example, in the characteristics of the migrant stream or the context of the migration decision. The concept of adaptation in the social process emphasizes the feedback dynamic of interactions which in turn shape future adaptation (Bennett 1969, 1976). The broader process thus must be understood through individual interactions.

The idea of considering migration as part of broader processes such as social change and urbanization is not new to anthropology. For several decades anthropologists have looked at migration from this perspective, as illustrated in community studies which consider the role of migration in more general processes of change and continuity (e.g., Barrett 1974; Arensberg and Kimball 1968; Fox 1962; Kenny 1962). Recent literature from other fields, including geography, calls for the conceptualization of migration as a process, not an event (Forman 1976), and as significant because rather than existing in relative isolation, it has a role in other social processes (Harris and Moore 1980). What is new in recent migration research is the recognition that a search for all inclusive theories is futile and that greater emphasis should be placed on the need to understand individual variation over time (Plotnicov 1976; Abu-Lughod 1975).

The basic concept of 'process' in anthropological literature is that the interaction of factors produces a given condition or governs the course of events (Bee 1974:3-4; Barth 1966:2; Hsu 1959:800). According to this view, to explain is to show what makes the cultural pattern. The pattern of migration, for example, is thus the cumulative result of people making decisions in specific processes of interaction. The study of process through individual decision-making is used by Howard and Ortiz (1971:215) as a conceptual frame which permits the investigation of both micro-level individual behavior and macro-level theory of social process. A decision-making approach to the study of migration can be used to ascertain variation at the individual level as well as to delineate the factors in changing patterns of migration over time.

Analysis of decision-making involves multiple levels of factors which impinge on evaluations of the relative attractiveness of migration and shape migration behavior. The level of regional and national relationships, the social structural level of roles and beliefs, and the individual and family level of relationships all affect the parameters of choice.   The   concept   of   migration   feedback   is incorporated in models of decision chains or trees for individuals in which the choice of a given strategy is colored by beliefs and past experiences (Heath 1976; Howard and Ortiz 1971).   These are models of sequential decisions made by the same actor.   An analogous model can be derived for the situation of ongoing migration such as it exists in São Miguel.   Decisions and satisfactions of migrants influence the subsequent behavior of other individuals in the home system.[9] Migration is thus part of an adaptive process in a widely defined social system.

The importance of the migrant-homeland link with respect to the consequences that migration at one point in time has for subsequent migration from the homeland is implicit in general theories of migrant selectivity and the reduced 'cost' of migration over time (e.g., Lee 1966; Zelinsky 1971) and explicit in discussions of assistance networks and 'chain migration', where migrants help relatives and neighbors from home join them abroad (MacDonald and MacDonald 1964).   Thus an historical perspective is integral to the classic models of migration, yet there is a dearth of specific case studies which look at migration over time. In order to understand what is going on at any particular point in time in the migration process an historical perspective is essential. One method is to use case histories over time to elucidate the migration process. This was done by Friedl (1976) in her work on Greek migration and by Schreiber (1976) in her study of Italian migration, while Douglass (1984) combined case studies with extensive archival research to produce an anthropological history of emigration in a southern Italian town. Brettell's (1986) study of a village in northern Portugal combines historical archival research, case histories and demography to discuss the effects of emigration over time on the home community. In this study of São Miguel a similar historical perspective is applied to explore how changes in migration patterns in the past two centuries have affected the way in which people now view migration options, embedded as they are in the cultural tradition. The focus is on interactions over time between the home region (not limited to one community) and destination areas. The approach thus permits analysis of a process which includes individual factors and factors at a broader level in the home system.

In the literature on permanent migration, as distinct from temporary internal migration, movement is generally viewed as a one time event and contact with the home region is discussed primarily in terms of ethnicity or retention of traditional culture in the new home and direct assistance to other migrants. When this study was written up in 1980 the notion of feedback as a useful concept for migration research and the need for an integrative approach combining micro and macro-levels of analysis were just beginning to emerge in the literature. Since 1980 there has been a clear move toward multi-level studies in the various disciplines involved in migration research, and a move away from the general models of earlier decades as the complexity of migration phenomena is recognized (e.g., Lee 1985; Kritz, Keely & Tomasi 1981; DeJong and Gardener 1981). The majority of these new works describe research on internal and international labor migration or what Chapman and Prothero (1985) call 'circulation.' The term circulation is used to describe reciprocal flows, the movement of people which ultimately concludes in the place where it began, or in other words temporary migration. However, Chapman and Prothero (1985:3) point out that French geographers first used the term circulation in the 1920's to include the back and forth flows of ideas, goods, services, and sociocultural influences as well as people. In this sense the concept of circulation is similar to what I have called feedback, the back and forth flow of information, goods, and money in association with flows of people. The importance of these other flows for temporary migration has been recognized in work, for example, on rural-urban migrant networks in Kenya (Ross and Weisner 1977); on 'wealth flows' of money, goods and assistance associated with migration in India (Caldwell 1976); and on the social and economic consequences of remittances in the Caribbean (Momsen 1986). In cases of permanent migration the links emphasized have been kin and community based networks to help kin migrate and assist them in the new area (e.g., Anderson 1974; MacDonald and MacDonald 1964). The data presented here suggests that other forms of feedback or circulation may have important consequences in the home society in cases of permanent international migration as well as in cases of temporary internal migration. The flow of money in the form of remittances is often viewed as the 'heart of the question' for impacts of migration on the homeland (Kritz and Keely 1981:xxv). For the Azores, a region where remittances are not large compared to other home societies, the consequences of circulation or flows are less easily quantified.

In 1977 in the villages of São Miguel people repeatedly

told me that everyone who can will emigrate. In the towns and among the better-educated I was told that only the poor people emigrate. A closer look at characteristics of actual migrants revealed that neither stereotype was valid. Some relatively well off people migrate, many of the poorest people are unable to, and many people who could emigrate choose not to. Why? What do these images of migration tell us about society's view of itself? I assumed that flows of communications between migrants and homeland were an important factor in migration behavior, but the question remained as to how communications flowed through the home system. Were the only significant links between migrants and their families or close friends? Did different kinds of information reach different people in the class-stratified society? Was that information used differently at varying social levels? This study is thus concerned with what influences people to migrate or not, how those factors are affected by previous migration, and how the patterns and context of migration changed in a twenty year period (1960 to 1980) of intensive emigration to North America.

FIELDWORK

The analysis of migration from São Miguel emphasizes the need for an understanding of migration in the home system. An important aspect of this is the interaction of factors in the home and destination areas. The study therefore includes research carried out in the destination areas as well as in a cross-section of the home society. One of the great strengths of the anthropological perspective is that it reaches beyond the quantitative data and provides qualitative analysis of individual and group behavior within their own contexts. However, one of the main criticisms of the traditional community study approach is that it may not be representative of the larger society. The limitations of focusing on one community are part of a problem central to the study of complex society: the integration of the study of the part and the whole in a social system. Leeds (1965) suggests that a cross-sectional approach enables the analysis of both the part and whole at the same time, made up as they are of basically the same social units. Such an approach is readily applied to the study of migration where the effects of people leaving may be experienced differentially throughout the social system.

The data reported in this study come from fieldwork done in the Azores in 1976-78 using traditional anthropological approaches of participant-observation, archival research, case histories, surveying and other techniques outlined in the Appendix. In order to reach an understanding of migration within the context of the larger society fieldwork was conducted in four different communities. The interconnections of these communities with the island as a whole, the Azores, mainland Portugal, and other parts of the world were also examined. The communities were selected to represent a range of types based on distance from the main town of Ponta Delgada, emigration rates, and general level of well-being. The four included one relatively prosperous village, close to the main town, which had sustained a moderate level of migration; one village close to the main town where emigration had dramatically reduced the population; one village distant from the main town where emigration had been intensive; and the main urban area. Short periods of time were spent in other villages, including four weeks in the favored vacation area.

The majority of Azorean emigrants come from villages, but what I wanted to examine was how migration over time had affected decisions about migration in the society as a whole, not in just one segment of that society. This broad research scope was feasible because of an insular location and a relatively small population. The nature of the location provided a unique opportunity to go beyond the limits of traditional community studies, or studies of one aspect of migration such as the effects of remittances on the sending society, and to look at the whole process of migration. Through interactions with the whole range of people in the society, elites and workers, young and old, migrants and returnees, people who didn't want to emigrate and those who did, it became clear that all of these categories of people impinge on or create part of the context in which migration decisions are made. São Miguel is bounded but not isolated by water. The smallness of the island and the remarkably efficient bus system meant that doing fieldwork throughout the home society was not only feasible, but in fact essential, due to the nature of interactions people have on the island. Fieldwork in the destination area was more limited, focusing primarily on Fall River, Massachusetts, but including short periods spent in surrounding areas and in parts of northern California.

The first six weeks of the research period were spent in Fall River, a former mill town turned factory town, where substantial numbers of Portuguese live, over half of whom are estimated to be from São Miguel (Gilbert 1976). Contacts established with emigrants in Fall River whose families I could locate in São Miguel proved to be invaluable in the initial months of fieldwork in São Miguel.

Thus I did not arrive in São Miguel as a stranger. My entry was via a network of ties that form a bridge between the Azores and America. Six months later when I returned briefly to Fall River, I became one link in that network, carrying gifts and messages to members of the emigrant community, and already preceded by news of my activities on the island. The only problem that I had with this role was to convince people that even though I was going to America this did not mean I would automatically come in contact with all of their dispersed relatives, and that during my stay in Fall River I could not easily deliver a package to someone in Toronto. I was also loaded with bounty when I returned to the Azores, this time for the relatives back home.

The fact that I was familiar with both ends of the system facilitated fieldwork in both areas. On my second trip to Fall River I was considered less of an outsider due to my recent residence in São Miguel. In São Miguel the ties to people in Fall River were helpful in establishing contact with a broad range of people in the home society. These ties also enabled me to participate in a wide variety of visitor activities when my friends from Fall River chose the summer that I was there to come visit the homeland. Prior to that time I had become well aware of the perspectives of people being visited, and those of the visitors themselves; but I was very fortunate to see both perspectives in the same situation.

While the study is mainly concerned with the homeland, it is a homeland tied to Azoreans in America through numerous and diverse links associated with ongoing migration. The dynamic nature of these ties makes it essential to incorporate data from both ends of the continuum in striving to understand the process of migration in the home system of São Miguel. The second chapter explores the dynamics of historical migration and how these ties between the Azores and America developed. Basic dimensions of the contemporary society as the home context of present migration are discussed in Chapter Three. This is followed by an examination in Chapters Four and Five of how migration associated flows of people and communications over a twenty year period affected the context in which people made choices about migration in 1978. Variations in factors which affect individual migration decision-making for people at different life stages and social levels is discussed in Chapter Six. The concluding chapter sums up what the past century's migration means for the contemporary home system in São Miguel.

CHAPTER 2
HISTORICAL PERSPECTIVES ON AZOREAN MIGRATION

Historical mobility patterns in São Miguel have affected the way in which present migration options are evaluated, and have influenced the opportunities themselves. This chapter examines the origins of migratory movement in the Azores, and the extension of Michaelense ties to America.[1]

In São Miguel, and in the Azores as a whole, there is no definable pure state of 'before' migration. Migration has been an element of the region's development since the peopling of the islands in the fifteenth century. There have been intensive periods of migration as well as periods when migration was minimal (see Figure 2.1), but the presence of migratory patterns pervades the past and the present. Historical perspectives are important in understanding the cultural orientation of present patterns. Halpern (1975:78) notes that in Balkan migration motivations for mobility are not based solely on economic opportunities but on opportunities which are perceived through a "cultural screen" which is strongly conditioned by historical perspectives. In São Miguel a strong mobility orientation is part of the cultural screen through which people evaluate their options. In the last two centuries that orientation has developed a class specific character which further influences present perceptions.

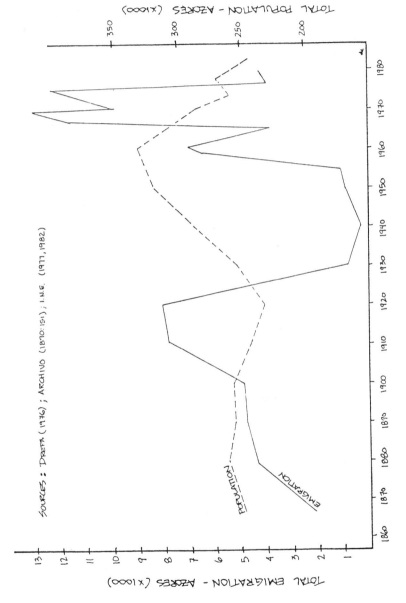

Figure 2.1. Azorean Emigration and Population, 1864-1982

In addition to the effect of historical patterns on perceptions, these patterns have affected the actual opportunities, both at home and abroad. On the one hand migration has been a traditional 'release valve' for excess population, helping to maintain sufficient resources for people remaining on the island, and a means of obtaining a better livelihood for those emigrants who returned with greater resources than they had when they left. On the other hand, the process of dispersal of islanders throughout the world, and specifically to North America, established an extension of the homeland which offered opportunities aboard. The history is similar to that of parts of Greece, where for centuries external ties have been established through the formation of 'urban extensions' (Andromedas 1967:274). For São Miguel, the extensions have been international, offering opportunities in both rural and urban areas.

Development of the current cultural screen through which the people of São Miguel view migration will be examined in the context of historical migration patterns, the character of extensions to North America, and changes in opportunities associated with migration. First, a brief picture will be drawn of the setting in which these processes of dispersal and extension have occurred.

THE SETTING

The history of Michaelense external extension is apparent to the newly-arrived outsider in visual forms. On the main city shopping street there are stores which, instead of using family names, are named after destination countries for emigrants, i.e., 'Brazil', 'America', 'Canada'. In villages, distinctively bright colored polyester clothes and miniskirts recall American fashions of a few years back. The ubiquitous T-shirt recalls American fashion of today and even the alter boy at Catholic Mass may appear in a 'Kansas City Wildcats' shirt. An old Buick, giant and lumbering, or a Scout travelvan with Massachusetts plates, looks oddly out of context on the narrow cobblestone roads which wind along the green hills and rocky coastline. Decorations for a Church celebration, *festa,* more often than not sport American flags or Canadian maple leaves, and dollars flutter among the *festa* donations. Newspapers carry stories about towns in southeastern Massachusetts and California that are not well-known even in the United States. Local coin collections boast ample arrays of five dollar gold pieces along with coins of Brazilian, African, and Asian vintage. Houses reminiscent of old residences in Brazil, Bermudian bungalows, and New England cottages are interspersed with the typical Michaelense dwellings. It becomes readily apparent to the outsider that São Miguel is not an isolated island. Beyond the visual clues, the way people speak about the world, words they use, and the ways they plan their lives all reveal the rich complexity of elements drawn in from other distant parts of the world.

Volcanic in origin, the Azorean archipelago is situated in the mid-Atlantic about 3800 kilometers from North America and 1450 kilometers from mainland Portugal. The nine islands, comprising a total area of 224.7 km^2, are strung across 500 kilometers of ocean, intersecting the prevailing westerly winds of the northern hemisphere and the southeast trade winds. The islands cluster from east to west in three groups based on geographic location, historical differences, and political designation as districts.

Although they are no longer officially districts, for purposes of clarity I follow the example of islanders and continue to refer to them as the Districts of Horta, Angra do Heroismo, and Ponta Delgada, which are named after the main cities in each region as shown on Map 1.

The westernmost group includes the island of Fayal, the simmering volcanic peak of Pico island, and the two smaller and most remote islands of Flores and Corvo. Fayal, with the port town of Horta, suffered from the effects of volcanic activity as recently as 1958. The last islands to be settled, they were the first to have extensive contact with North America through maritime activities.

The central group contains Terceira island, with a port in Angra, plus the two less accessible islands of Graciosa and São Jorge. It was this group of islands that was severely damaged by earthquakes in January 1980.

Ponta Delgada is located on São Miguel, which along with neighboring Santa Maria makes up the eastern and most southern district. These islands were the first to be discovered and settled by the Portuguese.

The three groups of islands have approximately the same amount of area, but the quality of land and size of populations varies (Map 2). São Miguel, the largest island, has the most fertile and accessible land and supported over half of the total population of 259,000 in 1974. By contrast, in the western District of Horta, almost one quarter of the land is above 800 meters, much of which is uncultivable, and only 14% of the total Azorean population lives in this region.

The individual islands vary in area, terrain, climate and population, and in sociocultural and historical background. Some of these differences will be discussed when they pertain to the context of migration in São Miguel, e.g., when data is only available for the Azores as a whole or

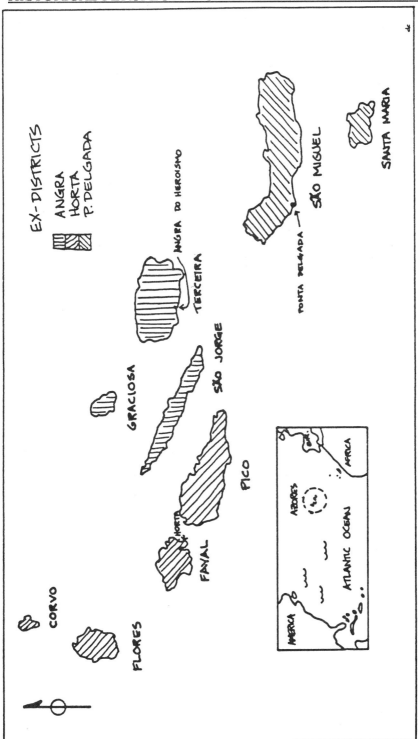

Map 1. The Azores: 'District' Divisions and Their Capitals

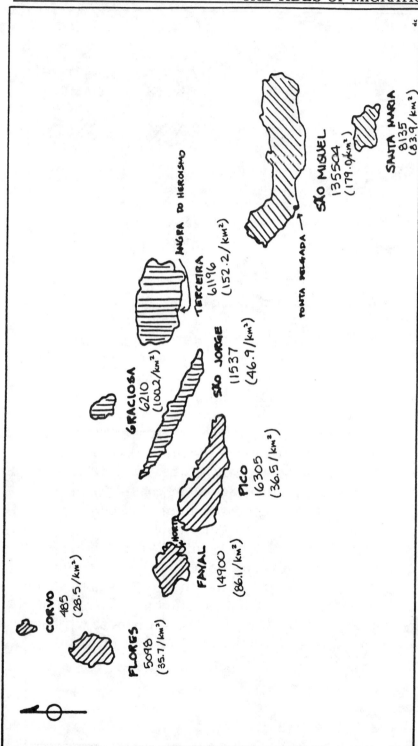

Map 2. Population and Density by Island, 1974

patterns of migration on other islands set the stage for Michaelense migration.

COLONIALIZATION AND EXPANSION

The Azores were originally unpopulated. Following their official discovery by the Portuguese in 1427, the immigration of settlers began in 1439.[2] Portuguese maritime exploration blossomed in the fifteenth century.[3] It was the era of Prince Henry the Navigator, and numerous vessels sailed off to seek and exploit new channels of trade with Africa, Asia and the New World. The currents and winds forced ships to swing west into the mid-Atlantic on their return route to Europe (see Map 3). It is in this path that the Azores are located. It was fortuitous for Portugal that Gonçalo Velho Cabral laid claim to the islands, which he named the Azores after the hawks, *azors,* seen soaring above the volcanic hillsides.

Immigration to the islands came under the auspices of local governors who were appointed by the Crown as hereditary captaincies. Many of these original aristocratic families maintained their dominant positions of power and influence well into modern times. According to one Portuguese historian, these 'first noble settlers' established the principal families which continued to flourish in the prominent positions in wine and sugar industries, management of different branches of business, political leadership and public administration and retention of 'rich estates' (Correa 1926:202). The burden of agricultural development which supported this continued prosperity lay on the peasant settlers.

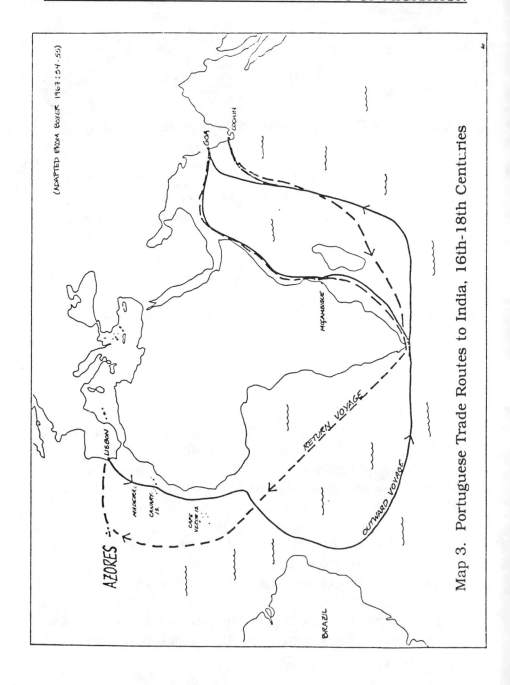

Map 3. Portuguese Trade Routes to India, 16th-18th Centuries

The Azores were originally a destination point for immigrants from mainland Portugal, Flanders, and later French Brittany. The first islands discovered, Santa Maria and São Miguel, at the eastern end of the archipelago, were originally settled by people from central and southern Portugal (Estremadura, Algrave, and Alentejo). Some immigrants came to São Miguel from Brittany during the early 1500's (Da Costa 1978:80-83). The central group of islands, Terceira, Graciosa, and São Jorge, were settled by people from northern Portugal and Flanders. At this time there were substantial numbers of refugees from the Flemish wars in Portugal and some of the early nobility on the western islands were of Flemish descent (Da Costa 1978:75). The four islands further east, Fayal, Pico, Flores, and Corvo, were settled last by people from the other islands, mainland Portuguese, and the Flemish.

A great variety of people were drawn to the Azores during this early period. A well-known contemporary Portuguese author, Vitorino Nemesio, wrote that many were avaricious but hardworking foreign adventurers while others, although strong and determined were not the 'finest flower' of Portuguese society. The largest number of these early settlers were agricultural laborers. For some of the shrewd bourgeoisie, migration to the Azores was an avenue to work their way into the rural nobility. For the majority, the peasantry, migration in the early years offered only a life of toil (Nemesio quoted in Da Costa 1978:63).

The settling of the Azores offered a number of advantages for the mainland. A letter written on the subject in 1443 stressed the economic importance of São Miguel as both a source of grain, wine, fish, wood and legumes and a support base for the nobility (Da Costa 1978:57). Of more long range importance was the fact that the islands could be used as a secure base in the midst of the Atlantic to provide supplies of food and water for maritime explorations and trade. With Madeira and the Cape Verde islands on the outbound route and the Azores on the return route from Africa and Asia, the Portuguese were well equipped with reprovisioning stations and ports of refuge from pirates. During this period, however, the Azores did not profit directly from the rich Asian and African shipments that passed through the ports, since unloading of any cargo was forbidden until the vessels reached Lisbon.

Even before the seventeenth century the islands were in contact with many parts of the old and new worlds. Fishing boats from the mainland passed through the Azores on their way to catch cod in the rich fisheries of Newfoundland and George's Bank (Terra Nova) as early as the 1500's. Trade between Portugal and Brazil, the Caribbean, Africa, and Asia further expanded contact as vessels passed through the Azores. Connections to continental Portugal were sustained by political, commercial, social and familial ties. The Azorean nobility frequently spent time in Portugal. Elite students were sent from the islands to Coimbra or Lisbon for their education (Da Costa 1978:294). Travel or correspondence by ship was slow, relative to modern transport, but connections were frequent and it should be remembered that for a nation that was sending ships as far as Goa for trade, the jaunt to or from the Azores was relatively minor.

Agricultural development proceeded rapidly during the early period. Land distribution was under the control of local aristocratic families, except for the cold and humid high brush areas which were originally designated as common lands on which the people pastured their livestock (Mendonça Dias 1940:419). Generally speaking, the distribution of property was most inequitable on the islands with the most fertile and accessible land, as, for example, on São Miguel (Da Costa 1978:173). The land on São Miguel lent itself to the cultivation of large fields on the part of the island with easiest access. This facilitated the production of wheat and pastel (woad, a dye), the two major cast crops in the fifteenth and sixteenth centuries.[3] The island was also suitable for cultivation of flax, another cash crop of importance, corn, the keeping of vineyards, and orchards. From the very beginning São Miguel was not only the largest producer of cash crops, partially because of sheer size, but also was relatively self-sufficient. This may have contributed significantly to the tight hold which elite owners kept on access to resources in later years.

Agricultural development was rapid after the first settlers arrived, and so was population growth. In the years between 1592 and 1640 the population doubled on São Miguel (Archivo 1890:145). The total population of the archipelago exceeded one hundred thousand. Shortly after settling the islands people were already moving out of them, both temporarily and permanently. Some emigrated for social and educational motives, as was the case with the nobility; some left as soldiers to help secure the colonies of Brazil and Africa, with those that survived bringing back tales of colonial wealth; and some went once again as colonists (Guill 1972:123-5). Information flow was facilitated by both internal and external trading patterns and the location of the archipelago on major sailing routes. The stream of ships into Azorean harbors brought news, people, and goods, and took out other people when they left. They also brought disease. Periodic epidemics took their toll throughout the islands. It was reported at that time that the Americas did not suffer from these plagues, a piece of information that may have influenced potential emigrants. More certainly, the allure of colonial opportunities was heightened by the fluctuations in domestic agricultural productivity which lead to periodic famines on the islands, e.g., a wheat crisis in the 1650's.

Portugal encouraged the development of the sugar industry in Brazil, offering incentives for contract settlers as early as the 1680's. Land, a cow, implements, seed, and transport for entire families was offered if the potential settlers contracted to stay in Brazil for the stipulated number of years (Guill 1972:128). In 1747 settlers were still being recruited. By then the enticements included cash bonuses for each person in a household, a practice that evidently led to a high frequency of fabricated kinship relationships to expand the numbers of the emigrant household and hence the number of bonuses (Archivo 1878:382).

The sugar industry and later the 'gold rush' in Brazil stimulated opportunities for persons involved in trade and commerce as well as for laborers. A large proportion of the immigrants went to urban areas. It was reported, for example, that in 1752 the first Azorean families in Rio Grande do Sul, founded and primarily settled in the town of Porto Alegre (Cardoza 1976:18).

During this period of colonization the social and occupational structure of emigrants from Portugal (mainland and islands) to Brazil differed substantially from that of later periods. The early emigrants were often not the poorest of the population, but rather a cross-section of the socioeconomic hierarchy. Some were nobility, or intellectuals, who established themselves in various official positions and professions. It is not surprising that some of the nobility emigrated, given a system of inheritance in which estates were entailed and went to the eldest son.

Younger male siblings commonly sought their fortunes or means of livelihood through the military, professional training, the clergy, and emigration. Other emigrants to Brazil included small property owners who either bought parcels of land to develop or engaged in business and trade in the town areas (Ferreira 1976:33-34). This is not to say that manual laborers did not emigrate. Many males who were not property owners or members of the elite did emigrate to Brazil. In the sixteenth century they also went to Asia in large numbers as sailors and soldiers. A Portuguese priest in the sixteenth century commented that if the outflow of men to Asia continued it might be necessary to bring back Asians to do the work in Portugal (Ferreira 1976:32).

The Azores were originally a destination point for migrants from the plague and poverty ridden provinces of Portugal, and refugees from the Lowland wars. By the seventeenth and eighteenth centuries, however, the Azores were no longer a destination point but had become a source of migrants for the colonies. At this time a new phase of the pattern develops with migration to North America.

MIGRATION TO NORTH AMERICA:
THE 1750's TO 1920's

The advent of the whaling era and the export of oranges from the islands to Europe and the U.S. were key elements in the development of a migration channel to North America (Map 4). Improved communications and transport between the Azores and America resulted partially from the increases in maritime movement associated with whaling, and partially from the intensification of other commercial networks between the two areas.

Whaling, Oranges and Sugar

Contact with North America (hereafter referred to as 'America') was not a new phenomenon, since for several centuries Portuguese and Azorean sailors had traveled to the fishing grounds of Newfoundland, known as Terra Nova. Contacts between the Azores and the new world had increased over time due to the islands' convenient location as a stopping point on major sailing routes. Direct trade with America grew during the 1700's, with items such as coarse linen and wine exchanged for gold, goods, and sometimes codfish (Da Costa 1978:204). It was whaling, however, that initially brought American ships to the islands' ports in large numbers, and facilitated the departure of Azoreans, on those same ships, when they left port. As already discussed, the main destination for emigrants was traditionally Brazil or other parts of the Empire. Up until the eighteenth century the movement of people to other parts of the world was part of a Portuguese national endeavor. After that time, however, emigration was more a matter of personal choice, unbiased by government pressure and incentives. The development of channels for migration to North America therefore marked the beginning of a significant change in patterns of Azorean migration.

In the middle of the eighteenth century American

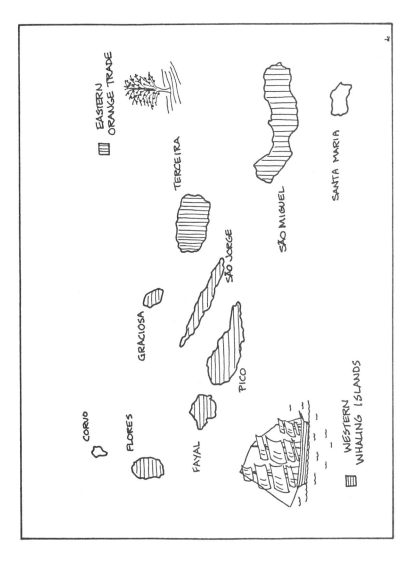

Map 4. Divisions in Azorean Commercial Orientation, 18th & 19th Centuries

whaling vessels began to reach the Azores. In the summer of 1768, for example, about two hundred ships from New England were reported to be whaling in Azorean waters (Da Costa 1978:207). But not all American ships that came to the islands were engaged in whaling. During the American revolutionary war privateers also provisioned their ships there. By 1795 a U.S. consul had been established in the western island of Fayal, due to the large number of American schooners that stopped there for provisions or to pick up export goods (Guill 1972:128). A century later the trade was still brisk. At this point there were estimated to be at least seven thousand islanders in the U.S. (Cardozo 1976:33), many of whom arrived via whaling ships. As time went on more and more of the whaling ships from North America that appeared in the Azores had Azorean masters (Amaral 1978).

American vessels came to the Azores for a number of reasons. The actual hunting of whales in the surrounding waters was the least important since the yield was comparatively low. The main intent was to reprovision and pick up Azorean crew members. Fresh supplies of meat, wine, and other foodstuffs were reputedly cheaper in the islands than in America. Although shore fishing and whaling were practiced in the western islands, in the early days most of the Azorean recruits were inexperienced sailors. Nevertheless, they had a good reputation for aptitude and hard work, and were undoubtedly a welcome source of replacements for a demanding occupation with high attrition rates (Martins 1976:126; Benjamin 1878:33). Ships stopping in the Azores for recruits proved to be critical in the development of future migration patterns. There was a small but steady flow of people from the western islands to America. Many of them found the means to stay in New England or

California, while others eventually returned to the Azores (Cardoza 1976:24; Da Costa 1978:207; Lang 1892:9). Towards the end of the nineteenth century the demand for Azorean crews increased as industrial prosperity in New England reduced the willingness of local young men to sign on as crew (Parry 1968:153). For well over a hundred years the pattern of refurbishing and remanning brought whaling ships to the western islands of the Azores, and thereby provided contacts with America that were to continue long after the demise of whaling.

The salient factors in the extension of migration channels between America and the more easterly islands of the Azores were the growth of the orange trade, improved transportation, and recruitment of contract labor for sugar plantations in Hawaii. The export of oranges established for the first time a major trade system independent of internal commerce or trade with the Portuguese empire. The bulk of the oranges were grown on the islands of São Miguel and Terceira. They were shipped from Ponta Delgada and Angra to England, and in lesser quantities to other parts of Europe and America. It was a flourishing business that resulted in the building of a small artificial harbor in Ponta Delgada to accommodate the increase in maritime movement. The trade developed in the 1700's and at the end of that century provided important income for the islands at a time when Portuguese trade in general was declining. Oranges were a prosperous business up until the 1860's, at which point the combined forces of disease and competition from Valencia oranges led to a drastic decline, the trade ending in the 1880's. The orange trade died out but the channels which had been established between the eastern islands and the U.S. and Europe remained active.

Transport and communications improved vastly during

this era. The transatlantic cable went through Horta in 1893, bringing with it an influx of Europeans and Americans. Steamships were operating in the 1840's, with regular schedules to Lisbon, other parts of Europe and New England established by the 1870's. In 1882 the Bartlett Steamship Co. of Boston had two boats which traveled every ten weeks to the Azores at a round trip cost of $110 for first class passengers (Correa 1924:85). The demand which supported these services was undoubtedly connected to the developing commercial networks, emigration, and tourism. Distances, in terms of communication or travel time, were being shortened as technologies improved and the flow of people increased. On the islands, internal communication systems were expanding with the founding of local newspapers in the 1830's, improved postal services, construction of better roads, and the eventual introduction of the automobile (the first of which came to São Miguel in 1901).

Officially documented emigration from the eastern District of Ponta Delgada to the U.S. began during the 1870's. It was characterized by a high proportion of males. Females generally did not follow, alone or with families, until the men were established. A relatively high percentage of the men listing a profession were in skilled or professional activities, with only one third listed as manual laborers (M.J.L. Trindade 1976:278).

The numbers of official emigrants from the District of Ponta Delgada to the U.S. were very small in the early years, one hundred and fifty, for example, between 1876 and 1880 (M.J.L. Trindade 1976:278). Total recorded emigration from the Azores during that period was about five thousand, most of whom were men going to Brazil (Furtado 1884:10). The number going to America increased rapidly in the next two decades, partly as a result of contract labor sent to Hawaii. It was not until the end of the nineteenth century that for the first time the total number of legal Azorean emigrants going to the U.S. exceeded the number going to Brazil (M.J.L. Trindade 1976:254).

Increased emigration from the eastern and central islands to North America was influenced not only by the development of commercial channels in the nineteenth century, but also by the implementation of a project which sent contract laborers to Hawaii in the 1870's and 1880's. The first recorded Portuguese residents in Hawaii, a total of seventy-five in 1853, were whalers and fisherman from the Azores (*Azorean Times* 1979:7). By 1876 the Portuguese population in Hawaii had increased to four hundred, mostly small farmers, dairymen, or workers on plantations. The rapid expansion of the sugar industry had created a critical demand for laborers. Chinese workers were imported, but could rarely be induced to bring their families, creating a surplus of males, a situation which the white landowners felt was undesirable (Young 1974:7). The planters sought alternative sources of familial labor. An enterprising German businessman, passing through the Madeira Islands on his return from Hawaii, engineered a plan for contract labor which brought island Portuguese to work on the plantations. In a letter to the Hawaiian government he stated his rationale for importing Portuguese families:

> In my opinion your islands could not possibly get a more desirable class of immigrants than the population of the Madeira and Azore Islands. Sober, honest, industrious and peaceable, they combine all the qualities of a good settler and with all this, they are inured to your climate. Their

education and ideas of comfort and social requirements are just low enough to make them contented with the lot of an isolated settler and its attendant privations, while on the other hand their mental capabilities and habits of work will ensure them a much higher status in the next generation, as the means of improvement grow up around them (Quoted in Young 1974:7).

Convinced by his eloquent argument, the Hawaiian government appointed the gentleman to supervise the project, which was jointly funded by the government and the planters. The first immigrants arrived from Madeira in 1877. The first Azorean contingent of over three hundred people left Ponta Delgada for Hawaii two years later (Parreira 1969:25). Subsequent voyages transported a total of eleven thousand people (mostly families) from the Azores and Madeira between 1878 and 1888 (Young 1974:8). After a decade the venture was abandoned, on the grounds that the cost of transporting the large number of children was too high and Japanese labor was less costly. Small numbers of Azoreans continued to arrive during the next several decades, many of whom proceeded on to California as work conditions on the plantations deteriorated (Cardoza 1976:55).

The flow of Azorean families to Hawaii for contract labor ultimately had a significant influence on the establishment of networks between the Azores and California. The earliest Azoreans in California had migrated there through fishing and whaling and in response to the gold rush in the mid 1800's. The opportunities in California included fishing, agriculture, and business. As in New England during the middle of the nineteenth century, emigrants frequently changed from one occupation to another, or from one aspect of an occupation to another, such as from whaling to a fish marketing business. This sometimes involved a change of locale, as in the case of one emigrant from the island of Pico who moved to California, then to whaling in New England, and finally back to California. By the early 1900's the Portuguese were well-known in California for their profitable involvements in both the dairy and fishing industries, some becoming wealthy businessmen (Pap 1985). The migration of Azoreans to Hawaii and later from Hawaii to California changed the character of the Azorean population on the west coast of America. While the initial flow of Azoreans to California had been individuals from the western whaling districts, the immigration via Hawaii was of families from the eastern and central islands whose background was agricultural.

Clandestine Emigration and Return

Although the preceding discussion focused on legal emigration to the U.S., clandestine emigration was also of vital importance. Whaling, trade, and improved transportation systems prospered in the nineteenth century, facilitating not only legal emigration from the islands but also clandestine movement to the U.S. Informal accounts and reports from the U.S. suggest that the rate of illegal emigration may have been as high as 20%. Many of the crew on whaling ships, for example, were clandestine emigrants who left the islands at a young age in order to escape the perils of military service. Accounts from the 1800's refer to the practice of Azorean lads taking 'French leave', often aided and abetted by their parents who made secret arrangements with a captain of a foreign whaling boat for a son to board the boat at sea and thereby avoid detection by customs officals (Amaral 1978:7-8). Many of these young men served as cabin boys and worked their way up in rank if they stayed in the sailing profession. Those who could not afford to make such arrangements, or were unable to, sometimes tried to stow away. Not all clandestine emigrants were penniless; many went with the sanction of their parents and with sufficient gold for a good start in America (Amaral 1978:75).

Azorean emigrants who went to the U.S. in the mid 1800's benefited from ties already established and from non-kin support networks that provided community focal points as well as financial aid. These non-kin groups were established with great frequency from the middle of the nineteenth century onwards, when there were sufficient numbers of Azoreans to support them. They took the form of fraternal organizations, financial aid organizations, and religious or musical clubs. The first recorded club started in San Francisco in 1868. A club for Azoreans from São Miguel was founded in Taunton, Massachusetts in 1895 (Parreira 1969:78-80). The Catholic Church was another important focal point for Azorean communities, the first Azorean priest arriving to establish a parish in the U.S. in 1869 (Parreira 1969:95). Another aspect of the whaling enterprise was that information flow between the western islands and the U.S. increased as the number of Azorean whalers going back and forth increased. Once illegal emigrants entered America and had obtained American papers, they were able to travel back and forth at will. In addition, many Azoreans Anglicized their names, whalers sometimes taking on the name of their Yankee captain, thus lessening the risk of legal problems when they returned (Amaral 1978).

Re-emigration, or coming back and then leaving again, was not uncommon. Both businessmen and sailors apparently traveled back and forth between America and the Azores. According to Portuguese data on passports issued in the late nineteenth century, 6 to 8% of the travelers going to the U.S. were born outside of the Azores. Most of these were born in the U.S. or Brazil, and in some families some children were born in one location and others in another (M.J.L. Trindade 1976:263). The same data shows that some of the emigrants had already been to Brazil and returned or had gone from Brazil to the U.S. Informal sources also provide data on the tremendous mobility of some of the islanders in the nineteenth century. One emigrant's life history records his migration to Brazil in 1864, his return to the Azores six years later and his subsequent migration to California to herd sheep. He later went back to the Azores to study for the priesthood and eventually returned to San Francisco to be ordained (Cardoza 1976:43).

The back and forth movement of Azoreans established a sense of proximity between the sending and receiving areas which is still an important variable in contemporary migration, as well as a factor in the development of Azorean communities in the U.S.[5] Since the beginning of the eighteenth century, in mainland Portugal the sighs of emigrants were expressed in literature and music as *saudades*, feelings of longing for the homeland. The undaunted expansionist mentality of the exploration period was transformed into the homesickness and longing of emigrants far from home. In the Azores, unlike the mainland, the separation was not so great, not so permanent, and a return not so unlikely. The sentiment that America was only an extension of home recalls the earlier mentality attributed to Portuguese explorers.

Return migration was an important aspect of what has been described as the 'migratory fluidity' of Azorean connections with the U.S. (Smith 1974:85). The intensity of interaction between the two areas continued in the early 1900's even though involvement in maritime activities declined and Azoreans found employment in the textile mills of New England. Smith (1974:85) cites U.S. census figures showing that between 1900 and 1920 about one quarter of Azorean immigrants returned to the Azores, and suggests that the figure may have been even higher. This is likely since the incidence of unrecorded clandestine migration was still very high according to informal accounts from the Azores.

The prevalence of clandestine emigration and return to the homeland is noted in one account, written in 1878, which refers to the voyage of a ship from Boston to the Azores.

> She had in the steerage thirty-one Portuguese, who were returning home, and the object of the voyage was ostensibly to secure a charter for an early cargo of oranges in November, but really to obtain, clandestinely, a haul of Azorean passengers flying in the face of the stringent prohibitory laws against emigration (Benjamin 1878:33).

The author reports that for that year alone the number of illegal Azorean emigrants going to America via British or American ships was over one thousand. Total legal emigration from the islands at that time, including emigrants destined for both North and South America, was about two thousand a year. As the account mentions, clandestine emigration was largely a response to laws that were enacted to prevent avoidance of the Portuguese military service through emigration. A series of restrictive laws were adopted throughout the nineteenth century as the Portuguese government became increasingly alarmed over the growing number of males emigrating to Brazil. In 1878 these laws prohibited a man under the age of twenty-one, who had not yet served his three year term in the military, from leaving without paying a bond equivalent to U.S. $300.00 to insure that he would return for service if his name was drawn in the lottery system. The bond was forfeited if he did not return (Benjamin 1878:33). These facts suggest that clandestine emigration was greatest among that sector of the population which had sufficient resources to arrange for a son to leave secretly but not enough clout or money to keep him from being drafted. Even if emigrants could afford to post the necessary bond it is unlikely, given the choice of forfeiting money to the government or taking that money to invest in a life in America, that many would have chosen the former. In the early nineteenth century arranging citizenship in the U.S. was not difficult, and afterwards the clandestine emigrant could safely return to the islands.   Illegal departure, therefore, did not necessarily mean permanent departure from the homeland.

The Changing Tide of Early Twentieth Century Migration

The earlier emigrants who went to North America were from a broad range of backgrounds. By the end of the nineteenth century, however, the pattern had altered.

Whereas the first emigrants were primarily males, by the 1870's there were already substantial numbers of Portuguese women in some regions. These women worked as domestics or did needle work if they were employed outside the home. The proportion of women emigrating increased towards the end of the nineteenth century. In a study of Portuguese immigrants in the U.S. during the early twentieth century it is noted that about 40% of this group were females (Bannick 1971:37-40). The author associates the high proportion of women with a pattern of family migration in which the male generally arrives first. The increase in female emigrants was certainly associated with the establishment of Portuguese communities and networks, plus the necessity of a family support group for those involved in tenant or private farming, and the demand for female labor in the mills both in New England and in California. The immigrants were primarily in the most productive age group , i.e., 69% were between the ages of fourteen and forty-four. Two striking features that distinguish this flow of emigrants from earlier patterns is their extremely high illiteracy rate, higher than any other immigrant group in the U.S. at the time, and the high proportion of unskilled workers. Compared to informal accounts and the information from Portuguese passport registries about forty years earlier, the emigrants had become a much less diverse lot. For the period between 1907 and 1916, of the Portuguese immigrants to the U.S. who listed occupation, over 90% were manual laborers or servants, with barely 7% listed as skilled workers and even fewer as professionals (Bannick 1971:40).

A shift took place in Azorean migration patterns in 1896 when for the first time the number of legal emigrants going to the U.S. exceeded the number going to the traditional destination of Brazil (M.J.L. Trindade 1976:254). This change in orientation was partly a result of new opportunities in America, but also a result of changing opportunities and perceptions of opportunities in Brazil. A Portuguese parliamentary inquiry of 1873 reported that hardships for emigrants were generally greater in Brazil than in the U.S. The exceptions in Brazil were those people involved in aspects of commerce. On the other hand, the successful ones who returned from Brazil were far more successful than their counter-parts returning from America.. The latter had led a more secure life but returned with fewer riches (M.J.L. Trindade 1976:245). Following the abolition of slavery in Brazil in 1888, the demand for agricultural labor rose and Brazil actively recruited immigrants from the Azores. However, tales of appalling work conditions also reached the islands. Some immigrants continued to go, primarily single males, and some returned.

One visible effect of the return of emigrants to the Azores from Brazil was the introduction of two-storied houses throughout the villages. The *brasileiros* who returned with money frequently invested in building new houses, *casas de balcão*, with two floors, an interior or exterior stairway, and balconies overlooking the street (Constancia 1963-64:24). The nobility and urban middle class had two-story houses much earlier, but the spread of more elaborate structures in the countryside is largely attributed to emigrants returning from Brazil.

Emigration affected the distribution of resources both through individuals returning from Brazil to acquire or expand property holdings, and through emigrants in Brazil sending money back if they were able to do so.[6] The flow of resources went both ways, with emigrants not only sending back money and presents, but with returned emigrants who had property in Brazil also receiving payments for rent and income from Brazil (Martins 1976:144).

In the Azores, among rural small landowners, it is quite common to find that one or both of the spouses have parents or grandparents, or even great grandparents, who were in Brazil at one time. Many of these people report that those relatives came back and purchased land after one or several sojourns in Brazil:

> My family was well off because my father went to Brazil three times. He had four siblings, all poorer than himself. He was the oldest, but his mother had died and his father remarried so there were even more children in the family. He returned from Brazil after he made some money and he bought land. He then married my mother who was just a young girl at the time and he was over thirty. She was the only child and her parents had some land so it was a very good marriage for both of them. They both had land, they were well matched, and they worked hard.
>
> (Fieldnotes, São Miguel 1978)

The mother added that even though her family was well off in the village she had to get married in men's boots because they were the only shoes available to borrow. This would have been about 1906.

Some who returned from Brazil had not managed to make a financial success of the venture. Writing in 1938, one Portuguese author asks rhetorically, 'Why do they still go?' His answer is that if you asked those less successful emigrants they will reply that the misfortunes of emigration are uncertain and it is always possible that great good fortune will be found, whereas at home it is almost certain that it never will be found (Herculano 1976:99).

The Home Society

For Portugal as a whole the 1800's and early 1900's were a period of agricultural expansion, with rapid commercial growth, and modest industrial development towards the end of the nineteenth century. Politically, the period was marked by the Napoleonic invasion of Portugal; the establishment of a constitutional monarchy; a struggle between liberalism and traditionalism; and the declaration of a parliamentary republic in 1910. Socially, a new oligarchy had developed, its members being drawn both from the landed aristocracy and a new economic and political elite. The sale of Church and most royal lands, after the defeat of traditionalism in Portugal, and the abolition of estate entailment in 1863, resulted in the transfer of a great deal of land. Increased fluidity in land availability helped establish a new middle level of landowners in Portugal. Despite changes in the upper strata of society, the traditional rural structure remained virtually the same throughout this period, often carrying the burden rather than reaping the benefits of economic reforms.

Up until the 1920's the pattern of who emigrated from the Azores closely mirrors the pattern of who benefited from development at the time. Opportunities for upward mobility among the commercial bourgeoisie and the educated middle class increased during the nineteenth century and the numbers of emigrants from those stratas declined. Opportunities for the rural peasants remained limited and the proportion of them emigrating increased. In the Azores the eighteenth and nineteenth centuries were an era when the rich were getting richer and an independent middle class was coming into its own, but by contrast the rural poor were getting even poorer (Da Costa 1978:211).

In the Azores the primary resource was land, and its availability was limited, spatially by the fact of being islands, and socially through the quasi-feudal system of allocations. A system of entailment and primogeniture meant that the oldest son inherited the entire estate and could not divide it. This was practiced until its abolition in 1863 and the introduction of the institution of equal inheritance. Typically, in one region on São Miguel in the 1920's most of the land still belonged to five major noble families and the Jesuits (Correa 1924:195-197). The families administered production on the land or rented out small parcels, generally being paid in crops, chickens, and wine by their tenants. The law of equal inheritance, and the influx of capital through emigration, to some extent helped broaden the limited distribution of property. However, as late as 1962 a local human geographer noted that the rural property in São Miguel was still concentrated in the hands of only a few families (Constancia 1962:9).

Access to land remained limited for the peasantry. But what about other resources? After the expulsion of the Jesuits in the 1770's, educational facilities in Portugal were expanded, specifically as a means of creating a much needed 'instructed middle class' (Livermore 1966:235). Azoreans, however, had to go to the mainland to take advantage of these facilities. As a result Azorean education was embedded in the Church until the closure of monasteries and convents in the 1830's. In the mid 1860's state schools began to be established, but the rural poor generally did not attend these public institutions unless they were sponsored by a patron.[7]

The nascent development of small industry and the swelling numbers of the commercially successful middle class provided another access to resources in the form of urban wage labor. The 1800's were a rich era for development of agriculture, industry, and commerce in the Azores. As the lucrative orange trade began to decline in the mid 1800's new export crops were introduced and cultivated. These included pineapples grown in greenhouses, tea, tobacco, and hemp (espadana).

Production, processing, and export of many products was centered in São Miguel in the late nineteenth century. The opportunities for employment and investment in the flourishing commerce appear to have encouraged several decades of internal migration during which people moved to São Miguel from other islands. In 1890 in the District of Ponta Delgada almost one fifth of the active work force was involved in the industrial, transport, and commercial sectors. The proportion working in industry alone increased to 18% in the next few decades but declined to lower than the 1890 level of 11% by 1930 (I.N.E.1973).

The commercial blossoming, centered in São Miguel, provided opportunities for capital accumulation. As in continental Portugal, the growth of the middle class developed among small businessmen and people involved in commerce. The effect this had on the lower classes was to provide service jobs catering to the growing middle classes and urban residents, and opportunities for wage labor in industry.[8] Wages were pitifully low and this meant

that for the majority of the peasantry the only visible
avenue to accumulation of capital was through emigration,
an unsure path but one where the dream might be
realized. The dream was to make enough money to return
and buy land, a desire that is still voiced among
contemporary emigrants. Obviously, many did not return,
and many did not acquire the wealth they had hoped for,
but some did return for temporary or permanent
residence, and enough came back with sufficient capital to
perpetuate the dream. The ties between the lower classes
and North America were becoming thicker as more people
gained experience in the U.S., more people had relatives
there, and more news was carried back and forth.

As the orientation toward the U. S. grew among the
Azorean peasantry, it decreased among the middle and
upper levels of the society. For them it was a cosmopolitan
era, with much movement and development and changes
in society. Culturally São Miguel was thriving with schools,
academies, libraries, and cultural societies. There were
theaters, music and opera; and foreign artists and literary
figures periodically took up residence in the picturesque
region. Tourists and travelers abounded, passing through
the islands by boat on vacations, exploring the carefully
manicured parks and 'natural' beauty of the volcanic
landscape, taking medicinal waters and baths and
purchasing local crafts. For the middle levels of society
opportunities flourished in the islands and there was less
incentive to emigrate than there had been in the earlier
part of the nineteenth century when the economy had
been more stagnant. For their children the path to
success lay through education, and institutions of higher
learning were found in continental Portugal and Europe.

Ideas, materials, and fashionable goods were being
imported from England through trade, and from other

parts of continental Europe through education and traveling. World War I brought foreign military personnel into the islands and services to entertain them quickly surfaced in the main centers.

Many of the elite lived abroad, as had been the pattern throughout Azorean history. Families went to Paris for some years, for example, to have their children educated. Even if the family was not abroad, children from aristocratic families were sent to Lisbon or Coimbra on the mainland for higher education. The elite and middle levels were thus culturally tied to the mainland and Europe while the less affluent continued to focus their outward orientation on America.

Summary: Migration Pre-1920's

Various interrelationships between migratory patterns and circumstances in the home and receiving systems are evident based on the preceding consideration of the historical context up to the early twentieth century. They can be summarized in terms of migration channels, flows of people, flows of information, and the connections between them.

1) The development of migration channels was connected with the contact and inflow of information resulting from commercial developments in Brazil and North America, such as whaling and new trade networks (see Map 5).

2) In conjunction with the development of channels, the migration flows of people were influenced by the flows of information concerning cost and benefit differentials at

home and abroad. Who migrated, in terms of socioeconomic status, depended on the structure of opportunities in both systems and the information flow between them. For example, while the demand for manual labor in the U.S. accelerated due to industrialization, opportunities were opening up for the middle class in the Azores. As a result, the proportion of peasant migrants increased and the proportion of middle class migrants decreased.

3) Emigration of families increased in response to greater information about the destination area and the establishment of family networks, clubs, and mutual-aid organizations. Emigrants also knew about the availability of jobs for women in the factories, and the security of contract labor for families in the case of Hawaii.

4) Migratory patterns gradually facilitated the inflow of resources, such as capital, to the Azores.

5) The inflow of capital and returning emigrants contributed to the development of a rural middle class in the islands as people returned with money to invest in land or business. This process was helped by prior changes in the home system, and prior migration flows, which effected the availability of property in the homeland.

6) 'Successful' emigration and return influenced subsequent migration by making it easier to use alternative home resources, such as education, and by demonstrating to others the feasibility of socioeconomic mobility through migration: the perpetuation of the dream.

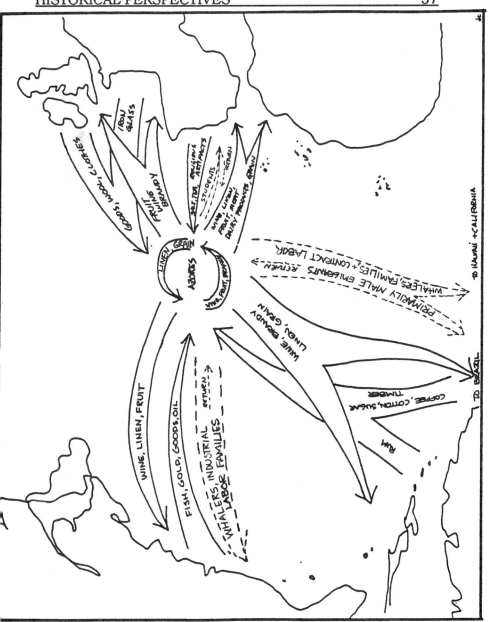

Map 5. Trade Patterns and Migration Flows,
Late 18th and Early 19th Centuries

CESSATION AND RENEWAL OF EMIGRATION:
THE 1920'S - 1960'S

The option of migration to the U.S. was sharply curtailed by restrictive immigration legislation passed in the U.S. in the early 1920's. The population of the islands increased rapidly during the following thirty year period, and the pressure of increased population on the limited land resources was compounded by economic   depression.

Economically, in the 1930's the Azores suffered from a slump tied in with the enormous financial problems on the mainland. In addition, the mainland restricted the entry of products from the Azores that competed with exports from the African territories and placed high tariffs on products being imported by the Azores. On top of this, the local economy lost an important source of foreign capital when remittances from America declined sharply following the U.S. imposed restrictions on migration (Leite 1940:445).   The extent to which emigration was considered integral to the welfare of the homeland is illustrated by proposals in 1938 to revive emigration by sending people to Africa (Leite 1940:449).

The World War II years were ones of moderate prosperity for the islands. The flow of foreign goods increased as did the flow of foreigners and the need to provide them with goods and services. Portugal remained neutral in the war, but gave Britain and the U.S. permission to use the Azores for crucial naval operations in 1943. After the war Portugal benefited from acceptance into the. Marshall Plan and the North Atlantic Treaty Organization.   The latter is represented by the U.S. operated base on the island of Terceira. People in the rural areas of of São Miguel still recall the World War II period and the years immediately after as a time when 'white flour arrived in bags from America'.

The sector of the labor force involved in manual labor, primarily agriculture, increased in the 1940's and the 1950's, reaching a high level of 64%. Educational facilities improved and compulsory attendance was instituted. The percentage of students in secondary school in the District of Ponta Delgada doubled in the eight years between 1956 and 1964. However, the unemployment rate for persons under twenty seeking their first job tripled between 1950 and 1960. These were not people seeking agricultural employment, but rather those with the basic level of education who aspired to blue collar and service positions, for which there was limited demand. The policy of raising educational levels in the Azores resulted, therefore, in the creation of a sector of people with skills for which there were few jobs. Here was a population ripe for industrial employment but there was little industry to employ them. The industrial sector actually had declined since the early part of the century.

Despite development programs, Portugal was still the poorest country in Western Europe in terms of per capita income. The Azores remained a few steps behind the mainland. Portuguese economic policy did little to raise productivity or stimulate development in the Azores. In addition, problems fermenting in the African provinces in the late 1950's led to an increase in military conscription to bolster the armed forces.

Emigration was curtailed severely by the U.S. quota system which allowed only a few hundred visas for the Portuguese, but movement between the Azores and the U.S. was not completely arrested. A much diminished flow still went to the U.S. with immigrant visas. Others went on temporary visas. Small numbers from the middle class and elite, continued to go temporarily to complete courses in such areas as engineering or medicine, or other specialized training. Others went as visitors, some just to visit, and some to try to get visas for permanent immigration. Still others went as visitors and stayed illegally, hoping to escape the attention of the authorities. Arranging a marriage or a specialized job, or getting a sponsor, were various channels open to the enterprising individual who wanted to stay in the U.S. Popular folk songs of the 1940's record this continuing, if not enhanced, desire to emigrate to the U.S. with phrases alluding to the 'call of America' and the hope that 'the sea will carry me there' (Parreira 1969:44).

During this period the only major legal emigration to the U.S. occurred under an emergency act for which John F. Kennedy will be forever glorified on the walls of Azorean cottages.   In 1959 an act was passed to admit one thousand household heads and their dependents following the volcanic eruptions that destroyed entire communities on the island of Fayal. The majority of these immigrants went to California to settle. A limited migration channel, temporary labor going to Bermuda, developed during this period. It is difficult to remain in Bermuda without a work permit due to stringent citizenship laws, but as noted elsewhere, the Portuguese were known for taking jobs that other people would not and therefore had little difficulty retaining work permits once in the country.

An important migratory flow for which there is no accurate documentation was the return of emigrants from America during and just after the depression years. Islanders say that during these years return from America was very common since even a small savings account went much further in the Azores than in the U.S. Many of those who did return reputedly had access to some property or a house, thus easing their living situation even more. Some people returned from the U.S. to the Azores for purely financial reasons, calculating that they could weather the depression better in the homeland where a little bit of land could supply your basic needs and where the American dollar went further than in America.   Others returned during the 1930's because they were dismayed by the advent of labor union organization in American industry and various professions.   The unions were threatening, particularly to the non-English speaker. Some older Azoreans who had been in America at that time expressed this sentiment with statements that 'the unions were Communist', and 'had to be avoided'. Of those who returned during the thirties, forties and early fifties, some intended to stay, but many hoped to return to the U.S. in better times.

Once in the Azores it was not always easy to return to America.   People who did not have citizenship or permanent resident status found that they could only return to the U.S. with a new visa.   Under the limited quota system getting a visa could take many years (unless you knew the right person in the right place).   Others were unable to return because they did not have the finances.   Travel from the Azores to the U.S. (and to Lisbon) was facilitated by the introduction of commercial air service in 1939, but steamers continued to be the cheapest form of transport.

One woman recounted how it had taken her nearly twelve years to reassemble her family together in Fall River, Massachusetts, after a return to the Azores during the depression.   She had been born in America but her husband was born and raised on São Miguel and wanted to

return to live in his father's house when life became
financially difficult in Fall River.

> We came back because you know it was easier to
> live in the islands than in America during that
> time.   There (in America) no one had work,
> people were hungry, but here we had our land and
> our relatives and with very little money we lived
> well. But then my husband died and I was stuck
> here with my three children and no money to pay
> the fare back.   The children were born in the
> islands so I couldn't get passports for them at that
> time and I knew I couldn't support them in
> America so finally I borrowed enough money to get
> a boat back and left the children with my
> husband's parents.   I got back to Fall River in
> 1940. The factories were bust then and I got a
> good job. In two years I saved enough money to
> pay off my debts and bring my children over.....And
> now here I am in the Azores again but this time I
> can go back to visit whenever I want!
>   (Fieldnotes, São Miguel 1978)

A very small number of returnees from Brazil also
continued to arrive up until the 1950's. So complete was
the abandonment of the channel of emigration to Brazil in
favor of the U.S. that in 1939 when Brazil was actively
recruiting immigrants from the mainland and Madeira no
propaganda was sent to the Azores. Just fifty years earlier
the Azores had been an important, although not enormous,
source of Portuguese manpower for Brazil.

During this period emigration was minimal compared
to preceding migration flows. There were a number of
developments in the sending and receiving areas,

however, that affected the nature of future migration. One development in the Portuguese-American communities was the increase of naturalized citizens. In Fall River, for example, only 7% of the resident Portuguese (mostly Azoreans) were naturalized in 1920. Ten years later the figure had almost doubled, and in the late 1940's the number of naturalized citizens was over 50% (Cardoza 1976:61). This trend had major implications for future migratory patterns. As the number of naturalized citizens increased the potential for future immigration to the U.S. increased because in subsequent years the determining preference factor in U.S. immigration policy was based on kinship ties to permanent U.S. residents. The Portuguese already in America prior to the cessation of migration were becoming more permanently settled. The fact that movement back and forth was curtailed may have had a bearing on this. The Azorean immigrants' increasingly permanent orientation, is reflected in the proliferation of Portuguese parishes, newspapers, benevolent associations, and clubs during this period. The associations and clubs provided substantial mutual-aid benefits as well as social and religious functions. In terms of future immigration this development meant that the receiving area had extensive infrastructures which reduced the psychological and even financial risks or costs of emigration for future flows. The path was paved, the way was lit. On the other hand, it also meant that future immigrants would arrive in communities where the hierarchies had been worked out and the adjustments made, placing them low in the pecking order as new immigrants or "greenhorns".

By 1960 the total population of the Azorean archipelago had reached an all time high of 330,000. In the following decade the population plummeted to 70% of its former total as the emigration flow of the 1960's gained momentum. By 1974 the total population was 259,000.

The tremendous flow of people out of the islands was associated with changes in immigration policy and labor demand in North America. Canada opened its doors in 1952, seeking immigrant labor to assist in new programs of economic development. Canada needed workers, and the word of opportunity spread quickly throughout the Azores. It was a selective migration.

> Emigration to Canada? I remember when it began it was just like it had been to Brazil in my grandfather's time. They took only the best, the young, the strong, the healthy men. They wouldn't take José because he had tuberculosis, but many men went. They worked hard, on farms, and sent money back to their wives and families.
> (Fieldnotes, São Miguel 1978)

The first seed group of men from the Azores arrived in Ottawa in 1953 to work on the railways and in market gardens. They gained a reputation as hard workers, somewhat timid, who kept to themselves and would take jobs that other people did not want. These combined attributes, echoing the characteristics ascribed to earlier emigrants in the U.S., made them desirable employees for Canadians.[9] By 1965 the Canadian government was encouraging the immigration of families, not just males, and many of the men who had gone in the first groups of emigrants brought their families over to join them. Others returned to the Azores, and new emigrants continued to come.

At this point, in 1965, the U.S. passed new immigration legislation   which replaced the restrictive quota system with a system of preference aimed at reuniting families. The Azoreans, with a strong base of relatives in America from previous emigration, began to emigrate in large numbers. The exodus exceeded any previous flow, and certainly was stimulated both by the high population density that had built up and the myth of American prosperity that had been nourished over the thirty-five years when emigration had not been a viable option for most people.

CONCLUSION

In São Miguel history permeates the present. Past centuries are brought into contemporary life in the continuity of family lines, in names, in daily customs, in architecture and in the attachments people have to the rest of the world. The history of attachments to America is characterized by expansion and flexibility, both of which affect the orientation people have toward migration in São Miguel today.

The process of expansion began shortly after the islands were settled and continues into the present. Azoreans dispersed to various parts of the globe. Ties to the homeland weakened in some areas, but in others such as North America they remained strong. The Azorean communities of North America are not, and never have been colonies, but nonetheless are extensions of the homeland in the minds of emigrants and islanders alike. The intensity of communication, return, and re-migration fostered the idea that emigrants were not lost to the homeland, but merely gone to another realm.

Psychologically the distance between America and the Azores was not insurmountable, as seen in the frequency of back and forth movement of individuals and communications. Ties to the destination area also perpetuated a pattern of 'chain migration' in which people already in America assisted other migrants to come from the homeland, a pattern also typical of migration from Italy to Britain (MacDonald and MacDonald 1964).

The flow of information, reflecting conditions in destination areas, sometimes altered the flow of people. Douglass (1974) discusses the Basque emigrants in Argentina who discouraged continuing emigration by disseminating information on the deplorable conditions they encountered there. Likewise, in São Miguel information discouraged the flow of people to Brazil and intensified emigration of people to the U.S. The flow of emigrants from São Miguel was subject to change in the past and still is today.

Changing destinations, socioeconomic variation in the emigrant flow, and variable perceptions of migration all illustrate flexibility in historical migration patterns. Migration was associated with colonial expansion and exploration. People from all levels of the home society explored and exploited resources outside the islands. Some came back from the adventure richer, some poorer, and others never returned. Migration was also a response to problems at home (earthquakes, famine, and poverty) which stimulated people from the lower levels of the home society to seek greater security elsewhere. In the twentieth century emigration became more associated with solving the problems of population surplus, i.e., it became a 'release valve,' and less associated with the idea of adventure and exploration. However, both ideas about migration are present in the cultural screen through which local people now see movement out of São Miguel. The interweaving of these two ideas shapes present orientations toward migration and provides the flexibility for change in those orientations.

Migration from the Azores has resulted in a network of ties that counteracts the geographical isolation of the islands. Over time and through space these ties have contributed to the development of São Miguel and its relationship to America. The feedback effect of ongoing flows of people and communications is also a part of the context of contemporary migration. This context will be examined in the next three chapters.

CHAPTER 3
THE ISLAND OF SÃO MIGUEL: DIMENSIONS IN THE SOCIOCULTURAL CONTEXT OF MIGRATION

The history of migration from São Miguel illustrates the development of two themes which are integral to the form of Michaelense society and migration in the 1970's. The first theme pertains to the cultural screen through which people perceive migration. Stratified evaluations of the relative attractiveness of emigration developed as emigration became associated with necessity rather than innovation. The second theme is how the structure of the society became associated with orientations toward migration. Current migration decision-making in São Miguel takes places in a context where the options open to individuals, and the way they perceive them, are influenced by perceptions of opportunities and the normative structures within the society. Three dimensions of the societal context are particularly important for understanding contemporary migration: Michaelense identity, social categories, and livelihood.

MICHAELENSE IDENTITY

São Miguel is a small territory (747 km2), and in some

68

respects small-scale, but it does not fit the orthodox definitions of peasant society. In São Miguel the idea that the village is the peasant's world (Shanin 1971; Redfield 1955) is a far cry from the complex reality of the social system. Small-scale attributes of role relationships are evident in São Miguel in that interactions are characterized by personal relations such as Benedict (1966) discusses for small territories. However, the society is a complex system with external interactions in many spheres which defy the spatial barriers of insularity. It is, in contrast to Kroeber's village 'part-society' (1948:284), a 'whole-society' tied into other complex systems.

International Ties and Regional Disparities

Just as the Azorean archipelago was a central node in the commercial shipping networks of earlier centuries, São Miguel is a central node in the web of active sociocultural affiliations which stretch out to the other islands, to the mainland, and to North America. On the one hand, residents of the island are part of a locally-centered, highly personalistic system of relationships, where 'everybody knows everybody'. On the other hand, they are part of a social milieu where people speak of events, persons, and values in American society or mainland Portugal with a familiarity which belies their spatial distance. Despite rivalries between the islands and differences in heritage, the islanders see themselves as Azoreans. Azorean identity comes into play, particularly in contrast to the mainland Portuguese.[1] Politically radical individuals say, 'We are Azorean, not Portuguese', while others merely say 'We are Azorean, but of course we also Portuguese'. On the mainland, the islands are seen as provincial, the 'poor country cousins' of Portugal. Azoreans complain that on the mainland they are discriminated against and that people ridicule their accents, but it reinforces their sense of regional identity. Islanders claim that being *açoreano* entails having a deep appreciation of the 'natural' beauty of the islands and an attachment to the sea, regardless of whether the individual is a farmer, fisherman, or businessperson. It is said that always being in sight of the ocean gives Azoreans a vital sense of the possibility of going somewhere, in spite of the smallness of the islands. In São Miguel this psychologically mobile orientation is given as an explanation for emigration, but almost always with the qualification that Azoreans never forget their homeland and will return eventually.2

Being Michaelense is culturally distinguished from being a resident of one of the other islands by both heritage and present behavior. The Michaelense are said to 'behave differently', they are more 'restrained', more 'family oriented', more 'closed to outsiders', more 'religious', and more 'somber' in their habits. They do not chase leashed bulls around the streets for entertainment or speak with a singing accent like more 'lively' people from the neighboring island of Terceira. The island of São Miguel is subdivided into six *concelhos* (municipalities) and fifty *freguesias* (parishes) whose residents are said to have their own distinctive attributes such as how superstitious they are, how hard they work, or how friendly they are.

There is a broad range of national, regional, and local identities that come into play for people in São Miguel, and emigration introduces an additional one. Michaelense emigrants retain the identity of being Michaelense. However, when they return to São Miguel, non-family islanders label them *americano* (American). The persons who emigrate are called *embarcardos,* literally, those who get on board a boat. When they return, they are Americans, while non-Azorean American tourists are generally referred to as *estrangeiros,* foreigners.

Town and Country

Within the island there are further distinctions made with respect to regional identity (as typified by accent and stereotypes of behavior), but the major distinction is between the town and countryside domains. The country people are called *povo* (the people, in the sense of peasants), in contrast to the more sophisticated town residents. Town and country are distinctive but they are not isolated spheres. As in other parts of the world, there is a range of interaction between town and country (Uzzell 1976; Buechler 1970:66). People frequently operate in both spheres, although there may be distinctive sociocultural characteristics in each.

In the rural community in São Miguel the degree of contact with larger towns and the city of Ponta Delgada depends in part on distance. Distance is not only a matter of kilometers, but also of bus lines and schedules. Since the island is less than one hundred kilometers in length and Ponta Delgada is located near the center of the southern coast, no locale is more than a four hour bus journey from the main city. 3

At one end of the range of interaction continuum, it is

not unusual to find older people, especially in the more distant villages, who have never been to the city, or have gone only once or twice. Excursions to the city often were made only to get to the hospital or begin a trip to America. As one woman in her eighties remarked about Ponta Delgada, "In Ponta Delgada I know only the airport, but in Fall River, Massachusetts, I have seen everything". At the other end of the spectrum, in villages that are located within an hour bus ride of the city, it is common to see people waiting every morning to take the bus into town to work. Occupations for villagers in the towns vary from industrial labor to secretarial and clerical positions in businesses.

Throughout the day people can be seen setting out by bus on missions that take them out of the village. For some it may be a trip to buy goods in the city stores. For others it may include taking a sick child to the doctor, consulting a social worker about insurance benefits, or obtaining the ubiquitous official stamp necessary for any official papers, such as a rental contract. It may be a luxury trip: an appointment with the hairdresser for the schoolteacher, a chance to run errands for a teenage girl, or a visit to a cousin's orange grove in another village to bring home some fruit.

Most daily business can be taken care of within the village. Letters can be mailed, dollars received from America can be changed for *escudos*, shoes can be mended, clothes can be made by a seamstress, and corn can be taken to be milled into flour for bread. Wheat, flour, salt, oil, sausage, and even frozen meat can be purchased in the local stores, along with a wide variety of sundries and clothing. A more extensive selection of items is announced periodically by the horn of a vendor who drives a well-stocked van of goods around to the villages.

It is possible for people to rarely leave the village, but then they depend on other people to do so. Town dwellers, by contrast, have less cause to go to the villages. Some do go to visit family, or take something to a favorite seamstress, and others own land which needs to be managed or country vacation houses.   In the latter case social interaction with rural residents is usually minimal. Town and country are intersecting spheres of activity, but it is the country that comes to the town more than the reverse. The exception to this is that emigrants who visit or return to rural areas are also town dwellers, but from towns of a different country. They are consequently more urban in their experiences than some of the town residents in São Miguel.

Although town and country interact in São Miguel, they are sharply differentiated by life style and material attributes. Over 70% of the island households are located outside of the urban areas (see Table 3.1). In 1960, 72% of the island's houses had three rooms or less, and in poorer residences as many as eight people sleep in the same room (Medeiros 1977).

Table 3.1. Urban and Rural Residence, District of Ponta Delgada, 1975

Residence	Percent of Total Inhabitants
City of Ponta Delgada	12.7%
Other Towns	16.0%
Rural Freguesias	71.3%

(Source: Medeiros 1977)

In the late 1950's and 1960's government projects were initiated to improve standards of living in the rural areas.   Electricity and water systems have improved significantly since that time, although sewage systems and

bathrooms with running water are still scarce in the rural
areas (see Table 3.2). Water taps at individual houses have
reduced the need to fetch water from centralized
fountains and wash clothes in streams or village wash
houses.

Table 3.2. Facilities in Houses, District of Ponta Delgada

Percent of Houses	Ponta Delgada		AzoresTotal
	1950	1960	1977
With bathroom	7%	12%	22%
With electricity	32%	39%	53%
With water	39%	55%	60%

(Sources: I.N.E. 1950, 1960 and DREPA 1977)

Some of the improvements in the standard of living
resulted from government projects. Others were and
continue to be made possible through funds brought or
sent by emigrants. Old stone cottages are newly plastered
and painted, water taps are installed indoors, bathrooms
are built, and roofs are newly tiled as the last of the
thatched roofs disappear. The modern new or remodeled
houses in the rural areas frequently belong to emigrants
who have returned or are planning to in the future. They
have 'American-style' kitchens, tiled bathrooms, and large
windows. New houses contrast even more with the
traditional form of housing (set close to the street and
with adjoining walls) because they are often set back from
the street with a yard. The older houses are protected
from the street with entry halls and shutters on the
windows, but the movement of people in and out, the

peeling of potatoes while sitting on the front stoop, and the visiting out of windows all integrate the house with the community. By contrast, the new emigrant homes tend to be isolated spatially by an open yard which deters casual interaction with people on the street.

In both towns and villages the number of television antennas is a striking sign of changing times. First available in 1975, televisions are now found even in poor houses and the antennas in the countryside jut into the horizon side by side with the tall pole frames used for drying corn. The high frequency of television ownership and viewing in rural areas is shown in Table 3.3. Fifteen years ago emigrants flooded the rural areas with radios, bringing and sending them back as gifts, but the spread of television has been a homegrown phenomenon.

Table 3.3. Television Ownership and Viewing Frequency in Two Rural Samples, 1978

Percent	Village A	Village B
Own TV	42%	42%
Watch TV at least once/week	79%	63%

Telephones, automobiles and modern appliances are still scarce outside of the urban areas. In villages televisions are more common than phones, which are considered less useful. There is always a nearby store where a call can be made if the need arises. The rural residents who do have phones or cars are usually the wealthier business people or professionals such as the priest or the schoolteacher. The number of telephones and automobiles has increased in the past twenty years (see Table 3.4.), but they are still luxury items. In the villages, refrigerators, freezers, and other modern appliances are rarely found outside the houses of returned

Table 3.4.   Telephones and Automobiles in the District of Ponta Delgada, 1956-1973

Average per 1000 Inhabitants	1956	1964	1973
Telephones	16	32	59
Automobiles	17	30	46

(Source: Medeiros 1977)

emigrants or professionals, but they are common in city residences.   The majority of village households have bottled gas stoves although many women continue to bake and cook using wood as fuel, saving the gas because it is expensive.

The gap in the standard of living between the rural and urban areas has been narrowing with respect to health and social services. Regional hospitals have been improved to provide a doctor in residence and basic care. Despite improvements, the number of doctors, nurses, and midwives (shown in Table 3.5.) is still inadequate for the needs of the District (DREPA 1977). Over a twenty year period starting in 1957, infant-maternal care dispensaries were established in thirty-one of the island's fifty *freguesias*. Since that time the birth mortality rate, the general mortality rate, and the rate of natural increase have all declined (Table 3.6.). Some of this effect is undoubtedly due to improved medical care and some to emigration, which has reduced the most fertile sector of

Table 3.5. Medical Personnel in S. Miguel, 1977

	Number	Inhabitants per Practioner
Doctors	88	1557
Nurses	207	615
Midwives	21	6522

(Source: DREPA 1977)

Table 3.6. Birth, Death and Growth Rates for the District of Ponta Delgada by Years

Year	Per 1000 Births	Per 1000 Inhabitants		
	Infant Mortality	Birth Rate	General Mortality	Natural Growth Rate
1960	111	36	12	22
1965	67	31	-	-
1970	71	28	11	20
1974	-	28	9	19

(Sources: I.N.E. 1970; DREPA 1976)

the population. Other social services have contributed to improved health through insurance and other benefits. Services include such things as subsidized medicine and visits to the doctor, pensions for the elderly and infirm, allowances for each child, and allowances for children in school for agricultural and other manual workers.

Nevertheless, social workers in São Miguel say it is still a region where infant and child malnutrition is not uncommon.

Educational facilities beyond the primary level were formerly monopolized by the city, but are now more equally distributed in smaller towns. There are four high school level facilities outside of Ponta Delgada, but the final two years of college preparatory work must still be taken in the city. Attendance at the secondary (high school) level has increased substantially in the last fifteen years (Table 3.7). During the same period the number of primary school students declined by 30% as a result of emigration and a lower birth rate. This necessitated the closing of primary schools in some rural areas.

Table 3.7.   Students graduating from High School Level (including college preparatory and technical schools) in the District of Ponta Delgada

Year	No. of Students	% of total Students	Per 1000 Inhabitants
1956/57	2293	7.6	13
1964/65	4627	16.4	25
1972/73	6082	19.8	38

(Source: Medeiros 1977)

Post secondary institutions (including a nursing school and a school for primary level teachers) are located in Ponta Delgada. Prior to 1976 university education was only available in mainland Portugal or abroad. The expense of sending a student to the mainland is a major limitation on access to higher education although small numbers of scholarships are available to cover tuition expenses. A college was started in Ponta Delgada in 1976 as part of a regional system with campuses in the three district capitals. This provides a local alternative, but its credentials are not equivalent to universities on the mainland. The Ponta Delgada campus of the Instituto Universitário dos Açores had two hundred and nineteen students enrolled in 1976/77. The following year thirty students from São Miguel received scholarships to study at the college, and an additional one hundred and eight received government scholarships to study in mainland Portugal (personal communication, Inspeção Socias, 1978).

Town and country domains in São Miguel are not isolated; the contrast in standards of living and access to services is less acute than it was twenty years ago and people frequently operate in both spheres. What this means for emigration is that people who emigrate now do so in a context which is even different from that of the 1960's. How people perceive their positions in the homeland, in terms of residence and standard of living, is one dimension of the context in which migration takes place. Integrally connected with this is a second dimension, the structure of social ordering.

SOCIAL DIFFERENTIATION

The local Michaelense categorization of rural *povo*, contrasted with the better educated of the towns, simplifies a more complex system of social stratification. There are six distinct social categories. I have used the local Azorean terms for four of the categories *trabalhadores, proprietários, novos ricos, and nobreza.* For the urban educated, sometimes referred to as the *classe média* (middle class), I have substituted two terms, *proprietário* educated and established educated, which distinguish between differences in recent social background. This classification into six categories is more complex than the traditional terminology which delineated three levels of society, the *nobreza* (the nobility), the *clero* (the clergy), and the *povo* (the people), and leaves out the middle levels even though it is clear from historical accounts that they existed when the islands were settled (Da Costa 1978). The six categories used here are distinguished by characteristics of stratification including life style, capacity to claim deference, capacity to initiate action, and access to strategic resources (Silverman 1970:212). I suggest that people differing in these characteristics have varying perceptions of opportunities and different values which shape their choices about migration.

People on the island use the concept of level, *nivel,* to indicate social status. Level often refers to social equivalence, i.e., someone is of 'our level', *nossa nivel,* emphasizing the horizontal aspects of social linkages. At the same time, since there is more than one recognized social level the term is used to describe what is basically a class stratified system. Characteristics of the social levels outlined in this section provide the underlying structures for a complex web of both horizontal and vertical social interactions in São Miguel.

Trabalhadores (The Workers)

In São Miguel almost 50% of the working population are manual laborers, *trabalhadores* . Since the 1950's *trabalhadores* have been the major portion of emigrants, and this has contributed to a decline in the primary sector of the active work force as shown in Table 3.8.[4]

Trabalhadores are workers whose rough hands and strong weather-beaten bodies keep the land and sea producing. They work for the small, independent landowners, the *proprietários*, and for the large aristocratic, landowners of the *nobreza.* They also work for themselves, raising what their families need. The land in São Miguel is rich volcanic earth, but it is the *trabalhadores* who make it bear fruit.

Trabalhadores live in the villages for the most part, going out to the surrounding fields and pastures by way of footpaths and dirt roads. Houses in these communities cluster along the main road, and are set close to the street. The Church and small stores form centers in the communities, with the small one story houses of the *trabalhadores* spreading out along the side roads. Furthest from the center, down by the sea, or up on the hillsides, are the poorest cottages.

The *trabalhadores* are *agricultores* who own or rent a small amount of cultivated land and work for someone else as well. They are the *camponês* who work for wages on the land; the *lavradores* who raise cattle as well as crops; the *pescadores* who fish for a living; and a few hundred of them are the laborers who work in towns on construction sites and in factories. The majority (96%) work with agriculture, and except for those who live in towns, they all raise at least their own subsistence crops,

Table 3.8. Percent of Active Working Population, by
Sector of Activity, for District of Ponta Delgada

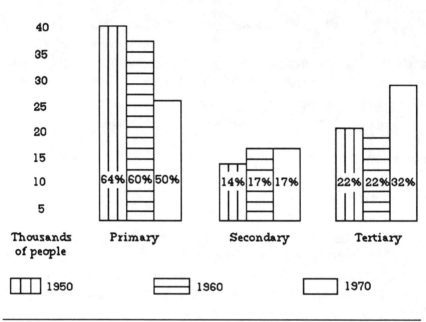

(Source: Medeiros 1977) [5]

even if they must rent the land to do so. The
trabalhadores are the salaried workers who form the
major portion of the agricultural work force as shown in
Table 3.9. Wages for *trabalhadors* have risen since 1960,
but they are still substantially less than those of other types
of employees (see Table 3.10) and less than those of
similar workers in continental Portugal.

Although wages have risen rapidly, and employers
complain about paying double the salary they paid five
years earlier (Table 3.11.), rises in the cost of living offset
some of the gains. In 1976, for example, the cost of living
rose 21% (DREPA 1977).

Table 3.9. Agricultural Work Force

Percent by Position	Ponta Delgada		Azores Total
	1960	1970	1977
Employers	3	.5*	1.4
Self-Employed	13	25.4	36.8
Salaried Workers	79	68.5	52.3
Family Members	5	5.6	9.5

* This does not include proprietários who hire seasonal or part- time
  workers.

(Sources: I.N.E 1965; Um Grupo ... 1977)

Table 3.10. Average Monthly Wages, Ponta Delgada

Occupation		Average Monthly Wage	
	1976	(escudos)	(U.S. $ equivalent)
Agricultural Labor		4000$00	$100.00
Cattle Herding		5200$00	$130.00
Construction and Public Works		5200$00	$130.00
Painters and Plumbers		5600$00	$140.00
Electricians		7000$00	$175.00
Office Workers, Clerks, Schoolteachers		4600$00-9200$00	$120-230.00
Professionals		10000$00-20000$00+	$250-500.00+

(Source: DREPA 1977)

Table 3.11. Daily Wages for Manual Laborers for the District
of Ponta Delgada, compared to Continental
Portugal, 1969-1977

| | Ponta Delgada | | Continental Portugal | | |
| | | | Under 15 Yrs. | | |
Year	Male	Female	Male	Female	Male
1969	38$00				84$00
1972	47$00				84¢00
1973	68$00				95$00
1974	88$00				126$00
1975	107$00				156$00
1976	125$00	65$00	74$00	40$00	179$00
1977	150$00*				

*U. S. equivalent, $3.75/day

(Source: I.N.E. 1977)

Among the *trabalhadores* are the very poorest of
society, and the least literate. In 1950 close to 50% of the
population of São Miguel was illiterate, and the highest
proportion of these was from the *trabalhador* sector
where even today some adults are functionally illiterate.[6]
Since the 1950's primary education has been compulsory
and virtually all young people are literate.[7] *Trabalhador*
families vary in their concern for children getting an
education, and there is only 70% attendance at the
primary level (DREPA 1977). Schoolteachers in the rural
areas complain that *trabalhador* families frequently take
their children out of school and put them to work in the
fields. This is illegal but there are few controls. There are
always ways to get around the regulations, e.g., not paying
certain fees, which means that a child cannot attend
school. Many families see little value in education for
their own children, complaining that when school starts it
is difficult to get work done without children at home to

care for the younger ones, run errands, and do chores. It is among the poorer *trabalhadores* that large families of over eight children are still found, although many couples now limit family size.

Proprietários (The Property Owners)

If villagers are asked, 'Who are the most respected people?', 'Who would people go to for advice', or 'Who are the wealthiest people?' a clear category of people emerges. The 'important' people are the *proprietários*, the people of property. *Proprietários* live off their own property without having to work for someone else. In the towns they are the small- scale entrepreneurs, who might own and operate a bar, a produce stand, or other small businesses. In the countryside they are the ones who own stores, or bars, run the milk collection station, or manage their own property, making a profit from cash crops in addition to raising their own food. In some communities, as shown in Table 3.12, *proprietários* make up almost one third of the residents and many of them are people who have emigrated or are already past sixty years of age. The proportions vary throughout the island and there are fewer *proprietários* and more *trabalhadores* in some communities, particularly where the land is still owned by a small number of large landowners.[8]

Most *proprietários* have at least a primary education, although some of the older ones are illiterate. In many *proprietário* families there is a diverse combination of education and occupation levels. For example, an illiterate father may have one son who teaches school in Lisbon,

Table 3.12. Total Household Heads by Occupation
Category, Village A, 1978

	Proprietários	Professionals	Skilled	Trabalhadores
60 years +	29 (67%)			
Under 60	14 (33%)			
Emigrated & Returned	4 (33%)			
TOTAL	43 (30%)	3 (2%)	4 (3%)	94 (65%)

N = 144

another who works in a factory in Boston, a daughter who works in a town, and a son who works with him on the land. The *proprietários*, more than the *trabalhadores*, consequently have ties to many spheres, internal and external.

The *proprietários* are distinguished from the *trabalhadores* by the greater amount of land owned (2-10 ha.), their role as employers and landlords, their level of education, and the less tangible quality of being from 'good' families. *Proprietários* are central to the rural social webs; their stores and houses are where people come to hear the news or sit and talk in the evening. They are the local level patrons, part of the 'family' of the community, but also the respected ones to whom people go for loans, jobs, information, and daily problem- solving. Additionally, they are the ones who are the most active in local political and church organizations; they are the town councilmen, and the organizers of *festas* who work with the village priest and sometimes with regional officials.[9]

Proprietário Educated

The children of *proprietários* who obtain higher education move into a different status level from their parents in the village. Some of the 'proprietários educated' are skilled workers, trained as mechanics, carpenters, plumbers, and electricians at the local technical school. They form the major portion of the 17% of the population employed in skilled, blue collar type occupations. This subcategory is referred to in subsequent pages as the skilled or urban sector. Others have received a high school degree and work as clerks, in offices, and as entrepreneurs. Other 'proprietários educated' have gone to universities and have careers in various levels of business, industry, and government. These better educated *proprietários* are generally referred to here as part of the urban educated. They aspire more to the social patterns of the established educated than do the skilled who often have stronger social ties to *proprietários* and *trabalhadores.*

The 'proprietários educated' have a higher level of education than their rural families and usually adopt an urban lifestyle. They aspire to a 'modern' life, with the outward signs of prosperity, a car, and a well furnished house, with all the appliances. Many of the younger 'proprietários educated' women work at office jobs, and with both parents working, couples frequently limit family size to one or two children. There is a wide range of income levels among the 'proprietários educated', but they are typified by a middle level status and the fact that they are still connected to their rural and unskilled roots.

Established Educated

The 'established educated' are the people from long established professional and commercial families which, along with the *nobreza* families, have traditionally controlled the island. They are the owners of large businesses, doctors, lawyers, and government officials. They are differentiated from the 'proprietários educated' by their long heritage of urban professional life, and are only connected to the rural areas as owners of summer houses. A tradition of association with the *nobreza* has led to some intermarriage between these levels. Furthermore, the 'established educated', through familial and commercial ties, are more closely connected to the mainland than the 'proprietários educated.'

Novos Ricos (The Newly Rich)

The *novos ricos* are an elite who have obtained status through newly acquired wealth, and not by virtue of birth. These families made money in commercial and industrial businesses within the last two generations. Some came from the ranks of the educated, and some from the rural *proprietários*. Their offspring are well educated professionals, but lack the cultural background of the established educated or the *nobreza*. Frequently they still have rural ties to family who were less fortunate in their enterprises. Some of these *novo ricos* families have established alliances with the traditional elite, through marriage and financial arrangements, but wealth is not a substitute for the inbred family connections of the traditional elite.

Nobreza (The Nobility)

The *nobreza* (nobility) are the traditional elite whose ancestors colonized the islands. Names from that period are still carried by the half dozen families who, intermarried for generations, have retained control over many of the island resources. They are the aristocrats of the island, the ones who traditionally controlled the land, the professions, and the politics. Many are still dominant in these spheres.

Some foreign families (i.e., British and American residents in the nineteenth century) and some of the established educated have been incorporated into the group by marriage. Children go to the mainland to study and some marry there, thus reinforcing strong mainland ties. The *nobreza* are not a completely exclusive group, but define their position in exclusive terms, based on a heritage where landholdings have been in the same families for almost five centuries and the family homes may easily be two hundred years old.

Social Interaction: Family, Community and Colleagues

São Miguel is a socially stratified society where economics and sociocultural aspects of status are interwoven but not coterminous. The stratified nature of status levels pervades virtually all aspects of the society, from etiquette on the street to choosing marriage partners.

The distinction has frequently been made between horizontal and vertical ties in stratified societies, and the emphasis is often on vertical ties such as patron-client relationships (Gilsenan 1977). In São Miguel patron-client ties, associated with a feudal tradition of elite-peasant relationships, are of decreasing importance for sheer survival. The pivotal ties within the society are based on horizontal 'informal structures'.10 This does not mean that two people interacting are exactly equal in status, but ties are referred to in equalizing terms. Variations in types of social interactions among the previously defined social groups will be discussed briefly here with respect to family, community, and colleague relationships.

As in other European societies, in São Miguel familial ties underlie the primary social relationships. The pattern is most distinctive for the *nobreza* and the established educated, who have maintained strong networks of immediate and extended kin which structure interactions. Socializing is primarily with immediate family and cousins, and marriage often stays within the circle of extended cousins. In business and professional enterprises kin ties are activated frequently.

For the urban *proprietários* and *novos ricos* the family is also the center of social interactions, but with part of the family in the country there are fewer instrumental kin ties. The Michaelense describe themselves as 'closed' and 'very close to the family'. Non-family are not readily invited into the home. However, the newly educated town residents who have emigrant relatives often find that when these family members come to visit they are less restrained about interacting with outsiders and even bring them into the home.

Among the *proprietários* and *trabalhadores*, in the villages the inbreeding which reinforces exclusiveness among the elite, fosters an ideology of shared status or relative equality in the idea that they are all part of 'one family'. Even in the larger villages real and fictive kinship ties connect a large portion of the residents within the community and between neighboring communities.[11]

Community and neighborhood ties overlap with family ties among the *trabalhadores* and *proprietários*. Even *trabalhadores* in the city interact closely with their neighbors. This is not the case for the town-dwelling better- educated and elite. These people may know every move their neighbors make and yet rarely have direct social contact with them. The fact that 'everyone knows everyone' among the educated and elite does not mean that they interact beyond formal greetings.

In rural communities and town neighborhoods there are invariably several locations such as the shoemaker's, the dressmaker's, a small store or bar, which are the focal points of social interactions for small groups of *proprietários* and *trabalhadores*. People gather to talk about the latest news, a recent event, or a letter from America. In towns the educated men go to cafes to meet over coffee and brandy, and women talk to acquaintances they encounter while out doing errands. This urban interaction is more selective and the intensity of contact with non-family is less than in the rural areas, where residents may even define a whole community as 'all family'.

The Catholic Church also plays a role in community solidarity, throughout the year organizing *festas* which unite the community in celebration and in support of the Church. Although more dominant in the rural areas, these *festas* are a time for freer social contact among youth in both town and country, a time when courtship blossoms. The elite and educated only participate extensively in the main *festas* of Ponta Delgada, but they do make donations for smaller *festas* in the rural areas where they have land or families.

In high school and post-secondary education institutions, higher education colleague ties are established which cross-cut social levels and provide horizontal linkages. Students who want higher education attend the one high school which provides that training, in Ponta Delgada. Students of various backgrounds interact intensively over a period of five years in a small group (less than 200 per class). They share a common store of knowledge about each other and though they go their separate ways, they share in common the status of 'educated', which sets them off from the *proprietários* and *trabalhadores.*

The strength of these contacts established in school can be seen in the case of one young woman who, upon returning after five years in America, consciously revived old school contacts whenever she saw former colleagues; within a matter of a few months she had reestablished an impressive network of acquaintances. Such contacts are essential in a society where the reinforcement of personal ties permeates every activity. It is said, for example, that 'without godparents there is no baptism', meaning that the personal tie is what gives substance to the action. It is also said that the only way to get things done is *'boca a boca'* (literally 'mouth to mouth') or in person.

Social mixing in the high school milieu creates important contacts that are utilized from then on as 'horizontal', if not exactly equal, associates. Social distinctions are less obvious with the veneer of modern dress, and the 'pop' culture of cars, movies, and the newest music from America and Europe. An elite boy may date a girl whose father is a plumber or a girl whose grandfather worked on his grandfather's land. Such unions rarely, however, lead to marriage. The recognition of differences and incompatibilities works both ways, as in the case of a skilled worker's wife who beat her high school age daughter for going out with a rich man's son. She thought it could only lead to disgrace; he would never marry the girl but might corrupt her virtue and ruin her reputation. The educational context thus creates horizontal ties cross-cutting social backgrounds; but these have not yet changed social categories.

Vacation areas are rising in popularity and provide a setting where colleague ties may overlap with social ties and where a new pattern of mixing with emigrants has developed recently. Since the early 1970's the once exclusive domains of the elite and foreign visitors have been encroached upon internally by the urban educated and externally by visiting emigrants seeking a summer retreat. The main resort on São Miguel is a village with hot mineral springs the medicinal waters of which drew foreign tourists as early as the beginning of the nineteenth century. The main attractions now are an elegant hotel where people sit drinking coffee on the veranda, a weekend nightclub, a hot springs pool, a nearby beach, and of course the people themselves. Parents keep to their own social groups, but the youth who come to spend the summer mix freely, reaffirming high school bonds and establishing new ties with visiting emigrant youth who bring with them the latest styles and mannerisms from America.

Status, Mobility, and Flexibility

The criteria for status in São Miguel include birth, education, property, and the intangible quality of moral and cultural 'good' which is separate from but can be associated with heredity.[12] Among the *nobreza*, education is important but the essential 'good' accrues to their descent; they carry the history of their lineages into the present with them. Among the educated status is associated with education and morality. Among the rural workers it is associated with productivity and morality. This difference in criteria is associated with different orientations toward social mobility; the elite and established educated see education as merely a confirmation of their status; the workers are oriented towards mobility through making money; and in between, the newly educated *proprietários* are concerned with attaining the visible signs of wealth to support their achieved status. Social mobility involves a number of types of movement within a society (Leeds 1965:388). The difference here is one that correlates largely with town and country distinctions, and is similar to what Pitt-Rivers (1960:225) characterized for a French village as 'two systems of social class' based on national versus local orientation. In the rural communities of São Miguel, the local orientation recognizes status through hard work and acquiring property, whereas in the towns there is a national orientation toward education as conferring status, and goods as a secondary support for that position, not the basis of it.

The social categories remain relatively permanent positions in the hierarchy in São Miguel, but the divisions are permeable to families and individuals through a process of gradual incorporation long established in social history. A person can move up into a higher status, i.e., through marriage, education, or acquiring property, but unless he can cultivate the relationships appropriate to that level he remains in a parallel but not equivalent position. For example, the primary criticism made of visiting emigrants is that they unsuccessfully imitate a higher status than they were born into. As one local saying puts it, 'You can see right away, who is, is', meaning that status is something inherent, something you have but cannot buy. However, children of returning emigrants, brought up in an educated status, do move up socially. This is similar to the process described in discussing emigrants returning from Brazil to Portugal in the 1930's, it was said that only after two or three generations did the family's social status really change (Monteiro 1944:47-48). The system in São Miguel has the flexibility over time to incorporate families at higher levels, changing the proportions of people in different social levels, without radically changing the hierarchical categories themselves.

LIVELIHOOD

The economic activities of the Azores are primarily associated with agricultural production. In 1965 the District of Ponta Delgada used 50% of the agricultural land for seasonal crops (e.g. corn, sugar beets, beans, etc), 9% for permanent crops, and 41% for permanent pasture. Since that time the amount of land in pasture has been expanded through the conversion of fields and the clearing of brush land to accommodate the growing dairy industry.

In the 1970's the government implemented a program to build roads to make crop land and potential pasture land more accessible. Improved access will facilitate mechanization of agriculture and the transport of crops, much of which is still done by hand and burros, horses or oxen. In São Miguel, with an average one tractor for each 98 hectares of agricultural land, there is more mechanization than on the other islands. The use of tractors, bulldozers, and trucks has increased steadily since the reduction in manpower in the last twenty years of emigration. For the smaller landholders, mechanization in many areas is limited not only by cost but by the lack of access, steep terrain and small, scattered landholdings. Pollnac and Carmo (1979) reported that in a sample of forty-five farmers in one of the flatter areas of the island, only 14% used any kind of mechanized equipment.

Most industry in the Azores is undertaken by artisans and 78% of the industries employ no more than four people. São Miguel is the most industrialized of the islands and 78% of the industrial energy used in the Azores is consumed in São Miguel. In 1973 industries in São Miguel employed about 11% of the island's active work force. The major portion of industry is located near the city of Ponta Delgada and in the central region of the island. The largest industries, which comprise over 50% of the total industrial production earnings, are in the areas of food production such as milk powder, butter, cheese, canned fish and meat, canned fruit, biscuits and vegetable oils; drinks such as beer, wine, liqueurs, tea, soft drinks, and fruit juices; and tobacco for the manufacture of cigarettes. Other products include wood; construction materials such as cinder blocks, pipes, and plaster; alcohol; soap; animal feed; ceramics; and linen (production stopped in 1978).

Most Azorean trade is with continental Portugal. In 1973 76% of the total imports were from the mainland and 88% of the Azorean exports were to the mainland. The remaining trade is primarily with the U.S., Britain, Italy, Canada, and France. Imports include gasoline, fertilizer, cement, machinery and electrical equipment, chemicals, corn, and food products. The main exports are milk products, cattle, wood, chicory, pineapple, and canned fish. In the late 1970's the regional government was actively exploring possibilities for expanding trade with other countries.

Land

Historically, agriculture has been the 'font of wealth' for the island. São Miguel, known as the *ilha verde* (the green island), has been in prosperous times a rich source of food for both the other islands and mainland Portugal. Land ownership is consequently a primary element in social differentiation. The present pattern of land distribution, shown in Table 3.13, arises from a history in which the noble families who were first granted rights over the land in the fifteenth and sixteenth centuries retained ownership, passing it on through an inheritance system of entailed estates and primogeniture. Large portions of land are at present still under the control of these families, as seen in the example of one family of four separate households who together own approximately one quarter of the total land in São Miguel.

Table 3.13. Landholdings, by Area, in São Miguel, 1965

	0-3 ha.	3-5 ha.	5-10 ha.	+10 ha.	Total
Percent of Holdings	88.3	6.0	3.6	2.1	100
Number of Holdings	15,443	1,046	630	375	17,494

(Source: I.N.E. Agricola 1965)

Equal inheritance, established in the late nineteenth century, has led to the breakup of some of the larger estates. Absentee landlords and professionals with little time to oversee the workers, began to sell off their holdings. Emigration further contributed to this process by reducing the available labor force and creating problems of production in the late 1950's and the early 1960's. A decline of 16% in the total active labor force between 1960 and 1970 compounded an earlier drop in the 1950's. Large landowners reduced their production of labor intensive crops during that period, and pasturage and cattle production increased (Table 3.14).[13] The demand for milk and meat products in mainland Portugal rose in the 1970's, partly due to disruptions in the Portuguese African colonies which reduced imports from these regions. By 1974, 90% of the milk produced in the Azores was used for industrial products such as powdered milk, cheese, and butter.

The gradual breakup of some of the larger landholdings increased the opportunities for *proprietários* to enlarge their properties. One of the traditional ways to acquire land is through working as an

Table 3.14. Cattle Production 1940-1976, Azores

Year	Number of Cattle
1940	112,697
1959	138,709
1965	147,904
1972	178,229
1976	211,100

(Source : DREPA 1977)

overseer, *feitor*, for a large landowner. The *feitor* is a 'trusted worker', who manages the other employees in return for a variety of favors from the landowners and sometimes a higher wage. One kind of favor is to sell the *feitor* land at an affordable price. Other small landowners often increase their holdings through emigration and return (see Table 3.12), or through buying land with loans from emigrant relatives.

People now complain that there is land for sale, but that only the emigrant *proprietários* and the wealthy elite are able to afford it. For an agricultural worker who earns little more than the equivalent of $100.00 a month, land that costs the equivalent of $200 to $1000 for one third of an acre (one *alqueire* or one seventh of an hectare) is not within reach. Houses in the rural areas are also difficult to arrange, not only because of prices but because emigrants seldom rent or sell their houses when they leave, preferring to leave the houses shut up in case they have future need of them.

There are basically two forms of access to property,

one is ownership, the other is rental. In 1965 the importance of rental property for agriculturalists in São Miguel could be seen in the fact that 63% of all landholdings were rented out, 36% were being worked by owners, and there was a fraction with workers in sharecroping (I.N.E. 1965). These figures are indicative of the high proportion of landless agricultural workers in São Miguel.

In any community, only part of the land is owned by local residents. Some is owned by people in neighboring communities since landholdings are often widely dispersed, and intermarriage between communities facilitates the dispersal process. More significantly, land is owned by urban residents and emigrants. The urban owners are primarily *nobreza*, and the emigrant owners are almost always former residents. In one sample community, for example, only half of the land was owned locally in 1968. 15% was owned by emigrants in America, over one quarter was owned by urban residents, and the remainder was owned by people in neighboring communities (Table 3.15 and Table 3.16).

Multibase Production

One of the basic principles of agricultural production and business enterprises in general in São Miguel, is 'Do not put all your eggs in one basket'. At all levels of society, this principle is seen in the way people diversify their investments, minimize their risks, and ensure a minimal subsistence. The pervasiveness of the pattern is seen in village production, in the 'penny capitalism' of small shops

Table 3.15 Village A Landholdings by Residence of Owner, 1968

Residence of Owners

	Number of Owners	Percent of Total	Hectares of Land	Percent of Total Village Land
Village A	132	64.7%	131.196	52.1%
Village A Emigrants	45	22.0%	37.441	14.9%
Other-S. Miguel Total	27	13.2%	82.958	33.0%
·Adjoining Freguesias	16	7.8%	19.351	7.7%
·Urban Freguesias	11	5.4%	63.606	25.3%
TOTAL	204	100.0%	251.596	100.0%

(Source: District Land Records Offices and Survey Data)

Table 3.16 Village A Emigrant Landownings by Residence, 1968

Emigrant Residence	Number of Owners	Percent Emigrant Owners	Hectares of Land	Average Productive Land per Owner	Percent Emigrant Land	Percent Village Land
U.S.	25	55.5%	14.180	.5924	39.6%	5.9%
Canada	14	31.2%	16.615	.8740	43.4%	6.6%
Bermuda	6	13.3%	6.6016	.9966	16.8%	2.4%
TOTAL	45	100.0%	37.441		100.0%	14.9%

(Source: District Land Records Offices and Survey Data)

in towns, and in the investment practices of the elite who own property not located on the island.

The pattern is also seen in the diversification of occupations within families. This reflects the traditional elite system of primogeniture where non-inheriting siblings were encouraged to diversify and go into other careers.   In São Miguel this pattern resulted in the dominance of the elite not only as landowners but as professionals who ran the commercial, military, Church, and political business of the island.   The inheritance system has changed but the pattern has remained among the elite and also among the small landowners who now have the problem of avoiding land fragmentation in a system of equal inheritance.

Among the *trabalhadores* the multibase orientation in production utilizes the manpower of the entire domestic group.   Income and food are produced from a variety of sources and all active members of the family participate, whether they are ten year old girls looking after younger children or eighty year old grandfathers tying up the corn to dry.   Crops are diversified, some are for subsistence, some for sale.   Most people have non-contiguous landholdings.   This is essential in order to have land appropriate to a variety of crops, including corn, grapes, fruit, vegetables, and land for wood. Landholdings are dispersed and often in small pieces.   There is an acute awareness of who owns what and there is a strong sense of private property.   The land produces the basic subsistence and a variety of other activities contribute to the family income.   Produce is sold in town, boys hire themselves out for wage labor, and women sell handiwork.

The system includes a network of reciprocity which distributes surpluses of perishable crops among kin and neighbors.   Reciprocal networks are also utilized in labor exchange where neighbors and families assist each other in agricultural tasks done near the house. Evenings spent tying together bundles of corn to dry, for example, become social events. More widespread reciprocal labor networks have died out as the labor force has been diminished and wage labor has become the standard, but older villagers still recall the important social role these labor exchanges played in past decades.

Proprietários also follow the multibase pattern. For them the diversification is less limited to the villages. It often extends to town markets and they even own shops and bars in towns where their produce and wine is sold. In such instances it is common to find one sibling working at the town enterprise and another one managing the land. For both *proprietários* and *trabalhadores* the multibase pattern leads to intensive utilization of family and community ties, and ensures that basic needs will be met.

Division of Labor

Within the rural domestic group both men and women perform a wide variety of tasks, together and separately. Men do the major portion of labor in the fields. They leave early to work on their own properties or to hire themselves out and spend much of the day away from the house. Women participate in harvesting the crops and do a great deal of the preparation of crops for storage. In the past women worked in the fields for wages and as sharecroppers for the *nobreza.* This kind of work is now considered undesirable and they only hire themselves out for brief seasonal jobs such as picking and sorting grapes. Women earn half the wages of men for these tasks and their labor is consequently in high demand at harvest time.

The only other ways that women have access to cash income in the rural areas is through selling crocheted and embroidered items, working as seamstresses, or if they are very fortunate finding a job in a factory within commuting distance when they are not needed at home (a rare combination). Some women do work as maids in the towns, but this kind of work is associated with being servants in *nobreza* households and, except for in the very poorest segments of society, women do not want to be servants. Within the home most household activities are the exclusive realm of the females. Time-consuming chores involving relentless cleaning, mending, cooking, and laundry, are things which the males do not engage in. The preparation of wild game or fish is the only task that the men do in the kitchen.

Only 10% of the active work force in 1977 was female (see Table 3.17).[14] The majority of these employed women are from the *proprietários* and established educated sectors and work as professionals and office workers in the urban areas or as schoolteachers and clerks in the rural communities. In the villages women point out that their work 'is never done'; the men come home to sit and talk and the women continue their labors. This is the informal unpaid labor of the household and these women do not show up in the official figures.

Social Status of Work Positions

In the last twenty years agricultural work has become increasingly devalued among the youth of the villages and positions in the urban sphere are much sought after. For the *trabalhador*, agricultural work is associated with past

Table 3.17. Percent of Males and Females in the Work
            Force, Azores, 1977

Sector	% Males	% Females
Primary	99.3	.7
Secondary	84.0	16.0
Tertiary	77.2	22.8
Total	89.4	10.6

(Source: DREPA 1977)

days when almost everyone worked for large landowners. It is now maligned as being dirty and low paying. Those without land of their own often look for jobs in the small factories of the island where the work is 'cleaner' and the wages higher. However, if they move to town the cost of living is higher without the subsistence base of rural life. *Trabalhador* women are interested in opportunities to work that are 'clean', but not in jobs that they associate with loss of status, such as housework.

The *proprietários*, who work for themselves, are less critical of agricultural work, stressing instead the independence of 'being your own boss'. The women in these families are often engaged in the business, e. g., minding the village store, or keeping accounts, as well as their daily chores, and are therefore less interested in work outside the house. Among the *proprietários* the path away from agricultural work is through higher education. Some become skilled workers and others obtain university degrees, both of these routes taking them into the urban job market. The urban jobs are not universally acclaimed, as the *trabalhadores* would believe. Skilled workers complain that many jobs provide little opportunity to get ahead. "I can work ten hours a day and still never get out of the hole...." is a sentiment frequently voiced, in this case by a taxi driver. Nonetheless, the skilled and higher educated who come from rural backgrounds do have higher status in their urban jobs compared to manual labor in the rural areas and in that sense they are already 'ahead'. According to the norms of society educated persons should not work with their hands like 'peasants' and urban jobs offer an alternative.

The dimensions of the sociocultural matrix which have been outlined in this chapter shape the types of opportunities perceived and the ways in which individuals evaluate their options. Perceptions of available opportunities depend largely on the distribution of access to strategic resources (such as land, education, and employment), and the pervasive pattern of multibase production. The elite of São Miguel have access to many resources while the *trabalhadores* are very limited in opportunities open to them.

Opportunities are evaluated through normative structures which also vary between social groups. Values associated with the town and country differences in modernization, with the strength of horizontal ties, and with the status of work and its potential for socioeconomic mobility, all affect the way individuals perceive specific options. A *trabalhador* who sees the socioeconomic mobility as possible through 'modern' manual labor has quite a different view from a 'proprietário educated' who sees success as getting away from manual labor.

The description in this chapter has been purposely wide in scope to present a broad picture of the context in which migration now takes place in São Miguel; it is not a total picture of Michaelense society. The dimensions discussed indicate that the context for people of varying social levels and areas of residence differs within the society. Furthermore, the context of migration has changed over the past two decades. São Miguel is a small territory but has a complex social system. The next two chapters will examine how migration since 1960 has affected the context of migration decision-making through flows of people and communications.

CHAPTER 4
THE EMIGRANTS: 'THEY CAN SEE THE OCEAN AND THEY WANT TO GO'

Since 1960 migration flows have had crucial effects on the present context of migration decision-making in São Miguel. Chapters Four and Five will examine how general dimensions of the home system matrix have been affected by these flows. Flows reinforced some aspects of informal structures and have also contributed to the flexibility that exists within the present stratified social system. These two chapters establish the general context of ongoing migration in São Miguel. Chapter Six will discuss the ways in which specific factors in the home system affect the migration decision-making process for individuals.

Most cases of voluntary migration involve movement back and forth between the home and adoptive areas. One of the migration 'laws' first proposed by Ravenstein (1885) is that for every main migration stream (movement of people) a counterstream develops. Expanding this concept, the term 'flows' is used here not only for people but goods, money and information that move between São Miguel and adoptive systems in association with migration (Table 4.1). In this chapter and the next information on flows (including counterflows) is examined to illustrate how these phenomena affect the sociocultural context of subsequent migration decision-making.

Table 4.1 Migration Associated Flows between S. Miguel
           and North America

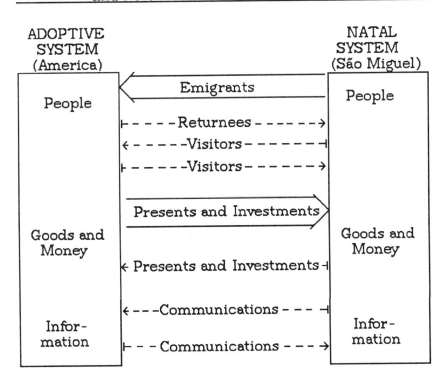

The changing nature of flows between the home and adoptive areas as migration proceeds results in a feedback system of interactions which contributes to a process of adaptation in the home society. In utilizing a decision-making approach to migration it is crucial to examine how links between home and destination area are established and maintained in association with previous migration and how these links alter the context of subsequent migration. At the level of individual decision-making the balance of constraints and incentives is continually changing, depending in part on a person's contacts with the destination area (DuToit 1975:66). At a broader level of analysis an ecological model of migration, such as that which Lomnitz (1976) employs, incorporates the idea of feedback in a consideration of the societal context. Lomnitz points out that the migration process affects the sending region not only by reducing the number of inhabitants, but by altering the 'imbalance' from which the process arises. In some cases information sent home by migrants may encourage further migration. On the other hand, new economic resources channeled home by migrants may stabilize the 'imbalance' for a while. Thus not only the people in the process of migration, but also the nature of what goes back and forth, provides a key to understanding the effects of migration on the 'donor' society (Lomnitz 1976:135).

The depletion of inhabitants through migration from São Miguel affects both the demographic and social structures and the informational context of subsequent migration decision-making. The effects of flows on the migration context in São Miguel will be considered in this chapter in terms of overall demographic alterations; personal contacts with America; and perceptions of demographic alterations. The first two directly affect structural characteristics of the home context; the population is now older and smaller than it was in 1960. At the individual level the overall demographic impact is translated into structural alterations in internal and external webs of relationships. Structural alterations affect both individual circumstances such as the presence of family in America, and information such as what people know about America.

The content of flows and how they articulate with the home society is influenced by dimensions of social stratification and horizontal ties in the home social system. Internal ties with the family and community and external ties to America are differentially affected by flows depending on an individual's social level. People of differing social levels in São Miguel have different degrees of contact with emigrants. Interviewing people in the home society revealed that contact differs with respect to the types of informal interaction with emigrants, the social context of that interaction, and the type of relationships people may have with emigrants in America, as illustrated in Table 4.2. Differential contact with emigrants in the homeland affects variation in perceptions of America, reinforcing both differences between social levels and patterns of flexibility in migration behavior.

The differences in contacts with emigrants according to social levels can be conceptualized in terms of multiplex and single strand relationships which Boissevain (1974:32) suggests are characterized, respectively, by more and less intimate relationships. In São Miguel the urban educated tend to have single strand, limited ties with emigrants, through one or two specific relationships such as a former employee, a colleague, or a distant relative. By contrast, in the rural areas, ties with emigrants tend to be multiplex in Gluckman's (1955:18-19) sense of serving many interests. The broad base of relationships in the villages is reflected in the nature of ties to emigrants; people are linked to their own emigrant kin and also to the kin of other community members, sharing the news and visits throughout the community. This fosters a more generalized pattern of contacts in rural areas than among the urban educated.

Table 4.2   Relative Degree and Type of Contact with Emigrants by Social Categories

Social Category:	Trab.	Prop.	PE	EE	NRico	Patrão
Locus of Contact:						
I. In São Miguel						
Informal Structures						
Family	++	++	++	+/-	+	-
Neighbors	++	+	-	-	-	-
Fictive Kin	++	++	+	+/-	+	+
Patron-Client	-	+	+/-	+/-	+/-	+
Colleagues	-	-	+	-	+	-
Social Contexts						
Household	++	++	+	-	+/-	-
Neighborhood	++	+	-	-	-	-
Local Festas	++	++	+	-	+/-	-
Public hotels, bars, etc.	-	-	+	+	+	+
II. In America						
Visits	-	+	+	+/-	+	+/-
Business	-	-	+/-	+/-	+/-	+/-
Sport groups	+/-	+	+	+/-	-	-
Bands	+	+	+/-	-	-	-

++ = high frequency of contact
+ = moderate frequency of contact
+/- = varying degrees of contact
- = minimal contact

Trab.= Trabalhador
Prop.= Proprietário
PE= Proprietário Educated
EE= Established Educated
NRico= Novos Ricos

A second feature of this difference among social levels is that contacts in the rural areas are generally along horizontal ties, whereas in the urban areas among the upper social levels the ties are frequently vertical, as in the case of emigrants who keep in touch with the former employer, the *patrão.*

Over the last twenty years the flows of people between São Miguel and America can be divided up into movements of 1) emigrants, 2) returnees, and 3) visitors. The first part of the chapter will examine these flows and the second part will look briefly at formalized flows such as visitors under the auspices of the Church or special interest groups. In São Miguel the basic flow of people (the migrant stream and counterstream) is supplemented by other flows such as information, goods, and money, associated with the human ties between home and adoptive areas. These latter flows will be considered in the next chapter.

OS EMBARCADOS: 'THOSE WHO GET ON BOARD'

As illustrated in Chapter Two, in the past the flow of emigrants out of São Miguel was an important variable in the development of the island. Curtailed by restrictive U.S. immigration policy for forty years, emigration to America reemerged as an influential variable in the island system in the late 1950's when Canada recruited immigrants to provide manpower for agricultural and industrial development. Since that time emigration has contributed to a significant decline in the island population, with emigrants going to the U.S. as well since the mid 1960's.

This section will examine Michaelense perceptions of past and present trends in migration; legal policies structuring migration; and demographic and social characteristics of migrant flows since 1960.

Views of Migration: Everyone but the Old and Sick?

The views of migration perpetuated in the homeland do not always correspond accurately to the reality, but they do reflect one basic effect that migrant flows have had on the attitudinal context of subsequent migration. Between 1960 and 1974 the population of São Miguel declined by 20%, from 168,687 to 135,504, primarily as a result of emigration.   The official view of this decline is that emigration has taken, and continues to take, the young and healthy, leaving the old and less productive behind.1 A joke that circulated in Azorean-American communities in the late 1970's and even appeared in one of the newspapers (Azorean Times 1980a:17), expresses the widely held view in São Miguel and the Azorean-American communities that every person who can emigrate does so:

> Suppose you were in the Azores and the government announced that all the Portuguese who wanted to were free to leave the country and go to the United States.   What would you do?- - - I would climb a tree.   Climb a tree! Why?- - - To avoid being trampled on by all the people rushing to leave!   (My translation)

The relative attractiveness of emigration is not as simple

as jokes like this suggest. Not everyone who can, leaves, and it is not only those driven by poverty who emigrate; less than 50% of the emigrants active in the labor force were engaged in manual labor in 1975. Views to the contrary are in part vestiges of earlier patterns of migration in the early 1900's and even as late as the 1950's when the poverty at home was more intense. At a more general level, views of migration as an exodus reflect the magnitude of emigration and the loss of people that is felt throughout society.

When the question, "Do you think that everyone who has the possibility of emigrating really does so?", was put to a sample of adult rural residents in São Miguel, over 80% answered in the affirmative.[2] People attribute a universal desire to emigrate to others, but this is contradicted by their own migration behavior. Further questioning revealed that of those respondents answering in the affirmative, almost 75% had never seriously considered the possibility of emigration for themselves. This was not solely because they lacked opportunities; over half of those who had never considered emigration had access to the legal prerequisites for obtaining a visa to America.[3]

Questioning urban educated residents showed that they too thought that everyone who could emigrate would do so; however, they often added the qualification that people who have 'a good job', property, or are 'important' do not emigrate. The general implication, sometimes voiced explicitly, is that emigrants are the ones who could not succeed in São Miguel. By contrast, in the rural areas people stress that emigrants are not necessarily poor but are ambitious and leave to obtain more money and success. Village discussions about departed emigrants frequently include statements about previous prosperity:

> I can't understand why they left! The husband had
> such a good life here---but he wanted to earn
> more, to have more things, like his brother in
> Toronto who came back here and rented a car
> last summer. In America he will make lots of
> money.
>
> (Fieldnotes, São Miguel 1978)

Attitudes about who migrates and the desirability of
migration clearly vary among people in the home society
although almost everyone agrees that it is a way to make
money.   How these differences are associated with
differential contact with migration flows is discussed
throughout the rest of the chapter.

Legal Constraints

The legal restrictions that have affected emigration
from São Miguel have been primarily policies in the
destination areas.   The one major exception is the
Portuguese law that any young man who has not served in
the army must apply for permission to leave the country
and, if granted, sign an agreement to return when called
for military service.

The usual destinations of Michaelense emigrants are
the U.S. and Canada, and to a much lesser extent,
Bermuda. The U.S. and Canada have preference systems
for immigration, and changes in policies affect the flow of
migrants. For example, after 1974 Canada adhered more
strictly to a point preference system, which partially
accounts for the decline in emigration to Canada shown in

Table 4.3 and Figure 4.1.

Table 4.3. Percent of Emigrants from the District of Ponta
Delgada by Primary Destination Countries,
1970-1977

	Canada	U.S.	Bermuda	Total %
1970-75				
(average)	60	38.5	1.5	100
1977	21	77	2	100

(Serviço de Emigração, n.d.)

It should not automatically be assumed that changes in policies are the sole explanation for changes in migration trends. Circumstances at home, or in the adoptive areas, may influence the relative attractiveness of emigration at a given time. For example, emigration increased during 1974, the year that there was a political coup in Portugal. This increase is associated with the political disruption on the mainland, but it is not clear to what extent it was a response on the part of the people in the islands, a response of the emigrants abroad, or a response of the U.S. and Canadian consulates. A 7% increase, from 59 to 66%, in   the   proportion   of   unemployed   (inactives)   and dependents among the total emigrants (I.N.E Boletim 1975) may indicate that it was the relatives in America, fearful of the effects of the leftist coup, who rushed to bring over family members still in the islands. Some of these may have been student age relatives who were unable or unwilling to study on the mainland because of disruption in the universities, some may have been younger children still in the Azores, and some were undoubtedly older people. The statistics do not specify but it is important to consider the range of possibilities rather than just assume that the stimuli for the increase came solely from the home system.   Such correlations must also take into account the significant effect of the way in which migration policies of a destination country are operationalized by the local consulate, and how this can change very rapidly.[4]

After an initial period of recruiting young male immigrants, Canada established a point system in 1967 which gave preference to people with family members already in Canada, higher education, and job skills.   One widely used method of manipulating this system was to enter as a visitor and work long enough to improve chances of being granted permanent immigrant status when it was applied for later on. Canada's 'non-policy' basically encouraged this manipulation (Anderson 1974:44).   From 1974 on, new acts were passed which tightened up the point system.   Extra preference points are now given to assisted relatives and experienced entrepreneurs.   This more restrictive legislation followed the period from the early 1960's to 1973 when immigration to Canada through either legal or illegal channels was feasible for most of the Azoreans who attempted it.

The second major channel for Azorean migration opened in 1965 with U.S. legislation enabling the immigration of immediate relatives of permanent immigrants or citizens already in the U.S. Like Canada, the U.S. has a preference system, but eligibility depends primarily on having immediate family ties with people in the U.S. The 1965 amendments to the Immigration and Nationality Acts (Pub. L. No.   89-236, 79 Stat. 911) provided an annual limit of twenty thousand for Portugal and a seven category preference system as shown in

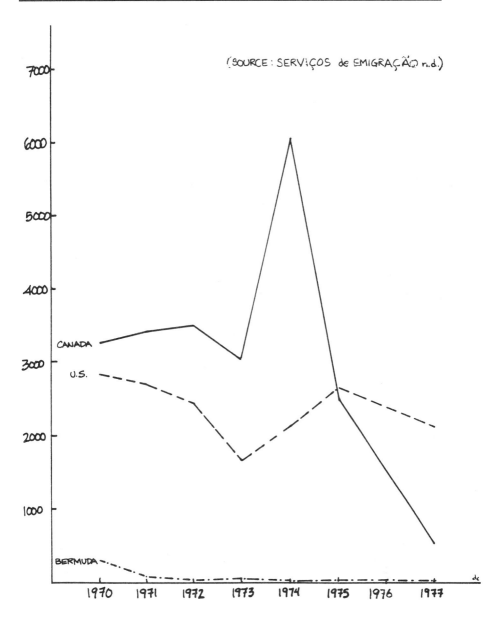

Figure 4.1. Emigrant Flow by Destination, District of Ponta Delgada, 1970-1977

Table 4.4.   The majority of Azorean immigrants to the U.S. enter on first or fifth preference visas.

An applicant for a U.S. immigrant visa must arrange to have an immediate relative in the U.S. who is already a permanent resident or citizen send a petition which is submitted to the local consulate along with a valid job offer from a business in the area of destination. Both the U.S. and Canada require medical examinations for the visa application.   A small number of immigrant visas are granted by the U.S. and Canada to individuals without close relatives in those countries who have obtained a job offer requiring a specialized skill (such as sausage stuffers and coffin liners). Marriage or engagement is another way of obtaining an immigrant visa for people who do not have immediate kin in America.[5] Generally the U.S. preference system has been less flexible for potential immigrants than the Canadian point system.

Table 4.4   The Seven Category Preference System
                    Established for the U.S. in 1965.

First   preference: unmarried sons and daughters of
        U.S. citizens. (20%)

Second   preference: spouses and unmarried sons and
        daughters of lawful resident aliens.   (20% plus any
        visas not required for first preference)

Third   preference: members of the professions and
        scientists and artists of exceptional ability and
        their spouses and children. (10%)

Fourth   preference: married sons and daughters of U.S.
        citizens and their spouses and children.   (10%
        plus any visas not required for first three
        preferences)

preferences)

Fifth preference: brothers and sisters of U.S. citizens and their spouses and children.   (24% plus any visas not required for first four preferences)

Sixth preference: skilled and unskilled workers in occupations for which labor is in short supply in this country, and their spouses and children. (10%)

Seventh preference: refugees. (6%)

Spouses and minor children of American citizens are exempt from the preference system.

(Adapted from U.S. Commission on Civil Rights, 1980)

Anyone can apply for a non-immigrant visa to the U.S. or Canada. According to consulate employees, people who seem the most likely to stay past the legal visit period or to work illegally, such as unmarried young men of limited income, are most frequently denied visas. A second type of non-immigrant visa, for both the U.S. and Canada, is a student visa. These are granted to students who have been accepted at institutions of higher learning; they are allowed to stay for the duration of their full-time enrollment, as verified by the institution.

In the 1920's a few emigrants from São Miguel began going to Bermuda. Entry there requires that a work permit be arranged beforehand. This means that it is almost essential to have a contact in Bermuda but at the same time there is no legal preference based on kinship. Citizenship is extremely difficult to obtain and immigrants cannot remain if they are not employed. The present flow to Bermuda is small, less than 2% of the total emigrants for 1977, but it is noteworthy because the majority do return and because it is an option for some people who cannot get visas for the U.S. or Canada.

With the exception of Bermuda, in recent years the legal policies of destination areas have strongly encouraged the emigration of families and the utilization of kinship networks between America and São Miguel. These policies are reflected in the demographic and social characteristics of emigrants.

Demographic and Social Characteristics of Emigrants

The population of the District of Ponta Delgada peaked in 1960 at 181,924, an increase of 40% over the 1920 population.[6] In the following decade, 1960-1970, the population plunged by 12% to 159,704, and reached a 20% decline by 1974. This rate of population decline was approximately double the rate of decline that occurred during periods of emigration at the turn of the century and it took place in a shorter time span than the previous decline (Figure 4.2).

The exodus of approximately 83,000 emigrants from the Azorean Archipelago between 1960 and 1970 had dramatic demographic consequences which throughout the islands were similar to those which occurred in São Miguel. As illustrated in Table 4.5, the District of Ponta Delgada, with the largest population, averages a higher proportion of emigrants than the other two districts. On the island of São Miguel, some municipalities lost over 30% of their 1960 population in one decade, and very few areas experienced any growth (see Map 6). The five (out

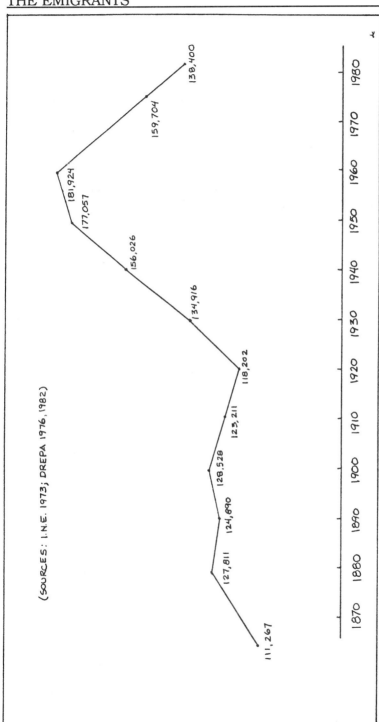

(SOURCES: I.N.E. 1973; DREPA 1976, 1982)

Figure 4.2. Population of the District of Ponta Delgada, 1864-1982

of fifty) *freguesias* within the six municipalities of the island which did grow during the same period are all suburban areas of the main city of Ponta Delgada, or located within easy commuting distance. The central area of the city declined 10%, indicating that although there was growth around the city there was probably some emigration of people from the city to America, augmenting the major flows of people to America from the least accessible regions of the island. There is little indication of any significant flow of residents from rural areas into the city to live and it was not until about 1976 that more young country people began seeking urban employment and residence.

Table 4.5 Average Percent of Emigrants by District Origin, 1950-1977.

District and Percent of Total Population in 1960	Average Percent of Emigrants		
	1950-59	1960-69	1970-77
Ponta Delgada (56%)	64	67	64
Angra do Heroisimo (29%)	12	20	25
Horta (15%)	24	13	11
Total %	100	100	100

(DREPA 1977; I.N.E. 1970; Gygox 1969-70)

Emigration was the major factor in population decline.[7] In the decade from 1960 to 1970 over fifty thousand people legally emigrated from the District of

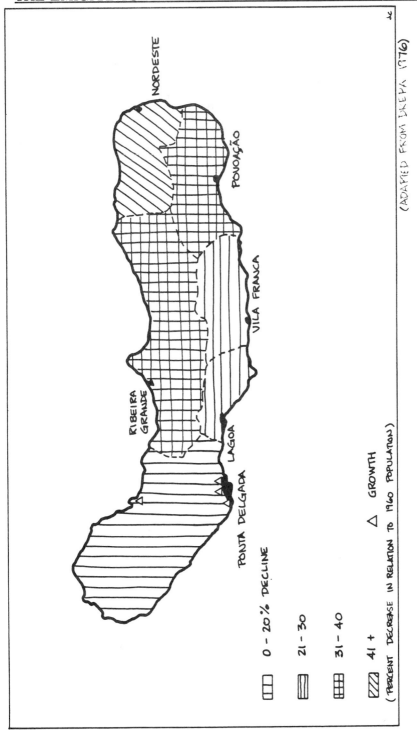

Map 6. Population Decrease: São Miguel, 1960-1974

Ponta Delgada. This total equaled 28% of the 1960 population of 181,924, and another 2%, 8,778, left the District without passports during that time (DREPA 1973). These people were presumably involved in internal migration that included students who went to the mainland. The population of the district declined another 10% between 1970 and 1974. Emigration has continued to the present, with the rate of emigration gradually declining from the 1960-1975 average of 22.1 per 1000 inhabitants.[8]

The age pyramids for the District of Ponta Delgada shown in Figure 4.3 reflect the impact of emigration on the age structure of the population. If the year 1950 is taken as a rough standard for the population at a time when immigration and emigration had remained minimal for several decades, it can be seen that the increased emigrant flow in the 1960's contributed to a striking decrease in the proportion of the population between twenty and fifty years and an associated drop in the percent of young children.

Changes in the home population are mirrored in the age and sex profile of the emigrant flow. Since 1960 there has been an almost equal distribution of male and female emigrants from the district. Since 1965 one quarter to one third of the total emigrants has been under the age of ten, with most of the adults in the twenty to forty year old range.[9] The emigrant flow has thus been composed of the most fertile and potentially fertile sectors of the population.

Demographic change at one level of the population has repercussions that move through the structure with time. Without emigration or substantial changes in fertility regulation the population in the district would have been

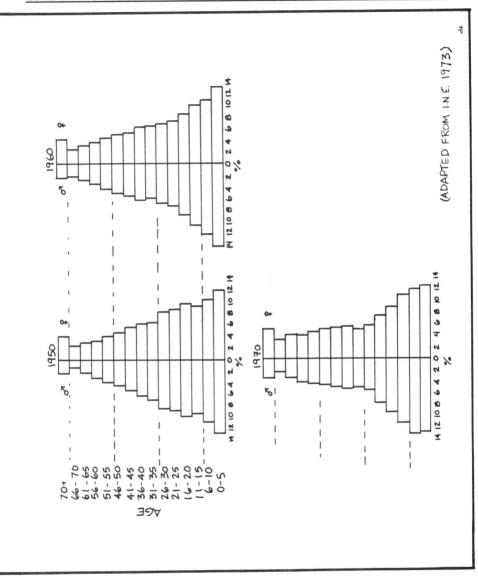

Figure 4.3. Age-Sex Pyramids, District of Ponta Delgada,
1950-1970

expected to expand rapidly in the younger age groups, accelerating the process as the female offspring became fertile in subsequent years.   Instead, the actual age pyramid for 1970 shows that the population is becoming older, with a decline in the younger age groups that will perpetuate overall population decline in years to come.[10]

As might be expected from the youthful age and equal sex ratio in the emigrant flow, 75% of the emigrants between 1960 and 1970 went in some form of family grouping, i. e., two or more people from the same nuclear family, siblings or parent and child, left at the same time. The continuing family nature of emigration is also illustrated in Table 4.6 which shows the high proportion of married emigrants for 1975.   These proportions, which include children, closely approximate the proportions by marital status for the home population as a whole.

Table 4.6   Marital Status of Emigrants from the District of Ponta Delgada, 1975, by Percent of Total.

	% Married	% Single	% Widowed
Male	40	59	1
Female	41	54	5
Total	41	56	3

(I.N.E. 1975)

As a result of the family pattern of emigration most villages have empty houses left by families who have departed for America.   They seldom return to use them. For example, in 1977, in one village where emigration has resulted in a 10% population decline since 1960, 9% of the houses were empty and belonged to emigrants in America. For the same year, of the total occupied households in the same community, 14% had at least one member living in America. Another 3% had someone in mainland Portugal. In other villages of São Miguel the proportion of empty houses and the number of households with former members in America is almost twice as high, while in the urban areas it is much lower. The effect of a predominantly family oriented pattern of migration is that very few households are severely depleted because of emigration (no more than they would be through the process of grown children moving out) but communities have suffered the loss of entire households.

Just as emigrants are not drawn equally from all age segments of the home population, they are not drawn equally from all socioeconomic backgrounds. According to the U.S. and Canadian consulate staffs the majority of emigrants from São Miguel are agricultural laborers who own little or no property. The fact that they do not report income or property holdings on their visa applications, however, may not reflect their actual financial status. One of the common 'folk wisdoms' is that one should not report substantial assets on the form. One reason is that it is illegal to take more than the equivalent of a few hundred dollars out of Portugal without government permission, which is difficult to obtain, and many fear that they will lose their rights to property if they declare it when they emigrate. Local social workers and priests concur that although the majority of emigrants have been agricultural workers, in most cases they are not the very poorest. This is supported by the fact that the municipalities (concelhos) with the greatest population decline since

1960 had the highest percentages of homes occupied by owners (Table 4.7).

Portuguese figures on emigrants from the District of Ponta Delgada between 1965 and 1975 show that about one third of the total over the age of ten had active occupations at the time that they applied for a visa. During this period 48% to 70% of these active emigrants were from the primary sector, which corresponds with the social category of *trabalhadores*. The primary sector covers a range of basically manual labor occupations such as agricultural work, fishing, unskilled factory work, construction and public works. As shown in Table 4.8, with the exception of the most recent years this proportion of primary sector emigrants exceeded the proportion of primary sector workers in the home system. The proportion of emigrants with primary sector occupations has declined in recent years.

Since 1966 there has been a striking increase in the number of employed emigrants who are skilled or secondary sector workers. The secondary sector designates a range of skilled, blue collar type jobs such as mechanics, carpenters, stone masons, bus drivers, taxi drivers, and high school trained clerks. This sector corresponds to the least well-educated part of the social category designated as *proprietário* educated. The secondary sector emigrants have increased to almost double the proportion found in the home population. This increase may reflect the opportunity structure in São Miguel, where educational facilities have been improved to produce more skilled workers but the job market for them in 1978 did not provide much opportunity for socioeconomic mobility. It may also reflect the opportunities in America for skilled workers. What these figures do not show is the level of training of individuals,

Table 4.7   Form of Occupation of Houses, by Concelho, for
            S. Miguel, 1960, and Percent Population Decline
            of the Concelhos 1960-70.

Concelho	Owned	Percent Rented	Other	Percent Population Decline
Ponta Delgada	53	38	9	6
Lagoa	59	26	15	5
Vila Franca	52	30	18	6
R. Grande	69	23	8	16
Povoaçao	69	18	13	24
Nordeste	75	18	7	21

(I.N.E. 1960; I.N.E. S.E. Regional #4 1970)

e.g., students and unemployed high school graduates, who are not actively working at the time of emigration. These people, along with self-employed property owners and housewives, are listed in the inactive category.

In summary, since 1960 emigration has contributed to a declining and proportionately older population in the District of Ponta Delgada. Age, sex, and family characteristics of the migrant flow have changed little since 1965, but the magnitude of the outflow has diminished. This decline may reflect a more restrictive Canadian policy combined with the effects of age-specific emigration. As the population has decreased and become proportionately older, the age pools which the majority of

Table 4.8 Occupational Structure of the Actively Employed
by Percent, for a) the District of Ponta Delgada
and b) the District Emigrants.

a)   District of Ponta Delgada

	1950	1960	1970
Primary	64%	61%	50%
Secondary	14	17	17
Tertiary	22	22	33

b)   Emigrants from the District P.D.

	1966	1970	1975
Primary	70%	53%	48%
Secondary	16	29	36
Tertiary	14	18	16

(I.N.E. 1970, 1975)

emigrants represent have also been reduced.

A second change in the flow has been the decreasing percentage of active primary workers and the concomitant increase in active skilled workers.   Prior to 1970 emigration was dominated by the less socioeconomically advantaged sector of the home society; now it is increasingly an avenue for more highly trained individuals. The view in the home society stated at the beginning of the chapter, that everyone wants to emigrate, is in one sense validated with these changes; emigrants are now coming from a broader cross-section of the society than in previous decades. On the other hand, the view that anyone who has a 'good life' in São Miguel in terms of job or property will not emigrate is becoming less valid as more people from skilled occupational backgrounds leave to seek their futures in America.

RETURNEES

Portuguese records claim that the return of emigrants from America constitutes less than 1% of the number who emigrated during the decade 1960-1970.[11] This does not include those people who do not reinstate Portuguese citizenship, and the figure is undoubtedly too low for São Miguel if all returned emigrants are included regardless of their legal status. In nine communities sampled in this study an average 3% of the households contained at least one emigrant who had returned from America since 1960. These returnees were of all ages (from school age to retired), almost equally male and female, and both single and married. According to the U.S. consulate about 500 returnees from the U.S. now living in São Miguel receive U.S. social security checks. This may indicate a slight preponderance of older returnees on the island. Return is at present a socially significant phenomenon, but even after adjusting the official numbers the rate is drastically lower than in previous eras of emigration when, for example, return from the U.S. for all Portuguese averaged 18% in the early 1900's (Taft 1971:101).

One of the greatest disappointments of researchers and development planners concerned with return migration is that the returning migrants in less developed countries do not become effective 'vehicles of social development' (Cerase 1974:261). They merely fix up their own homes and avail themselves of a comfortable standard of living (Baucic 1974). São Miguel is no exception to the latter point; improvements on the domestic front is a traditional pattern dating back to the houses built by returnees from Brazil at the turn of the century, and carried on at present with plate glass windows and modern kitchens.

With respect to returnees and development, focusing solely on American models of innovation may obscure some important phenomena of change. Returnees in São Miguel are creative in using and manipulating resources without working within or setting up totally new forms, and in doing so they do present new models to their fellow islanders. Two of the female returnees interviewed had managed to obtain office jobs for which they were not qualified by their level of Portuguese education. They did speak fluent English, one had graduated from an American high school, the other had taken some college courses in America, and both had work experience and confidence which evidently contributed to their success in obtaining good jobs. They were successful within the traditional system without having followed the traditionally prescribed path of obtaining Portuguese credentials. Other returnees have set up businesses which cater to the tourist industry, employing their knowledge of America as well as their capital to provide services, such as an ice cream parlor or motel, which both tourists and locals patronize. Many of them are involved in businesses as well as agriculture, thereby successfully exploiting specialized urban markets. These small entrepreneurs have become involved in a rapidly expanding domain of opportunities which was previously controlled by a limited number of more affluent business people. The enterprise of the younger returnees in São Miguel has provided examples which indicate that there is greater flexibility in the paths to success than the traditional view of the social structure would indicate.

VISITORS

    In São Miguel there is a long history of emigrants visiting the homeland on trips back from America. Since 1960 improvements in transportation, a migrant ideology of maintaining ties, and the American pattern of vacationing have combined to intensify the degree of contact between emigrants and homeland. The character of the flow has changed. Visiting emigrants in the 1960's came to see their families; ten years later they may combine the role of family visitor with that of tourist. This change has contributed to an expansion of contacts between emigrants and people in the home society.

    The flow of visitors to São Miguel from America has been facilitated in recent years by improved air service and relatively cheap excursion fares for two to six week visits. These excursion rates apply to flights leaving from major Azorean-American communities, such as Toronto and Boston, and in 1971 cost under $400 round trip.[12] Late spring through autumn is the season of *festas* in the Azores, the season of vacations in America, and the prime time for visiting in São Miguel. During this time welcoming family groups jam the small airport in Ponta Delgada as relatives and friends arrive for their vacations. According to the local populace, the *'americanos'* (Americans) are readily identifiable on the streets by their colorful clothes, strange accents, distinctive manners, and unrestrained spending habits.

The largest influx of visiting emigrants usually occurs for the island's major Church *festa* in honor of Santo Cristo in Ponta Delgada. In 1978, the newspapers estimated that twenty-five to thirty thousand tourists of Azorean descent attended this *festa.* Charter flights for the occasion brought visitors from both coasts of the U.S. and from Canada. Santo Cristo and Espirito Santo are the *festas* that involve the greatest number of tourists and the greatest direct or indirect participation by emigrants in America. Many emigrants send money to pay off a promise to Senhor Santo Cristo dos Milagres, the bejeweled statue of Christ that has been on the island since the 16th century and reputedly performs curing miracles. Others contribute to Espirito Santo, the celebration of the Holy Ghost which traditionally involves a procession and distribution of food to the poor. Large numbers of emigrants return at these times, many to march in the procession of Santo Cristo, and others return throughout the summer to participate in smaller celebrations in their own villages. Returning so that a child can take first communion in the natal community is a common *festa* oriented stimulus for visiting.

Some of the visiting emigrants still have their own houses to stay in, or the key to a vacant house belonging to a friend in America. Others stay with their families. Some, usually second and third generation Azorean-Americans or emigrants without relatives in town, stay in hotels. In the villages everyone has contact with visiting emigrants staying there. Observations from three rural villages showed that in 1978 about 5% of the households had at least one emigrant visitor from America stay with them at some time during the year. Still other families had visitors who did not actually stay with them.

The migrant ideology in America stresses the importance of not forgetting the homeland. This is reinforced by similar sentiments in the homeland. Although not all emigrants manage to go back and visit, and not all want to, many do. The typical pattern of priorities for new immigrants in America is to get themselves established, save money to buy a house and other 'necessities' such as a car, and then save money to pay for a visit to the homeland. Visiting is not cheap, and sometimes involves borrowing money in order that the emigrant is able to buy the right clothes and gifts to make the desired impression of success and well-being on the homeland family and community.

Emigrants visiting São Miguel are in some respects both 'at home' and 'on vacation'. They are generally visiting relatives, but at the same time they are often influenced by the American work place concept of having a limited period of leisure time, the coveted vacation, that they must use to good advantage. Some emigrant visitors put on their old clothes and spend the whole time working in the fields and the pastures. They are an exception, however, to the general pattern in which emigrants come back dressed in style for a leisurely non-work visit. Among the *proprietários* and *trabalhadores*, typical images of emigrant visitors as tourist are the family from America seeing the whole island for the first time in a taxi, or emigrants who rent cars at great expense to show off the local scenery to their kids and take relatives on outings. According to local taxi drivers, one outcome of this behavior has been the adoption of sight-seeing by villagers who save up to take the family out for a Sunday taxi excursion and see parts of the island they have never been to. Additionally, the emigrant visitor, as tourist, spends substantial periods of time in urban and resort areas, which communicates to the villages a clear preference for urban living and American-style modernity.

The traditional pattern of holiday outings was to walk or ride to a lake or a scenic view along the coastline and have a picnic. Often these outings took the form of *romarias* or pilgrimages to local shrines. Today, outings with emigrants visiting urban-educated families go to the same scenic spots, although usually not to the closest one, and on a scale of grandeur that far surpasses a simple walk. One such picnic involved an entourage of ten vehicles careening halfway around the island for a lunch of two dozen stewed chickens and innumerable bottles of local wine, all at the hosts' expense. In the villages the visitors treat the hosts, and if they stay for a long time they invariably contribute to their own support in the household. Among middle level urban residents, the hosts shoulder extravagent costs to entertain the 'rich Americans,' demonstrating their own well-being and capacity to succeed without leaving home. The visitors, for their part, often come laden with hundreds of dollars worth of assorted gifts for relatives and friends. If any of those friends or relatives go to America to visit, as well they may, the roles and costs are reversed.

Visitors from America who were educated in the towns or city before they emigrated, even if born in a rural area, rarely spend more than a brief period in the villages. If the natal village is close to the city, they may commute regularly into town and go on trips around the island. This frequently happens, even if the original plan was to spend the entire time in the village.

The visiting emigrants who adopt the strongest tourist role in São Miguel, spending time in the resort areas and going to the fancier bars and hotels for entertainment, tend to be the young and better educated, or more Americanized emigrants. Some are from educated backgrounds on the island, but many are not, and they reflect the social mixing that takes place in Azorean-America. Generally these visitors do not spend much time in the villages, as the case of one young man from Fall River illustrates:

> Louis went back to S. Miguel after an absence of ten years to visit his home village. He planned to stay six weeks but left after three because he said he was 'going crazy, there was nothing to do and I couldn't stand it.' He said he saw the boys he used to know but they were still going out with the cows and living in poor houses and he 'couldn't relate to them.' He plans to go back some day, but with a group of friends from Fall River, to go live near the beach, rent a car, go dancing, and have a good time.
>
> (Fieldnotes, Fall River, 1978)

For young people like this, the idea of going as a tourist for a vacation to São Miguel is appealing, but not the idea of returning there to stay.

The emigrant visitors-as-tourists have contact with sectors of the society that in many cases they were not associated with before they left. Girls who would not have gone dancing, go dancing along with the urban educated and elite. Men who would not have talked freely with the traditional elite, converse about their lives and jobs in

America in familiar terms. These visitors are the people who are tied into community and extra-community opportunities in America; they know about politics, education and non-factory employment. They come in contact with the educated and elite youth of the island who frequent the same resort areas, and night spots. These visitors socialize with friends and family, but also mix with people who have little other contact with emigrants except perhaps through a former employee or godchild.

The flow of emigrant visitors provides intensive contact between the homeland and America. It touches not only the rural areas, but also the urban educated sectors of the population. The idea of permanent return has diminished, but the ideology of maintaining ties is strong and is reinforced by the American pattern of vacations.

The flow of visitors also goes in the other direction, and has increased in recent years. For the U.S. alone, the number of non-immigrant visas granted to Azoreans tripled between 1970 and 1978. This increase reflects both a greater number of applicants and a lower number of refusals (see Figure 4.4). In 1977 non-immigrant visas to the U.S. numbered 25% more than the number of permanent immigrant visas granted.[13] Some of these visitors from São Miguel to America go to see family who have emigrated previously and therefore tend to stay in the Azorean-American communities. Others, usually the wealthier urban educated, go to visit, seeing the people they do know in America, but getting a broader picture of life in America outside of the Azorean-American communities and the factories. Ironically, it is the elite who often know no one except former employees in

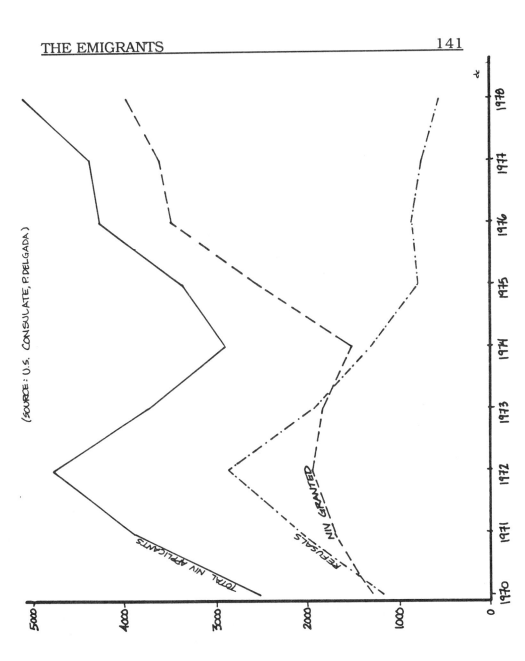

Figure 4.4. Non-Immigrant Visas to the U.S., 1970-1978

America and consequently may not get the deluxe tour that some of the urban educated non-elite get because of their contacts with better educated emigrants. Many of these visitors have motives other than that of vacationing; a visit to a medical specialist, buying a particular kind of contact lenses, buying property, or making other investments are just a few of the diverse reasons for these trips.

The intensity of contact between homeland and emigrants is greater than in previous eras of migration, due to improved transportation and a pattern of maintaining ties and vacationing that is fostered by the ideology of migrants in America. In their roles as tourists, emigrant visitors now have a broader range of contacts with people in the urban educated and elite sectors of the home population. People from these sectors also have increased contact with America through vacations, business trips, and visits to emigrants there.

FORMALIZED FLOWS: CHURCH, ARTS, SPORTS AND POLITICS

There are a number of formalized or group channels for flows of people between São Miguel and America. These flows are basically voluntary movements. The channels reflect the array of connections that have been built up between natal and adoptive areas throughout the history of migration, providing contact of different kinds for various social levels of the home society.

As early as the late nineteenth century clergy were sent over to America at the request of Azorean immigrant communities. This pattern is now weaker, but the ties between Churches, and between Churches and former members, have remained strong. Clergy on vacation from the island still visit Portuguese churches in America, sometimes presiding at a traditional feast day, and Azorean-American clergy sometimes return to the islands to participate in religious celebrations. In 1978, for example, the Archbishop of Boston returned to his homeland, São Miguel, to preside over the island's largest Church celebration. The magnitude of these flows is small, but the high visibility of such individuals fosters the ideology of extended social spheres and shared values between homeland and emigrant communities in America.

Most parishes in São Miguel have marching bands. The ubiquitous Azorean band is generally recruited through the enterprise of local priests wherever a community is large enough to support one. The recruits are of all ages and are drawn primarily from the families of *proprietários* and *trabalhadores* and skilled workers in the city. It is the dream of many a band to play in America. The best bands are apt to fulfill this dream, and likewise the better Azorean-American bands may find their way to the Azores. Bands are a limited channel of contact but one which enables people to visit who might otherwise not have been able to do so.

Soccer is another channel for visiting which takes team members to America, as well as to other islands and other communities on the island. Soccer teams are found in every sizeable community and members are drawn from a wide sector of society, but the teams that get a chance to go abroad are usually from the larger towns and often are recruited through the high schools. The members are therefore usually from *proprietário* or urban educated backgrounds. Teams that go to America generally play in several communities of the U.S. and Canada and may see more of America in a shorter time than do most people who go to visit family members. They are well paid and privileged visitors.

Cultural exchanges are another form of movement which enables people in São Miguel to see America without becoming emigrants. Some exchanges are sponsored by the government and some by private organizations. One amateur theatrical group regularly goes to America to perform in Azorean-American areas, and a folk dance group sometimes comes from America to be in *festas* in São Miguel. In some cases Michalense performers find opportunities for themselves in America and return later as emigrants. For example, a young woman went to America with an entertainment variety show that played in Azorean-American communities for a month. A year after her success as a singer on the tour she emigrated to New England and pursued a career singing the Portuguese style *fado*. There are various other kinds of groups which organize trips to America. In recent years various student groups returned with fewer members than when they had departed, as some used the tour as a vehicle for unsanctioned emigration.

A major form of interaction stems from the interest shown in Azorean-American communities by Azorean and Portuguese officials. The head of the Emigration Department frequently tours Portuguese communities in America, various ministers of the regional Azorean government give lectures at conferences and present programs at schools near Azorean-American communities, and various forms of political-cultural exchanges take place such as sister-city ceremonies and exchange visits of mayors. The government also sponsors organized cultural and scholarly events. In 1978 a Congress was held in the

Azores that brought participants from various parts of the world.

Thus visiting also takes place in the other direction, from America to the Azores. At times of crisis such as the recent earthquakes in the Azores, or reelection at home, it is not uncommon to see American politicians, regardless of their own ethnic heritage, but with Azorean-American constituents, in the Azores reaffirming their goodwill toward the islands.

With the exception of the clerical, all of these formalized channels have expanded as emigration has continued in the contemporary period and as the adoptive communities have become more interested in maintaining ties with the homeland. The process of maintaining ties thus works both ways. In America it fosters ethnic identification, and in São Miguel it nurtures the belief that homeland and emigrants are tied into the same social universe despite residence on different land masses.

SUMMARY

Over the last twenty years flows of people have had both demographic and sociocultural impacts on current migration patterns in São Miguel. The demographic impact of emigration on the population structure in São Miguel has important implications for the interpretation of future trends in migration. Emigration has resulted in a smaller, proportionately older population with a smaller proportion of people in the most fertile age groups than existed fifteen years ago. If the present pattern of emigration continues (young and equal sex ratio), a decrease in numbers of emigrants would be expected because the age pool from which they are drawn is shrinking, in part due to the effects of previous emigration. A decline in numbers of emigrants does not necessarily indicate a decline in the proportions of emigrants from specific age groups.

Examination of flows of people from São Miguel further illustrates that despite rapid population decline, the stereotypical images of 'everybody who can' emigrating or 'only the poor' emigrating, are not verified by the composition of emigrant flows. However, the emigrant flow does increasingly represent a broader cross-section of the home society as the percentage of skilled emigrants increases.

Persisting flows between emigrants and the homeland have resulted in more people in the home society having contact with emigrants. While the rural *trabalhadores* and *proprietários* suffered the greatest losses in family and neighbors through emigration they are not the only ones who interact with emigrants who came back to visit. The urban educated have contact with the young and better-educated emigrant visitors on vacation in São Miguel, and they also visit America on business and vacation trips. The large landowning elite suffered the greatest loss of workers because of emigration, but ironically these same domestic and agricultural workers who emigrated have provided the elite with channels of contact with America that they do not usually have through their own kin.

The sociocultural impact of different social groups in the home society having varying ties to people in America is also associated with the effect of emigration flows on the domestic group. Emigration of people in family groups, as is the pattern in São Miguel, is not as demographically disruptive for domestic groups as is the emigration of single males or unaccompanied seasonal laborers. Permanent family migration does not result in a system where vacant positions are kept open in the social fabric, awaiting the return of migrant individuals. In this respect migration from the Azores is very different from that from parts of mainland Portugal where the majority of emigrants are seasonal and a higher proportion are male. In some areas of Portugal this has resulted in changed patterns of agricultural labor and in attempts by the community at home to keep open the 'gaps' left by emigrants who often return (Brettell 1979; Smith 1975). This is not the case in São Miguel; whole families leave and they generally leave for good. This produces a different kind of effect in the rural areas from whence the majority of emigrants come; the loss of family and neighbor groups depletes the extended household support networks that are vital to everyday existence for both young and old. However, the very fact that these support networks do extend outside each individual household means that a certain degree of loss in the pool of households can be sustained as ties are strengthened with remaining households. The flexibility entailed in this kind of organization is not a result of emigration as has been noted for some other sending societies (Gonzalez 1969), but it is adaptive in a situation where emigration has periodically depleted the immediate family networks of many residents.

In recent years the formal and formalized flows of people have fostered an ideology of shared worlds, of belonging to part of the same social universe, of being 'tied to different ends of the same string'. People are the main variables in these flows between America and the homeland, and people are also the transmitters of a variety of communications. The effect of these communication flows on the migration context is the topic of the next chapter.

CHAPTER 5
THE SCENT OF AMERICA: FLOWS OF INFORMATION,
MONEY, AND GOODS

In São Miguel, all the things from America have a special smell. The people, the clothes, the dollars, they all have a very good scent!

(Fieldnotes, Fall River, 1978)

The processing of information by individuals about circumstances in the destination area is integral to migration decision-making. The communications associated with migration flows of people are an important part of the information that is processed. During the 1960's and 1970's the flow of communications between São Miguel and America increased in conjunction with an increased flow of people. The communications considered in this chapter are the informal and formalized flows of information, money, and goods between São Miguel and America.

The literature on migration, anthropological as well as economic, tends to assume that in the decision to migrate, people base evaluations on actual regional differences. Wright (1976:30), for example, in speaking of Mexican migration to the U.S., states that migration functions as an adaptive response to regional differences in economic, political, or social well-being. The implication here, which is also made in many other works, is that people respond to regional differences that exist in some objective reality. Regional differences do exist, but it is important to understand the framework that they exist in for potential migrants. Assuming or implying that people have accurate information about regional variation may obfuscate the specifics of a given process of migration.

Gonzalez (1975) suggests that the nature of the 'micro-environment' of the destination area is an influential factor in ongoing migration. Michaelense emigrants do not go to America in the same way that a non-emigrant tourist might visit 'the Azores'; they go to a specific community where Azoreans are already established. Communication flows back to São Miguel generally emerge from the particular 'micro-environments' of emigrant enclaves. Only a small amount of the information originates in the broader American society. What people know and perceive about differential well-being in the home and destination areas thus depends on what information they have access to. How that information is processed and filtered by individuals in São Miguel will be examined after the content of the information, where it originates, and whom it reaches, is sketched out for the home system.

The importance of migration associated flows of communications has been noted for other situations of migration. Brandes (1975:182-183), for example, lists alterations in knowledge of the outside world and of material aspects of life as among "the most profound changes resulting from migration." In São Miguel a similar process has occurred, but the alterations have varied for different sectors of the home society. Although people with the most direct contact with emigrants have been the most obviously affected by these flows, there have also been significant effects on other levels of the society.

INFORMATION

What are the specific types of information about America that circulate in different sectors of the home society? The following section describes what emigrants in America, and those visiting São Miguel, say about America, in person, through letters, and through other media of communication.

Informal Information Flows

As seen in the preceding chapter, contact with America is not limited to the families and neighbors of emigrants, but pervades the whole population. There are two general categories of information that reach two different sectors of the population. The information transmitted to the rural *trabalhadores* and *proprietários* and to skilled workers (rural and urban) is dominated by details of the modern standard of living in America; the information transmitted to the urban, better-educated sector focuses on educational and leisure time activities. These two categories reflect different interests and different opportunities in the home system for these two sectors. In the Azores perceptions of what opportunities are available in America are thus colored by the type of information that reaches individuals as well as by the normative structure in which they operate. Value systems associated with people of different social levels act as filters on the way information is perceived and transmitted, in the manner that Epstein (1969) has discussed for flows of gossip in central Africa.

In São Miguel the information about America that flows into the rural and skilled worker part of the society is largely transmitted through word of mouth, but also through letters, occasional telephone calls, and cassette tapes. These communications are characteristically community property; information is rarely meant for only 'one ear'. Absent emigrants invariably figure as one of the main topics of conversation, eclipsed in interest only by the latest episode of a Brazilian television serial. The current news of departed kin and neighbors is a comfortable topic, one that everyone has equal access to in a neighborhood or family gathering where everyone knows the emigrants. In addition, the stories and actions of visiting emigrants are swiftly transmitted throughout the community they are staying in. The arrival of letters and tapes from America is community knowledge and the recipients are expected to share the news. Telephone calls are rare, since few people have phones in this sector of the population, and calls often signify the death or illness of emigrants in America. Some people do have private phones, such as a woman whose husband works in Canada or a family with a business in the city. Phone calls received at a local store or bar are a community event. In these instances the call is made or taken in public, with a few people invariably standing nearby or in the doorway and discreetly keeping other people on the street informed of the course that the conversation is taking.

On the island and among emigrants in America, most

correspondence is managed by the women. In a sample from one Michaelense community, 79% of the households interviewed corresponded regularly (at least four times a year) with relatives in America and in 79% of those households which corresponded it was the wife or a daughter who wrote the letters. The idea that women are the primary nodes in the communication networks between America and the Azores is supported from the American side by data from Smith (1976) and Anderson (1974). This indicates that women are important instigators and contacts for emigration. Part of this female role is related to rural work patterns, which are similar to those discussed by Reigelhaupt (1967) for mainland Portugal, in which the women work near their houses and move throughout the community doing chores such as washing, collecting or purchasing food, and preparing food for storage. Women, therefore, have more intense daily interaction among themselves than do working males who go off to the fields alone or in small groups and return at night, missing most of the information that comes into the village during the day. The women of the household pass information on, but selectively in many cases. Women thus manage a large proportion of the external and internal information flows. Furthermore, because much of the information from America originates with women, it tends to concentrate on topics of interest to them. In contrast, property management is a male domain and males are the main correspondents about management of property belonging to emigrants.

The content of information received by the rural and skilled worker sector focuses primarily on attributes of the modern standard of living in America. The urban good life is a basic theme which is stressed in information about modern appliances, convenience foods, and the availability of clothes, or anything else a person could possibly want, at low prices in large stores. There is very little information about education and health care services. A second theme is job opportunities. Work is portrayed as hard, but it is said that there is always work in America. It is described as clean, secure, and well paid, compared to the dirty, irregular and low paid work of agriculturalists in São Miguel. Work for women is praised as being clean, modern, of good status, and as well paid as work for men. A third theme, related to the second one, is that anyone willing to work can save enough to acquire property. Stories abound of how emigrants started out with nothing and after a few years were able to buy their own houses. The possibility of successfully acquiring property is reinforced by the fact that some emigrants come back to São Miguel and buy land or houses. Other varied information about America finds its way to São Miguel, but most topics are hinged to one of these three main recurring themes. The three themes are usually portrayed in a positive light, but there are also negative aspects of life in America carried in the information flows.

Internal processing of information within a community, typically by *proprietários* who have lost or fear the loss of workers, people who decided not to emigrate, old people, and returnees from America, sometimes brings out the negative aspects of these themes, as seen in the following example.

> Fatima and her husband were talking about their plans to go to America where her older sister was already living. When I asked why they wanted to leave he responded that on the island he could 'work and work but never save enough to have anything' whereas in America 'anyone can earn enough to buy a house'.

Immediately the woman Fatima used to work for chimed in that in the islands a man could work and support his family, but in America everyone <u>must</u> work to make ends meet and there are lots of expenses, such as heat, expensive store bought food and winter clothes which they don't have on the island.

(Fieldnotes, São Miguel 1978)

Old people in particular stress the information about problems of isolation among strangers, not knowing the language, harsh weather, and family difficulties (such as lack of respect for elders and divorce). In general, the negative information is emphasized by the people who are most concerned with the benefits of staying in the home society. Emigrants in America report that this is a relatively recent trend in information; as little as ten years ago it was rare to hear anything but good said about America in São Miguel.

Some negative information that might be expected to be discussed is not mentioned. Many of the areas in America where emigrants go, such as southeastern Massachusetts and Boston, had relatively high unemployment rates in the 1970's, but this has not been stressed in the information about America, apparently because Azoreans continue to find employment there. As one young emigrant visiting from New Bedford stated,

My wife found a job, but I spent the first three months looking for work and watching TV to learn English. I finally found a job in a shoe factory. It was 1974 and many people were laid off, but anyone who really wants to work can find a job.

(Fieldnotes, São Miguel 1978)

There may be unemployment in America, but the information that emigrants send home is that there are jobs for those willing to work.

The information flow among the rural workers conveys the idea that life in America is good for anyone (except the old) and emigration is a positive opportunity. The words are reinforced by the prosperous image that visiting emigrants present through their appearance and behavior. In return, these visitors hear that life has improved at home, that nobody lacks for the basic necessities of life, and that although they are poorer than in America, life is not bad at home. These responses convey the idea that people in the homeland have managed well without emigrating, but do not contradict the sentiment that emigration is nonetheless an appealing opportunity.

Among the urban educated, information about America travels largely by word of mouth, but lacks the community property aspect of information in the rural and skilled sector. Patterns of information flow reflect differences in social interaction patterns among the two sectors. Information received by urban educated relatives, for example, is not freely transmitted to the larger community. Additionally, emigrants from educated backgrounds may suffer greater hardships through loss of status and unaccustomed work when initially in America, and these stories come back to their families at home. Information flows are thus more limited, and are also more likely to carry negative information. The limited one-to-one contacts, rather than community contacts, are also characteristic of information flows about America to non-kin, in situations previously discussed such as tourism and vacation and entertainment settings.

The type of information differs from that passed within the rural and skilled sector. The urban educated generally ask and hear about selected aspects of life in America such as educational institutions, what life is like for students, urban night life and entertainment activities, and investment possibilities for someone who is not living in America. Usually they are also informed of the hardships of emigration and, unless they are family, are not encouraged to contemplate permanent residence in America.

The urban educated and elite have to some extent always received limited information about America from former employees. This information about factory work and material goods did not provide an incentive to emigrate. When specific persons are channels for information, the prestige of both the transmitter and the receiver may affect its impact (Eisenstadt 1966). In this case the high status patron receives information about America from lower status persons who have different ideas about socioeconomic mobility, and the disparity in status affects the way in which the information is perceived. Unlike their employees, the patrons do not need outside channels for economic mobility to improve their status. They interpret the information in a negative light as indicative of the 'fact' that only those who cannot succeed at home need to emigrate.

In recent years information reaching the urban educated via better-educated emigrants pertains to opportunities that the urban educated see as useful to them. This information flow conveys the idea that there are opportunities in America, but that emigration is not necessarily a good thing for people of good standing at home. In return, they respond with information about how difficult it is to get anything done in a country where everything is expensive and no one wants to work, thereby giving reasons to leave but at the same time deflecting emigrants from the idea of coming back to compete with them in the homeland. The emigrants, for their part, are deflecting competition for themselves there while reaffirming the worth of life there by saying to the urban educated, 'don't emigrate, just come to America to study.'

Formalized Information Flows

Public communications media and the government and Church sponsored Emigration Service (Delagação de Emigração) are the two main channels of formalized information flows which affect the context of migration decision-making.

Television programming from America is varied; the 'Muppets' and 'Star Trek' are among the favorites. Shows about America fall into two categories; those about Portuguese-American regions and all others. For most people, only the former are a factor in the informational context of decision-making. The latter are about America, but not the same world that people in São Miguel think of as America. A news clip on a huge snowstorm in Boston, where there are many Azoreans living, arouses great interest, but a show on the Rocky Mountains does not.

Portuguese newspapers from America can be purchased in São Miguel and vice versa. The papers are read mostly by the urban educated and a few rural proprietários, and therefore reach a more limited audience than television. A sampling of the content of local papers showed that they frequently carry news of America, mostly focusing on emigrants and events in their communities, adding to an increasingly realistic picture of life in Azorean America.

The Emigration Service, started in 1977 to extend pre-existing services of the Catholic Church, assists emigrants by making visa applications (a task performed gratis by travel agents), organizing basic English classes (usually taught by returned, better-educated emigrants); and providing films and other educational materials on America. The films are often out of date, but the radio shows produced by the Church address current social problems of emigrants such as the confusion created by the permissive sexual mores of America that young emigrants encounter.

In summary, increased information flow has resulted in a broader, more realistic, range of knowledge about America for a broader cross-section of the island population. The urban educated now have access to information on education and leisure time activities which is evaluated in a positive light, rather than just having access to the negatively evaluated information they received in the past through lower status emigrants. The rural and skilled sector has greater access to both positive and negative information about life in America, in contrast to the simple 'streets paved with gold' image that dominated their perceptions in the early 1960's. In addition, the rural and skilled worker image of modern urban life is cast in terms of American characteristics of modernity, rather than the European model prevalent among the urban educated. In villages a freezer is a "freeza", whereas in town it is referred to by the Portuguese term, *congelador*.

MONEY

In the literature on migration, remittances generally have been treated in two ways. First, they are considered as a form of ongoing commitment of the emigrants to their homeland, especially if they intend to return, and secondly, they are treated by recipients as a source of subsistence which contributes to modernization in the home communities, but rarely to radical change (Manners 1965).[1]

Flows of money associated with migration will be considered here in terms of the extent to which remittance monies support people in São Miguel, how they are utilized, and who receives them. These patterns are discussed from a temporal perspective; the magnitude and type of flows have changed since since 1960 as have the uses they are put to in the home system.

At present emigrant remittances are less a viable economic resource for people in the homeland than a form of expected 'prestation' on the part of those who leave. The expectation is reinforced by a long tradition of money sent and brought back from America. Coin collectors in the Azores probably have an easier time getting hold of U.S. gold pieces than those in the U.S. The tradition of remittances has two persistent features: people continue to send money back, and part of the money is usually saved as a small form of personal security.

The sum of dollars coming into the Azores as official, i.e. reported, remittances from America, is significant for foreign exchange but does not represent a major source of income for the majority of residents. In 1976 the Azores, with a total population of approximately 292,000, reportedly received 282,000 *escudos* worth of official remittances from America. In U.S. dollars this comes to about $28 per person. This is one third of the average amount received per person in mainland Portugal during the same year. The mainland, with approximately 9,200,000 people, received 26,566,000 *escudos* worth of remittances, much of which came from France.[2] Combined remittance figures for the 1967-74 period indicate that on average Azoreans received about half of what mainland Portuguese received in formal remittances (Chaney 1986:132). Remittances in the Azores are also less than they are in other migrant sending societies in Europe. In Italy, for example, remittances in the 1960's were more than double those for the Azores (Lopreato 1967). However, when the large outflow of emigrants from the Azores began in the mid-1960's, remittances were a critical source of money, even in small amounts, for the cash-poor lower status levels of the home society. At that time there were no monthly benefits from the government and wage labor was less prevalent in a system that depended heavily on patron-client relationships.

Today emigrants from São Miguel typically send dollars back to close family for Christmas and birthdays. Sometimes a few dollars are sent in letters to former employers or *proprietário* patrons in a gesture that displays the emigrants' new found affluence. A Christmas card from America usually brings a few dollars, as witnessed by an American teacher's cleaning woman in São Miguel who admired the ample array of North American cards and exclaimed that her employer was very fortunate to receive so many dollars! Not everyone receives dollars from America, however, and the amounts that are received are often less than $10 and seldom more than $50. Local rural stores with bank outlets reported cashing substantial amounts of dollars in 1978, particularly

at Christmas time.   Propreitors of stores in two
communities estimated that the total averaged as much as
ten to twenty dollars per resident in the months of
December and January.   They reported that considerably
less money was received throughout the rest of the year.
The store proprietors also reported that these small sums
of dollars are frequently cashed without the use of a bank
exchange.

These small remittances are saved by some, and spent
by many.   They are used for 'extras' like a new shawl for an
older woman, perfume for a younger one, sugar, special
foods for a *festa,* or something to improve the house.3
The latter use was particularly prevalent in the earlier
years of migration.   In the 1950's the houses were
reputedly mostly white and blue, but now they are green,
and pink, and orange, 'painted with American dollars.'
The inside often remained the same, but the outside was
'spruced up' thanks to remittances from America.   It is
thus said that emigration has 'changed the colors' one sees
in São Miguel.

Among the *trabalhadores* remittances rarely exceed a
hundred dollars, i.e., less than 7% of an average annual
income for a family during a year. *Proprietários* are more
likely to be involved in larger cross-Atlantic cash
transactions, such as loans to buy property or the securing
of funds outside the country as a way of diversifying their
investments.   Distant kin, and kin who have been gone a
long time, tend to send less money, so the amount
received by any family depends on whom they are related
to in America and how closely the ties have been
maintained.   The general pattern of remittances fits the
model typical of much of Europe in that people who
emigrate with family and stay permanently rarely send

back remittances of a magnitude sufficient to support the relatives in the homeland (Parenti 1967).

The official remittances are relatively small, compared to monies from temporary migrants, but there is another source of money associated with migration that does not enter the official records. In studies of migration, remittances are frequently considered solely in terms of the relatives receiving them or the relatives sending them (e.g. Barrow 1977; Philpott 1973). One assumption implicit in such studies is that the primary impact of remittances in the homeland is directly through the sectors of the society from which emigrants originated, i.e.,their families. But if the dynamics of the overall system are taken into account it becomes evident that in São Miguel official remittances are only one aspect of the flow of money associated with migration, and that a second aspect, that of illegal flows, must be taken into account in order to fully comprehend the effects of emigration in this sphere.

The previously mentioned flow of visitors between São Miguel and America facilitates the illegal movement of black market dollars to and from the island. Dollars come into São Miguel with tourists, as cash or as travelers' checks, which may be sold, usually at a slight profit or as a favor, to friends and local business people. Some Azorean-American tourists use this as a means of subsidizing the trip back home, bringing extra undeclared dollars expressly for the purpose of selling them, frequently to people who send them out of the Azores, undeclared, for investment abroad. Customs officials are instructed to check for dollars being taken out, but the ingenuity of people smuggling them (for example, inside sealed cigarette packages) outstrips the enthusiasm for checking. In 1973 another variant of making the trip back home pay off was for emigrants to bring American clothes (declared as 'used' in customs) back home with them when they came to visit and then to sell them.

Official remittances in the Azores, as in the rest of Portugal, dropped markedly after the political unrest of 1974 (Chaney 1986). This partly reflected the fact that some emigrants decided to invest in banks and property in America, rather than send money back to what had previously been considered a 'good investment' in Portugal but which they feared no longer would be. Other factors which Chaney (1986:141) suggests were operative for mainland Portugal were the increases in minimum wages and social security reforms that were implemented after the revolution and which improved general well-being. This factor may have been less influential in the Azores, where remittances were not a major form of family support. Political and economic fluctuations in the homeland therefore do affect fluctuations in the flow of official remittances. Remittances began to rise again in 1976, going up over 40% in 1977 (*Azorean Times* 1980:1), and continued to rise as shown in Table 5.1. These remittances come primarily from the U.S., Canada, and Bermuda.

Table 5.1 Official Remittances to the Azores, 1976-79.

Year	Value in Escudos	Values in Dollars Approx. Equivalent
1976	282,000	9,097 (31 per $)
1977	418,000	11,943 (35 per $)
1978	718,000	17,950 (40 per $)
1979	755,000	18,875 (40 per $)

(Source: *Azorean Times* 1980:1)

Dollars are occasionally solicited in the countryside by townspeople who go from house to house. The urban educated and elites now seek dollars from emigrant visitors, and the visitors come prepared to oblige them. One exception is the emigrants who own income property in São Miguel and have been unable to smuggle the profits to America; they come back to spend *escudos*, not to bring dollars.

Dollars coming into the system, particularly dollars that are not declared in customs or changed through official channels, facilitate the extra-legal movement of money out of the islands. A critical characteristic of the black market dollars is that they tend to enter at commercial and educated levels of the society. These levels include the people who have the capital and the sophistication with finances to be interested in making investments outside the country. The uncertain political situation in 1974 was one stimulus for this, as was the poor condition of the post-revolution economy in general. A further stimulus has been the desire to have children obtain higher education abroad. For various reasons people from the educated and elite levels have wanted to make investments outside Portugal, and since it is illegal to take much money out without special government permission, the subterranian economy in dollars brought in by emigrants has enabled the illegal flow of investments out.

When simply going on vacation outside of Portugal, not necessarily to invest, it is helpful to gather dollars to take out surreptitiously that will supplement the government allowed minimum, which in 1979 was less than the equivalent of $200. People also collect dollars to send as presents to people in America. For all the various incentives to collect dollars, contact with emigrants makes it easier to obtain U.S. or Canadian currency and to transfer it out of the Azores. Many of the urban educated and elite who lack emigrant relatives are still in contact with former servants, former employees, or godchildren who have emigrated. In a reversal of the traditional patron-client roles, some former patrons have used these contacts to spread their resource bases to investments in America. In one case an Azorean landowner transferred substantial funds to Canada to buy a farm. The transfer of dollars and the purchase of the farm was facilitated largely by a former tenant farmer who had emigrated in the early 1960's and had kept in touch with his former *patrão.*

The pattern of money flows and increased importance of dollars is seen in payments on property sold. In the last decade people selling land to emigrants increasingly demanded that payments be made in dollars which could be deposited for them in America. Property is also sold in the other direction, by emigrants to people at home or to other emigrants. In both São Miguel and Azorean-American communities newspaper advertisements appear regularly offering property on the island for sale by owners in America. The sellers now ask for dollars, or a higher *escudo* price, making it difficult for people without access to dollars to buy land.

In summary, dollars enter the homeland as remittances, as loans paid back, as land payments, and as funds brought by visitors. Some of the money enters via official channels, is cashed in banks, and contributes to the foreign exchange. The people who receive remittances, primarily *trabalhadores* and *proprietários,* are rarely dependent on them, but use them for luxuries and household items. An undetermined amount of dollars enter the black market economy. This facilitates the transfer of funds out of the island in the form of smuggled dollars, which are used both to make investments and to pay the returns on investments that emigrants still have in the homeland.

There are also social and political causes which stimulate the flow of money into the island from America. One of the most common stimuli is the plight of a family or individual. Money is frequently solicited in America by radio and newspapers for aid to a homeless family or help in a case of catastrophic illness, which may even require funding for medical treatment in the U.S. Donations are made for political causes. During the 1970's the illegal Azorean independence party (FLA) sought funding throughout Azorean-American communities, and for a period received strong support. Later the leaders were accused of pocketing the funds and financial contributions declined. The stories of high level financial contributions from emigrants to the independence movement live on, sustaining the idea of a strong support base in America.

GOODS

Although it is sometimes overshadowed by the emphasis on remittances found in migration literature, the value of goods that emigrants send back to the homeland can be very significant. In São Miguel, according to the accounts of older residents, the gifts of clothing sent back by emigrants from the 1950's on had a major effect on the overall well-being of rural residents.

One indication of what life was like prior to the contemporary period of emigration is given by a Portuguese geographer, Soeiro de Brito, writing in 1955 about rural life in São Miguel. He describes the majority of the population as having a very low standard of living, being poorly fed, poorly dressed and without comfort in a situation which had become progressively worse since the turn of the century (Duncan 1972:113). This view was confirmed by many of the older people in São Miguel, including one moderately well-off, literate, sixty-five year old village woman who had this to say about the conditions prior to emigration in the 1950's:

> People then had lots of children, and many of them had the swollen bellies which means they did not eat anything but bread. . . . There was no butter, no cheese, none of the things that we have now. Chicken was only cooked for a special *festa*, not like now when people eat meat or chicken almost every Sunday.
>
> My daughter was the only one in the school who wore shoes, except for the three children of rich people. She had shoes because my husband made them for her. It was cold in winter, but people had no coats, they wore corn leaves instead. What misery, what poverty! The young people can't understand, but if it had not been for emigration the islands would have gone to ruin.
>
> (Fieldnotes, São Miguel 1977).

Stories abound in São Miguel about how crucial the clothes and money sent back by emigrants were to the recipients in earlier times. The first emigrants of the 1950's sent back clothes, fabric and shoes to their families. It didn't matter if they were used clothes (which they usually were), they were warm and free. In later years they began to send more luxurious goods such as radios, but the clothes kept coming, and the material comfort of those remaining at home improved. The need today is not as dire, but the gifts are welcomed even if the used clothing is sometimes disdained by the more affluent.

Used clothing is still a major item sent from America. Large sacks of clothes arrive by boat in Ponta Delgada where they must be redeemed from customs for a fee. As gifts sent to individuals the sacks are less common than they were in the 1960's, but some used clothing is also sold commercially. Although commercial use is not separated out, the magnitude of the influx of clothing can be seen in the 1976 figure showing that over $96,000 (U.S. $) worth of used clothing was sent to Ponta Delgada from the U.S., Bermuda, and Canada (I.N.E 1976b).

For the wives of the rural *trabalhadores* used clothing is still a valued gift, regardless of style and color. The sentiment was expressed as follows by the moderately well off wife of a *lavrador* (owner of dairy cattle) who has two small children.

> How much will ten dollars buy here? Not even a good pair of pants for my husband. But the clothes they send are strong and last a long time. Work clothes is what we need, things to wear everyday at home and in the fields, not things to wear in town, so they don't have to be the latest fashion. In one sack my aunt sends me more clothes than I would ever be able to buy here with the ten dollars she might send me instead.
>
> (Fieldnotes, São Miguel 1978).

In the towns people are less enthusiastic about the frequently outmoded or imperfect 'factory seconds' clothing that is sent by relatives in America, preferring to receive fabric which they can fashion as they wish. They criticize their relatives for thinking that nothing has changed since they left. The idea of 'dire need', perpetuated in America, no longer fits the conditions in São Miguel for most of the people. For example, one well-meaning emigrant who left in 1958 sent a sack of clothing to his niece which contained articles so outrageously outdated that the family would not even think of using them as work clothes. The rural *trabalhadores* and *proprietários*, whom the emigrants don't hesitate to label as ignorant, marvel in such instances at the well- intended but unforgivable ignorance of those who have emigrated.

While it is primarily the rural *trabalhadores* who receive gifts of used clothing, even the sophisticated, well-educated town dwellers who own cars, televisions, and stereos, occasionally receive shipments of presents from family in America. A family with emigrant parents, for example, may be sent a crate of American goods for Christmas, despite the fact that the younger couple visits America every few years. Typical gifts include canned foods, pans, pyrex dishes, appliances, and fabrics. All of these things are available in São Miguel, but at greater cost and in some cases lower quality. The cost of sending the package, however, offsets any cost differential.

For more recent emigrants the tradition of sending presents and money takes on the aura of ritual. As soon as emigrants are well established in America they send back presents and money, as if to prove success and affirm loyalty to the family back home. One young woman in Fall River recounted how with her first paycheck she went out and bought clothes from the factory store, candy, and watches to send to her sister-in-law's family at a cost of well over $300. Such gift giving is in most cases disconnected from any necessity in the homeland. The recipient of the above mentioned package, for example, exclaimed over the good fortunes of her sister-in-law while sitting in the modern kitchen of her large, well-kept house in Ponta Delgada. Clearly the 'thought' far exceeds the utility of the actual gifts, as exemplified by the fact that Nescafe is frequently sent both ways -- from America to the Azores, and from the Azores to America.

Emigrants who visit from America generally bring gifts to distribute among their relatives. The characteristics of these gifts are fairly universal, with the quantity and quality depending on the actual or hoped for status of the giver. In the rural areas, stockings, scarves, and cosmetics are given along with clothes, fabrics, candy, and other foodstuffs or knickknacks for the family. Radios were a common gift in the past, having now been replaced by watches and cassette recorders. The presents that are sent back via the emigrants, for those who did not visit, consist primarily of local handicrafts, such as embroideries or small replicas of rural cottages; local liquors; candy; and miscellaneous religious artifacts.

Formalized Flows of Goods

Used clothing is still sent through churches, which collect it and send sacks of clothes to parishes in São Miguel for the priest to distribute among those with the greatest need. Some of the very poorest families without close relatives in America benefit from this practice.

Another form of charity is the collection of goods for specific causes. In 1978, for example, a local Fall River radio station organized a campaign to raise funds for sending bicycles to an orphanage in São Miguel. The 1980 earthquakes, although not serious in São Miguel, are another instance of this type of charity emerging in response to need. Funds and goods were assembled in Azorean-American communities and sent over to assist the victims.

As recently as the late 1960's the goods sent back from America significantly alleviated individual poverty in rural São Miguel. Those functional goods are still valued by the *trabalhadores*, but the presents to the urban educated and *proprietários* tend to be expressions of the emigrant's status through a traditional channel rather than an actual response to need in the homeland. There is a ritualized aspect to the expression of success and generosity on the part of emigrants, but the content of that expression sometimes reveals a deficient understanding of transformations that have taken place in the homeland since their departure.

The majority of American goods reach the rural *trabalhadores* and *proprietários*. The people who have the greatest need, *os pobres* (the poor folk), are often the ones who, lacking close relatives in America, have the least access to that bounty except through formalized channels of charity. The traditional elite, on the other hand, also lack access except through an occasional gift from a former employee or lower status godchild.

In summary, over the last twenty years in São Miguel there have been profound changes in knowledge of the outside world and material aspects of life among the rural and skilled worker sector of the population as a result of information, money, and goods flowing in from America. These migration associated flows have contributed to an improved standard of living, primarily in the rural areas, and to a more realistic picture of life in America.

The communications between the rural and skilled worker sector and America are largely conditioned by a migrant ideology of sustaining ties with the homeland and reaffirming the success of emigration. Information emerges primarily from the 'micro-environment' of Azorean-American communities. Generalized information about America, for example that concerning unemployment, is therefore not necessarily conveyed to or considered relevant by the rural and skilled worker sectors in the homeland.

The intensity of communications between rural areas and America has resulted in increased familiarity with American characteristics of urban modernity. The categories of goods are similar to those found in European models of urban modernity, but the specifically American characteristics set them off from those familiar to the urban educated in São Miguel.

One of the greatest changes in these flows over time has been in the expansion of communication flows from America to the urban educated, many of whom do not have close emigrant relatives. This information flow is in part stimulated by the increase of better-educated emigrant tourists. The information they transmit, e.g. about colleges, is drawn not only from the 'micro-environment' of Azorean-American communities but also from the macro-environment of America in general.

During the 1960's-1970's period of migration in São Miguel, the structural context of decision-making about emigration has been affected by improved standards of living associated with flows of goods and money, and internal development. Communication flows, particularly since 1960, have affected the informational context through both expanded content and expanded communication networks. As also seen in the previous chapter on the flows of people, past emigration has been part of a process which has produced alterations in the context of decision-making for subsequent emigration. The effects of particular variables from this context on contemporary migration decision-making in São Miguel will be examined in the next chapter.

CHAPTER 6
MIGRATION DECISION-MAKING IN TIME AND SPACE

Voluntary migration is a dynamic process which occurs as a result of decisions formulated at particular times and in particular contexts. Choice of the migration alternative is influenced by economic, social, and cultural constraints and incentives emerging from various levels of the system. An analysis of past flows of people and communications between São Miguel and America was presented in the previous chapters to illustrate the feedback characteristic of migration at the regional and local levels. This chapter examines how historical and ongoing flows articulate with contemporary migration decision-making. The main constraints and incentives which affect the relative attractiveness of migration for individuals in different social levels of the home society are discussed within a life cycle framework. A cursory analysis of migration statistics indicates that young families compose the bulk of Azorean emigrants, but there are two other stages in the life cycle which are critical points for migration decision-making; the youth and the elderly, and particularly students who have not yet established families and the elderly whose families are grown-up. Analysis of specific attributes of individual circumstances based on case studies of migrants and non-migrants in these three stages in the life cycle thus augments the preceding aggregate perspective with an examination of individual variability.

175

A DECISION-MAKING PERSPECTIVE ON MIGRATION

Migration studies have tended to focus on the largest categories of migrants, paying less attention to numerically less significant groups whose behavior may affect the overall pattern over time. A decision-making approach allows for description of the variation within migration flows. This is critical for an understanding of the migration process which attempts to elucidate changing patterns and the potential for change. Incremental changes in decision-making at the individual level are what make up the broader patterns. The broader patterns thus reflect alterations in either circumstances or the process for evaluating options (Barth 1967:667). It is therefore essential for a fuller understanding of the migration process to examine how the interactions of circumstance, perceptions and information vary throughout the home society.

In this study I assume that people try to maximize a wide range of satisfactions, including economic and social gains, and that choice is colored by beliefs and past experiences. The fact that people do not always maximize income, as Bennett (1969) illustrates with respect to North American farmers, does not negate the idea that they maximize a range of satisfactions; cultural values and social relations which act as checks on maximizing economic gain may themselves be maximized in a decision to live more modestly.

The concept of maximization raises the question of whose criteria is used to judge rationality. I follow the positions of Heath (1976:83) and Barth (1967:668) in formulating rationality of migration decisions in subjective terms, relying on judgments expressed by the informants. Migrants follow the course which seems best to them under certain conditions. They may realize that better jobs can be obtained in other areas, but their choices make the best of what they know, taking into account conditions such as where they have relatives who will ease the transition to a new life.

Decision-making analysis can be used with a wide range of models and permits analysis at both macro and micro levels (Howard and Ortiz 1971:215). Decision-making analysis is not confined to the actor's, i.e. the decision-makers, conscious perceptions. Factors which appear to influence decisions without the awareness of the actor must also be taken into account. It is thus the postulation of factors which affect decisions that is the aim, not the imputation of motivations (Howard and Ortiz 1971:215).

There are four main types of data incorporated in the discussion of decision-making which follows: what migrants say about their decisions, what non-migrants in the same context say, how people behave with respect to migration, and my own observations about the context of that behavior. By combining these viewpoints I have attempted to approximate the 'insider' view of migration and integrate it with my own 'outsider' perspective.[1] The explanations I offer for what is going on in the process of migration in São Miguel are not the insiders' explanations, they are an outsider's interpretations based on evaluations made by the actors.

In many discussions it has been noted that stage in the life cycle is an important determinant in the propensity to migrate (see, for example, Leslie and Richardson 1961; and Bishop 1976).[2] In this chapter life cycle stages are used to discuss different propensities to migrate at specific transitional points. The framework is also used to explore the varying perceptions people of different ages and personal histories have of migration.

This chapter discusses emigration from São Miguel for the three life cycle stages of older people, young families, and students. Who makes the migration decision, at what point, and what factors act as constraints or incentives are discussed for each life stage. Constraints and incentives are assumed to be both principles and circumstances: individuals evaluate information and make a decision influenced by their own cultural values and beliefs as well as by specific conditions in their lives (Howard and Ortiz 1971:220). The flexibility of the migration option over time can best be understood in terms of the influential role of migration feedback on individual circumstances and perceptions, as illustrated in Table 6.1

Studies which focus on general attitudes toward migration in the homeland (e.g. Moustaka 1967) are limited as to what they say about specific factors in decision-making. The reasons which people give for emigrating often involve the same categories of factors as those given for not emigrating. In São Miguel, the reasons for not emigrating are because life is better at home, work is better at home, or people do not want to be uprooted from the community of family and neighbors.3 Those who have already emigrated or plan to emigrate state that they migrate to have a better life, to obtain better employment, and to be with family who have already gone. The critical variations in migration decisions are not found in these general reasons but in the specific attributes of factors which shape them. These specific sociocultural and economic constraints and incentives are examined in this chapter with respect to the quality of life, work, and family categories.

Table 6.1   The Migration Process in Time and Space

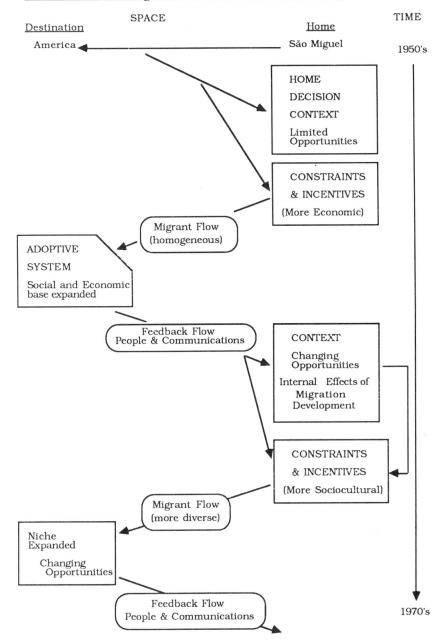

Economic factors are important in migration decision-making, yet are not the sole determinants in many situations of migration.   If wage differentials or other income factors were the decisive factors in Michaelense migration, then it would be expected that everyone who could would leave. They do not. Sociocultural factors such as kinship, social roles and values modify and supplement the economic factors.   The following examination of migration decision-making therefore focuses on specific attributes of factors at specific life stages rather than on aggregate categories such as wage differentials.[4] The first life stage discussed is that of the elderly, those who have experienced many of the changes wrought by migration. The chapter concludes with a discussion of the youngest life stage of migration, the youth whose migration behavior may have the greatest future effects on the homeland.[5]

'OS VELHOS' (THE OLD ONES)

Starting with the elderly end of the life stage continuum may appear unorthodox, but it is chronological. The positions and perspectives of older people reflect the cumulative changes throughout the most recent decades of migration, the history which to some extent affects people of all ages.

The concept of retirement is relatively new in São Miguel. The elderly carry on the basic activities of life as long as they are able to. A ninety-two year old widow lives alone near her seventy year old daughter, looks after her own chickens, does agricultural work such as sorting grapes brought back to the village by her son-in-law, and takes care of her own cooking needs. The seventy-two year old son-in-law has a business selling wine and other crops and oversees the property of his three emigrant children. He hires a seventy-two year old man who can climb up on the twenty foot high drying rack to hang corn with the agility equal to that of the twenty year old youth who also works for him. One of the decisions that these older rural people often face is whether or not to emigrate to America where the work/retirement distinction forces them into relative inactivity.

In São Miguel older people frequently stay alone in their own homes and are usually cared for by family and neighbors in rural communities.

> Maria and I used to live on the same street when I was a girl. We are like sisters, and if she gets sick now I will take care of her and lots of others will help.
>
> (Fieldnotes, São Miguel 1978)

Priests and others in villages throughout the island, however, note that more and more of the old people have very few or no family living nearby. This is not surprising, given the rise in the proportion of people over sixty-five in the population due to emigration since 1960. The local priests often actively watch over the older residents, advising them about government benefits[6] and alerting others to their needs. The priest in one community, for example, organized a youth group where the girls spend a few hours a week helping people, particularly the aged, who are in need of their attentions. Those who do not remain in their own homes or do not go to live with family, are cared for by the state in a hospital or facility for the elderly in the city. Although the local government is now

planning to build a new home for the elderly, the one
facility in existence is considered as a last resort, not a
real alternative.

For those who have immediate family in America,
another option is to emigrate, i.e., to retire in America.
Because of the previous patterns of migration this means
that the majority of older people who emigrate are drawn
from the *trabalhador* and *proprietário* levels of the
home society. There is no breakdown in the Portuguese
figures on age distribution of emigrants except over and
under ten years old. In the over ten category, between 14
and 20% of Azorean emigrants since 1965 have been listed
as 'inactives'. The proportion declined from 20% in 1965
to 14% in 1973 and rose again in 1974 (I.N.E. 1970,
1977). According to U.S. and Canadian consulate staff in
1973, a high proportion of those listed as inactives were
elderly people (personal communication, Ponta Delgada
1973). Inquiries made with parish priests in three
communities indicated that in the last ten years between
15 and 20% of the elderly who went to America to join
family in the last ten years returned to São Miguel.

Old people, more than those at any other stage of the
life-cycle, usually consider migrating because of strong
urgings from families abroad. There are two periods when
the elderly are particularly subject to these pressures:
first, if they are widowed, and second, when their
productive activity decreases.

> A seventy-eight year old woman stood in the travel
> agency conversing with the agent and myself. She
> explained that she had gone to Canada last year to
> join her son and his family. Two of her other
> children also live in Canada. For years, she said,
> the children had written asking the parents to

come, but they had not wanted to leave their house on the outskirts of Ponta Delgada, where she knew all the neighbors and her husband could go down to the small bar in the afternoons after taking care of the crops. Then her husband died and the three offspring in Canada sent her an airplane ticket and arranged for her visa to be processed. Under this pressure, 'What could I do?' she said, and she shut up her house and went.

(Fieldnotes, São Miguel 1977)

Others resist these pressures, saving the dollars they are sent for the time when they are no longer independent, hoping that such savings will forestall being uprooted from the island.

Frequently the family in America will 'call over', i.e., send a petition for a visa, a grandparent or grandparents because both parents are working and they need someone to take care of the house and the children while they are gone. The alternative to this is often for one parent to work a day shift and the other to work a night shift, a plan which has obvious drawbacks for family life. On the island, child care (or more accurately, just keeping an eye on the children) is part of the daily life of most older people whether the children are from their own family or those of someone else in the community. Children also do their share of looking after each other and an adult is rarely engaged in exclusive surveillance except in the case of small babies. In the emigrant household in America the island grandparent is likely to find that childcare is not the same as in São Miguel. The same woman as above continued her account to explain why she had returned to the island from Canada after just eight months there.

My son and his wife were both working in
factories. It was too hot to be outside when I
arrived and I didn't know anyone to visit so I never
left the house. I stayed with my grandchildren
and I watched television. After a while I could
understand but I still don't know English and even
my grandchildren spoke English. The children
over there are different, they do what they want to
and go everywhere by themselves... The food is
different... And the weather, terrible. First too
hot, and then too cold. After the Christmas
celebration I said 'I am going back to the island'.
Here I have a good life, the weather is good, I
know everyone, I have everything I need. I will
never go back to Canada. I am afraid even to visit
because I want to die here, here in my own land.

(Fieldnotes, São Miguel 1977)

There are many tales of this sort, the old men and
women who went to America to join their children and
found themselves lonely, without transportation, away from
the people they knew and the familiar daily interactions, at
home with the grandchildren, confused by their behavior,
watching endless soap operas without knowing English,
hot in the summer and cold in the winter, and with
nowhere to go even if the weather were fine. Some, like
the woman in the travel agency, return. Others stay, and if
literate, write home about their troubles. One such woman
after two years in Canada with her son and daughter, wrote
to her brother that "I came to hell in America". Even
though she is financially well off, the children don't want
her to return to the village because she is in her seventies
and in poor health. On the other hand, she does not want

to die in America. Her brother, the only one of eight children who never left the island, laments his sister's fate, fearing she will die far from the homeland. In the meantime he rents out her land, putting the money in a bank, keeps watch on her closed-up house, and hopes for her return.

Information about emigrants is a major topic of daily conversation among islanders, particularly the elderly. There are two major topics: one, the good life in America and its counterpart, the woes of old people in America; and two, the benefits emigration has wrought for the island contrasted with the view that soon only the sick and the dying will be left. News is passed from one person to another and discussed extensively in small gatherings throughout the day. Life in America is undoubtedly good since emigrants have been able to work and save and become richer than they ever were in São Miguel. Older people are proud of their children's achievements and boast about their clever grandchildren. Many have been visited, and others have themselves gone to America to visit. Stories about these interactions are retold endlessly. Not all of the stories are positive; the tales of the misfortunes of the old and the unhappy also filter back to the homeland. People hear of the old woman whose children pressured her to come live with them in Winnipeg after her husband died, and then was shuffled from child to child every few months until after two years she became ill and they put her in a nursing home. Old women in shawls shake their heads and men say it is not for them, they will never go now, it is not for the old. But some do go. The families insist, it becomes more difficult to be without children to lend a hand in daily activities, and they go. Sometimes they sell their property, convinced that life in America really will be better for them. Sometimes they are less sure of their fate and keep the property as a place to return to if need be.

The loss of old people through emigration is not as vocally decried by the people who remain as the loss of the young, but it is felt nonetheless. They are lost kin and neighbors, lost for the old with whom they spent their time, talking over the wall, shelling beans together, and they are lost for the young whose children they watched and who sought their advice. Those who leave are often the *proprietários* and the better off *trabalhadores.* Many of their siblings left years before to make lives in Brazil and the United States, but they were the ones who stayed, or returned, accumulating property over the years as others left. The ones without much property, the poorest, are the ones who do not have relatives abroad or whose relatives do not press for them to emigrate. In Ponta Delgada young educated families are sometimes ashamed of the illiteracy and backwardness of the parents, and for this reason do not bring them to live with them in the city. There is a similar sentiment in America where such elders too clearly define the emigrants' more humble origins.

From the perspective of the community at home, the ones with property and respect are a loss to the community as leaders, advisors, and the modest patrons of the less fortunate. They are the ones with enough margin to lend money and rent land to those who need assistance. As dependence on the large landowning traditional elite declines, such village elders are the only alternatives for many rural people seeking capital. Bank loans have become easier to arrange in the 1970's, but even so it helps to have an affluent sponsor or cosigner. These losses account in part for the growing concern with the fate of the elderly in São Miguel.

The emigration of older people is connected to the

needs of their families abroad, but also depends on their own views which are influenced by contact with emigrants. In the countryside, it is a rare old person who has no parent, sibling, child or grandchild who has emigrated in one of this century's waves of migration. For many, the very land they own was in part obtained through the money of or sale of land by migrants. For others the new houses, and a variety of improvements such as modern kitchens and bathrooms, are the benefits associated with emigrants. These people experienced the poverty that existed in earlier decades, the poverty that made life bitterly hard not so many years ago. They understand the magnitude of improvements and praise migration as a salvation for the island. Many sentences begin with the phrase 'If it were not for migration...' and speak of how much worse conditions used to be. On the other hand they see the young leaving and their grandchildren growing up through pictures or an occasional visit; and they feel abandoned, left behind, and increasingly useless.

> Everyone who can leaves. They don't want to stay here and work. The young people want to earn more and more and the life here is not good enough for them. It is only us old people who can't go who stay here. Soon there will be no one left on the island.
>
> (Fieldnotes, São Miguel 1978)

These are the people who have managed their lives without emigrating, and now when they should have some peace at the end of their lives they are often placed in the dilemma of choosing between life in the familiar home, and a life in unfamiliar America. They hear that America is not good for old people; yet it may have been good to their own offspring and if they stay in São Miguel they will suffer the separation from children and grandchildren. Part of the information they are exposed to emanates from the return flow of older people who came back from America to retire in São Miguel. These people both praise the life in America for the young, and reinforce the idea that life in the island is really better for the elderly.

> Lourdes, known as Lou in New Bedford, sat with her apron on waiting for a cake to come out of the gas oven in her modern but not ostentatious kitchen and told how she had enjoyed life in America. She said that life was good there for anyone who could work, because you had to work hard but you could make a lot of money. She had come back to the island because her husband liked to have his own land and do his own work and they were old enough to live an easier life now. She protested that of course they both worked here, taking care of the crops and selling a little surplus, but it was for themselves. She liked the peaceful life, and the fact that people were not in such a hurry as in America. And with their social security check coming every month from the U. S. they didn't worry about money as they did in America where everything is expensive.
>
> (Fieldnotes, São Miguel 1978)

The older people who voice the most positive opinions about life in America are the ones who went there while they were still able to work a few years before retirement. Regardless of how well they like the work, it makes them more independent and enables them to meet other people. In contrast to those elderly immigrants whose only work is child care, they gain a sense of what the community and America are like.

In summary, there are two transitional points at which the elderly are likely to emigrate: upon being widowed, and at the point of decreasing productive activity. The decision-making process is affected strongly by the situation of the family in America, who are more likely to urge them to emigrate if they can be useful in child and household care. In addition, the process is influenced by the perspectives of the family in America, who in many cases feel responsible for their parents and do not think they can properly care for them just by sending money. These Azorean-Americans have been conditioned to the American emphasis on retirement and think that their aging parents should not have to work. On the other side of the picture, the old people, who are the other element in the decision-making process, may see that capacity to do a little work as essential independence. They are often torn between the desire to take part in their grandchildren's upbringing and share in the family support networks, and the fear of losing the independence and dignity of their lives on the island. Thus for the elderly migration poses a choice that creates conflict between traditional social positions and cultural values, which in the homeland are harmonious.

YOUNG FAMILIES

Migration studies show that the highest mobility is generally found in the 25-44 year old age group. This suggests that the family formation stage of the life cycle and the early stage in labor force participation affect the extent and character of migration in various European countries (Goldstein 1964:1131). In São Miguel statistics on emigration show that on average, since 1965, migrants are one quarter children under the age of ten, and three-fourths of the total leave in family groupings. This indicates that the great proportion of migrants are in the life stage of young family.

A broader range of influential factors come into play for people at this stage than is the case for the elderly. At this middle stage, the onus of deciding lies primarily within the homeland domestic group. Three categories of factors are associated with young family migration in São Miguel: 1) family ties, 2) quality of work and quality of life, 3) and family allocations of opportunities. The three main transitional periods important in young families' migration decisions are at the times of setting up a family, expanding the family, and arranging access to property or a secure base for family livelihood. As with the elderly, the people who emigrate with greatest legal ease are those with immediate family in America.

Marriage is said to 'free the child from the parents'. Ideally, married children stay nearby, but history has accustomed people to the idea that marriage, education, and emigration can take them away. Marriage and emigration may combine when single emigrants come back to the island to find a good spouse, a 'pure', 'obedient' girl or a 'hardworking' family man. Young men and women visiting the island on vacation are joked with about looking for a spouse. One young woman who returned to stay was constantly asked when she was going to marry because no one believed that she returned from America for any reason other than marriage. The fact that emigrants, even though they are better off in America, still value the above qualities reinforces the idea that such virtues, intimately associated with the concept of good family life, should be maintained. Virtues are not always the central consideration, however, and marriage to an emigrant is sometimes only a means to a passport.

Some people marry an emigrant and in that way obtain a visa to the U.S. or Canada. Others get engaged when one member of the couple is about to emigrate, planning to reunite and marry later. These plans do not always come to fruition, as seen in the following case.

> Rosinha was engaged to a man from the village who emigrated with his family to Fall River about four years ago. They were supposed to be married two years later, but the month before he was going to return to marry her he married someone there. Her employer told me that it was very bad for this to happen to a girl because once she has been engaged and jilted her reputation is tainted. Rosinha, she added, was a very good person and everyone knew she had never done anything wrong; nevertheless she was very lucky when Luis wanted to marry her.
>
> (Fieldnotes, São Miguel 1978)

A family in São Miguel may try to emigrate at the point when they have several children if it becomes clear that they will have difficulty arranging a good livelihood for them all, or if they miss the support of family members who have already emigrated. In the past the husband went first and later either returned or called over the rest of the family.

My father went to America in the 1950's because he
had a brother there who arranged it and we were
very poor. He used to send us letters with dollars
and always a few sticks of gum. I was a kingpin in
the village because I always had gum to chew. After
another five years we all went over.

(Fieldnotes, Fall River 1977)

This rarely happens now, unless a family is very large. In
such cases one parent and the older children may go first
to set up a household and earn enough money to bring the
others over.

It is not simply the individual couple's family situation
which must be considered in decision-making leading to
migration. It is also the interactions of the new family
with other families, with natal families of both members of
the couple, and with unrelated families in the community.

Family Ties

    The viability of kin and community support systems in
America affects the migration decision-making process
when support systems in the homeland are depleted or
attenuated as a result of previous migration or other
causes. Informal structures, such as the extent to which
assistance in child care can be activated, affect the well-
being of individuals. Family ties extend well beyond the
physical boundaries of the household. Households are
ideally independent, and newly married couples should
move into a separate domicile to start their own family.
Yet the actual interactions between households of family

members in both social and economic spheres are often intense, obscuring the boundaries between household units.   Specific societal and personal values about the qualities and responsibilities of extended family relationships thus influence perceptions of migration choices.

Emigration has touched the lives of many residents in São Miguel by thinning the support networks. Within the community, reciprocal exchanges of everyday goods and favors include food and childcare, both of which are basic to the welfare of the family. Siblings and grandparents are enlisted to keep an eye on children. Neighbors help out, entertaining children with stories and sending them off with messages to deliver or errands to run. A child readily spends a few days with cousins or grandparents, even if they live in another community. If a wife or couple goes to America to visit, cousins or siblings can be asked to cook for and look after the remaining household. The range of reciprocal support extends far beyond the immediate household and may even include caring for land belonging to an urban sibling or housing a rural nephew who comes to the city to study. As people continue to emigrate these vital support systems are diminished for those who remain. The greatest impact is in the countryside, but effects are felt in the towns as well

The loss through emigration of supportive kin is particularly acute because of the values associated with close family ties. The household is a basic social and economic unit, but the system of extended kin ties is the context in which it operates. One of the most frequently mentioned condemnations of emigrants is that they forget or neglect family in the homeland. In Azorean-American communities the Portuguese newspapers and radio shows are full of reminders not to forget the *terra natal*

(homeland).   Advertisements stress the desirability of
going back for vacations, to see the family or attend *festas*,
and articles solicit donations for victims of various
calamities or other needy persons back home.   On the
other side of the ocean the priests in Michaelense
parishes preach about remembering 'our emigrants,' and
'our families' in America, and stress the contributions
these emigrants have made to their home churches and
communities.   All of this supports the ideology of
maintaining strong family ties in both natal and adoptive
systems.

The value placed on maintaining family support
networks is further reinforced by patterns of older
returning emigrants.   Many of these returnees who come
back to retire after years in America do not stay long in
São Miguel because the separation from children and
grandchildren is too painful.   One elderly *proprietário*
recounted how his daughter and her husband had just
returned to Boston after eighteen months in   São   Miguel:

> My daughter's husband returned a few years ago
> and they sold their house and came back here to
> live.   They remodeled a house in the city.   She
> brought everything from America, all the bathroom
> things, only the tile they got from Lisbon... After a
> few months she began to cry about missing her
> daughter and she cried more and more every day
> until last month they decided to leave.   They sold
> the house and moved back to Boston.
>
>   (Fieldnotes, São Miguel 1978)

When this story was told four fairly young women standing
nearby all agreed that it was a great hardship to be far away

from your family, and the old man, who had other children in the village, concurred.

Family ties and associated values have been influenced by past migration and they affect migration decision-making in the present. The importance of family considerations in decision-making is illustrated in the following case of a couple who were arranging visas to the U.S.:

> The husband, aged thirty-four, said that he had a very well-paid job as a clerk in town which gave him a lot of contact with foreigners. He enjoyed the work and, not having a high school education, it was a very good job. His wife and he had just had their third child and hope to have one more... His wife's widowed mother went to the U.S. five years ago to visit her sister who had been there for many years. While there she met a widower who lived in the apartment building and she went back the next year to marry him. Two years later the wife's only sister emigrated to join the mother. After they left the wife said she was very lonely and the mother kept writing and telling them to come. When she got pregnant again they decided that they should go after the baby was born so they could be with her family. She realized that they will both have to work, but she is a seamstress and thinks that it will be easy to get a job where her sister works in a clothing factory. Her husband is less sanguine about working in a factory, but since he has learned some English he hopes later to find a better job.
>
> (Fieldnotes, São Miguel 1977)

Although the husband in the above case is more highly skilled than others in such families, other aspects of their situation are typical. The family assumed that both adults could earn a satisfactory living in America. The type of work was not an incentive since it involved a loss of status for the husband, from clerk to factory worker. Wages were an incentive but did not throw the balance in favor of migration. The important factor in the decision-making process was the desire to be close to the wife's mother and sister, augmented by the presence of the aunt as well. Information about possibilities came directly from the mother and the sister. The decision was made with the interests of the wife dominating, and at a transitional period when the family was expanding. The arrival of a new baby meant that family support was needed more than ever from non-household kin. The wife's perceptions and her family relationships were thus critical in the decision-making process.

At certain transitional times in the development of a family, ties to other relatives and family support systems become decisive factors in the migration decision-making process. Families with young children are particularly prone to influence by these factors. At this time family ties take on more weight in the migration decision than do isolated economic factors. However, the familial and economic factors are not completely separable. A family may emigrate in order to be with other family members, knowing that the support network will enable both parents to go out and work for wages.

At an individual level this pattern mirrors MacDonald's (1964) structural model of chain migration in which kinship relationships are viewed as one of the basic mechanisms for perpetuating the migration flow from Italy to the U.S. In the case of Michaelense migration to

America the family relationship is not only a mechanism for the actual move, but also a stimulus for migration as family support networks at home are diminished by previous migration.

Quality of Work and Quality of Life

Evaluations related to the quality of work and life involve personal ideational perspectives. What information people have to process is influenced by the informal structures, such as kin and community, to which they are linked. The perspectives which are basic to evaluations of the relative attractiveness of work and material life in America relate to ideas about independence, modernity, and social mobility. The importance of these ideas, and the information about America with respect to them, varies among different social levels in São Miguel.

Despite the intensity of family ties in São Miguel, there is also a strong value placed on independence. The emphasis placed on nuclear family households as the ideal is one example of independence already discussed. Property ownership and 'being your own boss' are two facets of independence which strongly influence migration decision-making. One great dream of many emigrants is to own property, either in America or back home, but property of their own. Some who buy property in São Miguel later sell it when they realize that they will only leave America for visits, not to return for good. Others accumulate funds to buy an apartment tenement or house in America, part of which can always be rented out. Some families manage to buy property within a few years of arriving by pooling family earnings.

> When my family arrived here seven years ago we all found jobs in the factories, even my little brother worked after school, and we dreamed of making enough money to go back to the island and buy a big piece of land. We pooled all our earnings and after two years bought this house which has three apartments. Then we were going to start saving for the land, but we needed a car, and then I wanted to own my own car, and my mother wanted new furniture, and we never did save for the land. I think my parents realized then that they were never going back to stay.
>
> (Fieldnotes, Fall River 1977)

In the homeland owning property becomes a particular concern when families expand.

> João has been working in town in a factory. He got married last year and they are now expecting a child. He is concerned with 'getting a little something', land to work for their own needs and a little extra income, and a house of their own. He says they could maybe even buy up the one they rent now from an older woman in the U.S. and fix it up. He wants to go to Bermuda and work for a year or two to save some money, saying that here he earns relatively well but the most he ever managed to save was for the television, and now being married, he can't save at all. He knows from his parents who went there that in Bermuda he

> would have to work hard but could save a lot.
>
> (Fieldnotes, São Miguel, 1978)

For the property-poor workers it is difficult to 'get a little something' unless they do emigrate, and without a little something they sometimes see themselves as destined to a life lacking basic independence.

For women independence is connected to their desire to work for wages. There are very few opportunities for rural women to be employed. There is only seasonal labor such as grape harvesting, for which they are paid half of what men receive. Young women in particular are attracted by the idea of earning regular wages. They complain that the only money they can make in São Miguel is through the pittances they earn from handicrafts and the month or so of seasonal labor.

> Why don't they (the government) build factories here? Most of the women would like to work if they could earn well. Don't you remember how all those women were applying for the one job as a janitor in the school a month ago? They want to work. Especially the young ones who aren't married yet, they have nothing to do but embroider.
>
> (Fieldnotes, São Miguel, 1978)

The woman speaking wanted to emigrate but the closest relatives she had in America were only cousins who had not offered to help her. The *proprietários* are generally quick to point out that in America both the husband and the wife have to work to make ends meet, and that this can be very hard on the family. Yet the homeland model for Michaelense women working outside of the house is set by well-educated professional women and provides a respectable example. Women in São Miguel are well versed in the benefits and types of work in America. They know that housework and family care must be done, in addition to the job, but that modern houses and appliances make this an easier task. The wealth of domestic information is connected to the fact that it is the women who maintain most communication between the homeland and adoptive areas.

Like owning property, 'being your own boss' is a valued status in São Miguel. In emigration the latter is sometimes forfeited for the former. For the *trabalhador*, who is used to working for someone else, employment under a foreman in an American factory provides access to independent ownership of property and goods. According to local conversations, a nice house and a big car are obtainable for anyone who works hard in America. In São Miguel they are not. For the *proprietários*, who are already property owners or will inherit property, 'being your own boss' may outweigh the profits of supervised factory labor, unless they themselves can rapidly attain foreman status. Dislike of factory work is often a reason given for return to São Miguel. As one small property owner who spent two years in Fall River put it, "Here I'm my own horse, my own boss. There (in Fall River) I was everybody's jackass."

For those with professional education who say emigration is always an option 'if things get worse', the getting worse is described as curtailment of their opportunities as independent businessmen. Some of these people, rare as they are as emigrants, express the view that the economic policies of the mainland government have made it very difficult recently for their businesses to expand. Faced with limitation, one such person emigrated to California, where he set up an import-export business handling products from the Azores and was rapidly expanding the business into areas outside the state. Others arranged for visas but not all have decided to make the move.

'Having a little something', which everyone wants, but not everyone has in São Miguel, confers independence within a status system that recognizes the worth of that independence. In the less hierarchical status system of America there is more perceptable social mixing and competition, which muddles the status distinctions. For this reason some of the elite claim that anyone with property does not emigrate from São Miguel where their life is comfortable and their status clear. However, people with property do emigrate, which indicates that for them other aspects of independence and other values and circumstances are operative in the decision to go.

Modernity in work and life has rapidly gained value, both with improvements in the standard of living in the homeland and the flow of information about amenities in America. Behavior patterns are influenced through the return and visiting of migrants. In one case a young returned male took the half dozen girls who had worked for his father during the grape harvest for an excursion picnic on the other side of the island, and they stopped to see a movie on the way home. The outing itself, with no adult chaperons, was not fully approved of by the community residents. Even more upsetting was the idea that occurred to the other *proprietários* who hire girls to harvest grapes that they might now have to provide some kind of treat in order to obtain workers. They were not at all pleased with such newfangled ways. Furthermore, with other more general actions, migrants influence values and behavior. Young emigrant visitors go out on dates without chaperons or other young people, and even kiss local youth in public, convincing adults that 'modern values' are not all good.

Visiting emigrants both praise and condemn island life, calling it 'backward and unprogressive' and 'healthy and peaceful' in the same breath. Older villagers echo these refrains, apologizing to visitors for the limited employment and entertainment options, the clothes dirtied from daily chores, and the lack of amenities such as fine foods and appliances. Village women carrying burdens on their heads take them off and carry them in hand so as not to appear backward when tourists pass them on the main road. The young people complain, wishing they had the material goods of American and European cities, but they do not apologize.

In São Miguel it is often said that the more people have the more they complain, and the more they have the more they want. The saying is frequently applied to emigrants, who from the perspective of the home folk are no longer satisfied with the simple life once they see modern life in America. Yet with respect to migration, in São Miguel it is the people with the least who glorify the amenities of America the most and who most want to emigrate in order to have those things. *Trabalhador* women in particular sing the praises of modern life in America. Their husbands are not always in agreement, as in the following case of a thirty-five year old mother of five, whose husband, employed on the public road crew, argues against her desire to emigrate to Canada but cannot dampen her enthusiasm.

Maria exclaimed over and over again to the assembled neighbors about the good life in America. She knew it from her cousin, she had seen it in pictures, and she was a believer. She would get a gleam in her eye, a determinedly optimistic flicker of a smile on her round face, and hold forth on the virtues of some American wonder such as being able to do errands in your own automobile, storebought bread that was like cake, and frozen food that had only to be heated for dinner. She wanted to work in a factory and earn as much as her husband, in fact, she would joke, maybe she could even go there and work without her husband if he was so obstinate. She was aware that some things were costly, pointing out the high price of beef, but shrugged it off, saying that her family didn't eat much beef here, why should they there.

(Fieldnotes, São Miguel, 1978)

Such women have seen the kitchens of returnees, heard the stories of emigrants, viewed photographs of full refrigerators, and although they realize that their own island is modernizing they believe that it is happening too slowly for themselves to reap the full benefits.

The women whose husbands are *proprietários*, or well on their way to being such, talk about the modern advantages of America but in most cases these couples who have worked to establish themselves, and have land or a business, do not want to emigrate. They are therefore usually quick to concur with the older people who point out to younger enthusiasts that although anyone in America can buy food at the store, the food made at home is healthier and better. Or they assert that amenities do not necesssarily better life, pointing out that people in the village who do not have bathrooms often bathe better than those who do have them.

The picture of America that emerges in daily conversations in São Miguel is rosy, but not totally so. Returnees, visitors, letters, and the news bring word of problems with crime, drugs, and divorce that concern the listeners in the island. One woman who returned from Canada with her two daughters after ten years explained that she had left her husband working there while she came back to the village because of the isolation and her fears that her daughters would be corrupted.

> Life there is like living in rabbit holes. No one comes out of their houses except to go to work, there is never anyone on the street, you don't even know your neighbors... My younger daughter was born there but I didn't spend much time with her because I worked a day shift. My husband worked a night shift and we traded off taking care of the children. America is no place to bring up children. I was afraid for my daughters so I came back when my mother was dying and I decided to stay. There are drugs in the schools there and boys and girls go out alone together... It's not good to teach young people about everything (the facts of life) because then they think they are able to do anything and they do it.
>
> (Fieldnotes, São Miguel, 1978)

Divorce is another topic of concern for the islanders, and they note with dismay that even Azoreans are now getting divorced in America, whereas in São Miguel it is a rare occurrence and then usually only among city folk. Young marriagable people also talk of divorce, saying that it is better to marry someone from home because a spouse from America (i.e., an emigrant) might want a divorce later on. Those who have been to America also point out that rural emigrants have a very hard time in America because they are not used to the ways their children begin to act; they see 'bad things' in modern behavior and this causes conflict in the family.

Ideas about modernity are also applied to the relative attractiveness of job opportunities in America. Traditional evaluations, such as degree of independence, and recent political doctrine further influence evaluations of options in terms of modernity. The image of modern work is clean factory work, i.e., you can go to the job and come home in the same clothes and still look respectable. It is not dirty work like field work, pays higher wages than field work plus benefits, and is not associated with the degrading image which young people have of working like serfs for large landowners. The image of 'modern' is associated with the factories in America, although there are some small factories in São Miguel as well. The increasing disdain for agricultural labor is connected partially with post-1974 policies and rhetoric which have addressed the plight of laborers and heightened their awareness of low status and oppression as things they should strive against. However, agricultural work, if it is for yourself, takes on a new light. It is 'healthier' than working inside all day, and gives a person more time to stop and visit or do something different. These are the sentiments of those who have their own property; they are not the sentiments of those who are propertyless.

For rural women, who complain of the dirtiness of daily work, the work in America is very appealing. Even housework, which very few will now hire themselves out for in São Miguel, looks good in America. The difference is that in São Miguel housework is associated with the low social and moral status which in the past was given to the maid for rich people. It is not well-paid work compared to what men earn, and the women consider it demeaning. The only women who work as maids are the ones who have done it for years, the ones who are very poor and have few alternatives, and the ones who do it 'as a favor' for families that their family has worked for in the past. However, according to many emigrants, in America the maid is not seen as socially inferior to the employee, the pay is high, and the work is easy because of modern equipment and conveniences. Factory work is cleaner than picking grapes or doing the daily chores, pays almost equal wages to those of men, and provides women with their own funds for purchasing the coveted items of the modern world. Women believe that when men and women share equally in the support of the family women have more independence, and the emigrants tell them that this is modern.

There are both positive and negative aspects of modernity which influence migration decision-making, and the way these are evaluated depends in part on the position of the decider. In the previously mentioned case of the clerk who reluctantly anticipated working in a factory, the modern aspects of such work did not offset the traditional idea that people who work in offices, people who are educated should not do manual labor. Yet for these same people the material goods of America may be very appealing. For example, a skilled office worker repeatedly told me that if he and his wife emigrated (his wife already had immigrant status in the U.S.) he would buy a Corvette to cruise around in. But for the *trabalhadores* just the idea of working in a factory, or owning any kind of car, is very appealing. Nevertheless, people are aware of the other side of the coin of modern life in America:

In America it is possible to become rich, but if you do not work it is also possible to starve. In São Miguel no one who has family or neighbors dies of starvation.

(Fieldnotes, São Miguel 1978)

The differential appeal of modern qualities and types of employment is related to a third area of values, those associated with socioeconomic mobility, which influences evaluations of relative attractiveness of work and life in migration decision-making. In São Miguel the stratified social system has a built-in flexibility that enables a slow trickle of families to be incorporated into higher social levels over time. Improvements in educational facilities over the past twenty years have made the possibility of moving up available to a broader range of people. In the past, emigration and return was a more accessible upward channel than education for rural residents. The upward mobility for rural families through acquisition of property gave their children greater chances of obtaining education. Emigration is still a viable channel for upward socioeconomic mobility, but for the emigrants, who rarely return, it is mobility outside of the home system. However, for those who remain behind, emigration has affected opportunities for mobility; consequently, it has shaped current perceptions of socioeconomic mobility and these perceptions, in turn, influence migration decision-making.

Acquiring higher education is the primary route to the middle levels of Michaelense society, and hence collegial contact with people of the higher levels. Accumulation of property raises status in the villages, but is not comparable to education, partly because education endows a person with the right contacts as well as the right credentials.

Land, on the other hand, is only a credential and confers limited status unless accompanied by the appropriate network of contacts within the aspired-to social level.

For the *trabalhadores* education has been and continues to be a limited option because of limited access and finances as well as conflicting demands on the student's energy. Emigration is a more viable alternative for people who aspire to higher levels but do not have substantial resources to draw on. Further, emigration is associated with the 'American dream' of rags-to-riches socioeconomic mobility through hard work. In the eyes of the emigrant, status in America is measured more by the accumulation of wealth and property than other criteria. This means that they can achieve a higher level <u>without</u> education. Young families who perceive limited opportunities to amass more than they already have in São Miguel are therefore attracted to the possibilities in America where the unobtainable education is not seen to be a factor in mobility. The viewpoint of a thirty-eight year old wife of a farm laborer is typical of many young emigrant families.

> We have nine children, the youngest is two and the oldest is eighteen. My husband has a sister in Fall River and we are going there as soon as the passports are ready. My oldest two children will work in the factories and my sister-in-law says they will make more than my husband makes now. America is a good place to make money... when all my children are working we will be very rich!
> (Fieldnotes, São Miguel 1978)

Education is not considered useful by many *trabalhador* emigrants in São Miguel and some see education in

America as equally useless or even a bad influence. They prefer to have the children go to work without finishing school, because in America it is clear to them that 'you do not need an education' to make money.

Michaelense emigrants of *proprietário* and more educated backgrounds recognize and use education as a channel to higher status occupations such as teaching, even if the wages are lower than that of factory work. This trend has been stimulated by the demand for educated Azoreans in local and state positions and in bilingual education. These opportunities are now talked about in the villages, as well as among the more educated in the homeland.

In the past people of higher status, the urban educated, generally emigrated at times of crisis. Financial loss on a poor investment, misuse of company funds, an impending maternity suit against a married businessman, the upcoming draft of a son during the war in Angola, and political oppression are a few of the reasons that stimulated these people to emigrate in past decades. In most cases emigration involved a loss of status, both in terms of property and social position. A woman accustomed to having servants ended up working side by side with her former employees in a clothing factory, and a man who had taught high school worked in a shoe factory until he could obtain American credentials through night school. As one teacher in the city explained when asked if he had ever wanted to emigrate,

> ... in America everyone thinks they are equal. But the fact that they make a lot of money doesn't mean that they are the same as me. I do not want a former hired man coming up and slapping me on

the back as if we were equals!
(Fieldnotes, São Miguel 1973)

Nevertheless, for some people the initial loss of status in America is more desirable than a threatened loss of status at home.

The allure of 'city lights' as a major incentive for migration has been refuted many times, but the attractiveness of modern living is nevertheless one variable that interacts significantly with others in the migration decision process in São Miguel. It has been suggested by some researchers (e.g. Graves 1966; Friedl 1967) that rather than 'city lights' *per se* , it is an orientation toward material goods, or having more than before, which motivates people to emigrate from home areas to more modern destinations. In São Miguel such orientations are conditioned by evaluations of independence and socioeconomic mobility, expressed differentially among the various social levels.

Among the urban educated, American mobility is most appealing to the *proprietário*-educated who have moved up in status but are limited by not having close ties with the elite levels. For them status is clearly associated with material goods because they do not qualify for status by right of heritage. If they feel that they can not gain further status in the home system, some are stimulated to emigrate to America where their access to wealth-based status is greater. One strong deterrent is the possible loss of status in America if they cannot immediately transfer into comparable occupations. Knowledge of non-factory job opportunities in America thus increases their propensity to migrate.

Emigrants who have only a high school education (technical or non-technical) see greater mobility in

America primarily because of the factors mentioned above, but there are also difficulties associated with employment in São Miguel. Those with technical training for skilled jobs such as mechanics, electricians, house painters, plumbers and carpenters, have little trouble locating a job but complain that there is no chance to get ahead for many years unless they have sufficient capital to start their own businesses. The homeland offers them jobs if they are patient enough to work their way upward, but America offers them more rapid financial and social mobility. In São Miguel those with non-technical high school education face a different employment problem, i.e., primarily underemployment rather than unemployment, for which there was a low official rate of 1% for 1977. However, the majority of these unemployed are young people, and over one third of them are high school graduates seeking their first job (*Os Acores* 1978).

Skilled workers compose 17% of the active work force in São Miguel. In 1975, 36% of the total active emigrants were drawn from the skilled sector. The proportion of skilled level emigrants has more than doubled since 1965, while the proportion of skilled workers in the home population has remained relatively stable. More are being trained, and more are emigrating. Informal interviewing of emigrants bound for America and interviews with the travel agents who arrange passage for them indicated that skilled emigrants are generally under thirty-five years old. Migration of these skilled workers has an element of what Kasdan (1965), in his study of Basque emigration, calls 'anticipatory socialization'; the high school graduates are already trained for a type and level of work, i.e., trades and secondary production, which is available in America at better wages. Philpott (1973) notes a similar situation for the emigration of high school graduates from the West Indies.

The *trabalhadores*, who have the least access to modern goods and services, are the ones who through their contact with emigrants have the most intense daily knowledge of the material aspects of life in America. They are also the ones who express the strongest desire to have the modern way of life themselves. The women in particular are enthusiastic about those modern aspects of American life which contrast sharply to their own daily activites. Yet *trabalhador* families are not very concerned about educational and health care services in America, contradicting the views of some researchers who suggest that these are major incentives for emigration from São Miguel (Monjardino 1968; Rogers 1979). The propensity of families with school age children to migrate, as indicated by the large proportion of children under the age of ten in the migrant stream (on average 25%), might be explained partly by the incentive to educate children in America where higher education is thought to be more readily accessible to people of any background. Yet analysis of what families say in São Miguel about the attractiveness of migration and what they do once they are in America suggests that education is not a major incentive. In New England educators are concerned over the high drop-out rates among Portuguese immigrant children (personal communication McGowan 1978).[7] A primary incentive, however, is that children earn well without having education past the mandatory level. Emigration is advantageous for families with children approaching the legal age at which they can begin work, which is 16 years in most states, because those children soon will be able to contribute an adult's share to the total family income. In some cases younger children also work part-time. Families with children, therefore, have a greater potential family income in America than in the Azores even though their costs are also higher. To reduce that immediate income potential by keeping children in school is not an appealing alternative for many emigrants.

In terms of independence in lifestyle and work, the *trabalhadores* have few possibilities in the homeland for owning a substantial piece of property or being their own bosses. In America, the women see that they can have greater independence through earning cash income, and the men see the possibility of saving enough to buy their own houses. For those with young families especially, emigration offers greater independence and upward mobility than they can hope for at home.

The *proprietários* own property and have greater access to modern goods than *trabalhadores*, but many of them also emigrate. For them too, the familiarity with modern goods and life described by emigrants is a factor, but it combines with other evaluations of life in America. *Proprietário* families have more sophisticated experience with other sectors of the society because their members often include not only emigrants but urban educated individuals, who are more aware of the problems of life in America. As little as fifteen years ago the appeal of greater financial independence and opportunities in America was more of an incentive for *proprietário* families to emigrate, but now they have greater security and opportunity at home and young families more frequently decide to stay than to go. In the case of *trabalhador* families, the improved material conditions at home, combined with information about America, have not dampened enthusiasm for emigration, but for the *proprietários* the same conditions have led them to stay once they are established. *Proprietários* most likely to emigrate now are those who have not yet settled firmly into family life and arranged access to or ownership of property.

At the stage in life when young families are establishing the resource base which will sustain them in the future, definitions of a 'good life' based on attributes of independence, modernity, and potential socioeconomic mobility, are determinants in the shaping of perceptions on migration. These definitions vary for individuals at different social levels. The importance of material orientations for evaluations of migration is thus conditioned both by access to goods and by the degree to which material wealth is associated with status.

Family Allocation of Opportunities

Diversity and multibase production, important in the livelihood patterns of large sectors of the Michaelense population, are also factors influencing the migration decision-making process. This is particularly so at the stage in life when people are establishing and maintaining young families. Access to property, training in skilled work, emigration, and higher education, are all opportunities which may be allocated within the family. Access to property and training are largely determined by allocations within the family. Those allocations, in conjunction with ideologies of property consolidation and the household 'right to subsistence,' influence the relative attractiveness of emigration for individuals.

Slightly more than a century ago the Portuguese

practice of property allocation through primogeniture and estate entailment was revised in favor of equal inheritance. The law changed but the family-held livelihood units remain. Equal, but not necessarily equivalent, distribution of property is combined with an ideology of diversification within the family; this provides greater security and is aimed at keeping property from fragmenting into diverse, small, and separately used holdings. For small landowners the problem of keeping the land together in a profitable holding is particularly acute, and it is important that not all offspring make immediate demands for their rightful portions. Decision-making about migration, as one alternative which reduces immediate demand on limited resources, is thus integrally tied into ideas about family continuity in family-held property. Family-held property is that which is still owned by the parents at the time the children are of an age to need their own production base for their own families, but which is being allocated through rental, joint use, or even sale, to those children. These allocations influence migration decisions and vice versa.

The effect of migration on property holdings in the past, and how family allocations affected the decision to migrate, is evident in families where migration decisions are being made today. The extent of property held by a family is often connected with the emigration of previous generations of relatives, who left whatever property they had to a sibling who remained on the island, or who returned with capital sufficient to increase their own property holdings. A high proportion of *proprietário* families had parents or grandparents who obtained or increased their property in this manner. In one community, for example, over 50% of the *proprietário* families had forebears who had resided in Brazil or North

America and had contributed to an increase in the family landholdings.

Families in São Miguel do not operate formally as corporate groups, but there is a strong sentiment that it is necessary to diversify so that everyone is able to set up a household with a viable livelihood. This is illustrated in the following case:

> João's father owns almost forty *alqueires* around the village and a recently remodeled house. The oldest of the four brothers did well in school and the mother, with only primary education, urged him to study further. He went to the university in Lisbon and is now a teacher there and engaged to marry a mainland girl. The second brother was in the army, then went to Bermuda to work for two years, and now has returned. A third brother emigrated and is married in America. João, the youngest, never liked school and doesn't much like working but at nineteen he is now thinking of getting married. He likes farming better than anything else and although he has talked about emigrating, his returned brother and father have convinced him that he would do well to pool his energies with theirs on the land. The land all belongs to the father but the returned son and the youngest son each rent some for their own uses. The returned son has used his savings to buy a small store in the city and has invested with his father in a produce selling business. The younger son will presumably take over the village end of the business as the father gets older. At the moment he is fixing up a house that his uncle left under their care when he emigrated and will

probably sell to João.

(Fieldnotes, São Miguel 1978)

Who emigrates is not a matter of seniority but rather of opportunity at a particular point in the individual's life. Hence the younger son in the case cited has chosen not to emigrate, in part because the opportunities for him at home are good as a result of other brothers emigrating. The new household's right to subsistence, therefore, may be achieved through a variety of channels, including migration or higher education, which ensure a basic livelihood without necessarily making direct use of the land.

Once an individual has established a family and is working family property he is less likely to choose to emigrate than someone who does not have access to property. As one father of four put it, "My family had nothing, and I have nothing, so why should I stay here?" The ones who want to stay are exemplified in the following case:

> Luis manages a village store and sells produce in the city. He inherited land from his father and uses the land jointly with his mother's land and that of his sisters. One younger sister lives in New Bedford. She emigrated ten years ago when her mother went to join a sister and work during the period after the father's death when they were having financial difficulties. An older sister is married and works in the city. Luis went to America to visit, but says he has no reason to emigrate: "I have everything here, my family, the people I know. It is more beautiful here than in America, my sister loves it there, but why should I

go? I have my life here."

(Fieldnotes, São Miguel 1978)

An important concept that is illustrated in the above case is that equal inheritance of property by all siblings does not mean that the land is actually divided. The siblings who are using the land may pay use-rent to those siblings who are not actively using their part. In other cases a sibling in Lisbon or America, or even in Ponta Delgada, may sell all or part of an inheritance to a sibling in the village who is working the land. The inheritance itself may in part depend on who was making what use of the land prior to the death of a parent. For example, a son who is building up a dairy herd may rent the pasture land from his father and buy some of it if he is able to. Previously purchased property no longer figures in the inheritance. The land being used is most likely to be inherited by the person using it. The son with cattle inherits equally with a child in America, but the former is probably going to obtain the pasturage and cropland needed to sustain the *lavrador* household, whereas the child in America might inherit the house and nearby land. This portion may be used on vacations or even sold. It is in this sense that inheritance tends to be equal but not equivalent. The person emigrating prior to inheritance does not give up rights to the property but may lose influence on what part of the property will be inherited. The sibling who stays often gains from the absence of others by being able to use their land, either as renter or as *procurador* (overseer). Those who leave retain some of the benefits of the property at home while they gain the benefits of work elsewhere.

Occupational skills are another means of diversifying within the family and ensuring that ends meet. Obtaining craft skills partly served this function in the past. One man explained that he had become a shoemaker, even though he owned enough land to survive on, because he never wanted to be forced by necessity to work for someone else or to emigrate. Today one can train as an apprentice or in the technical school. Carpenters, electricians, mechanics and other skilled workers are in high demand, but this does not necessarily deter them from emigrating. It does lighten the burden on any property the family may own. Training, as already mentioned, may in fact increase the likelihood of emigration and reduce direct demands on the land.

> Hermano explained that as an electrician in São Miguel he could always find work, but that he would be working for someone else for years before he could hope to have his own business. His father was young and there was not enough land for all the sons to farm and he didn't want to farm anyway. So when his sweetheart's family emigrated last year he became engaged to her and he plans to go to the U.S. There, he says, he can use his training to make more money than he ever could here.
>
> (Fieldnotes, São Miguel 1979)

In this case the young man from a *proprietário* family felt that his training would bring him greater benefits in America. He was taking the government sponsored language class while waiting for his visa, so that he would have a better chance of getting the kind of job he wanted right away.

In a situation where the resources are limited and the demand on them is great, emigration has served as one means for channeling people away from direct use of the land resources. Emigration has, in the process, contributed to the consolidation of land among small property owners in São Miguel. Ownership is consolidated as absent owners eventually sell off their holdings to those who remain. Use is consolidated as some of the owners turn to other occupations. To a lesser extent, emigrants also contribute to land consolidation by buying land at home. For example, in one family the husband and brother-in-law both worked in Canada and sent money back for the wife and her brother to invest in family-held property. Their property holdings have quadrupled in the past twenty years.[8]

Changes in inheritance patterns a century ago have affected the dispersal of land, but emigration has contributed to maintaining a degree of cohesiveness in that distribution. This has primarily affected the *proprietários*, the small landowners. For them the ethic of a 'guarantee for subsistence', which Wolf (1970:102) associated with 'impartible' inheritance is embodied in 'partible' inheritance, through the concept of doing what is necessary to sustain a household at a given stage in its existence. Among *proprietários* there is rarely sufficient property for all offspring to set up viable households based on the land's production. Consequently, a pattern has developed, mirroring the aristocratic tradition of past generations, in which some offspring find alternative sources of livelihood which remove their direct use demands from the land. This pattern means that for those who remain on the land the right to subsistence is guaranteed. At the same time it allows the property to be consolidated in use if not in actual ownership when the inheritance occurs. It is thus similar to the former elite pattern of primogeniture and estate entailment and results in similar continuity in small landholdings through an informal process of family allocations.

Emigration is one of the alternatives to staying on the land which supports this pattern of informal limited partibility despite partible inheritance. Integral to this process is the division of land into what Weinberg (1972:129) calls 'equivalent quanta' rather than into 'same quantities'. Not only do emigrant heirs rarely use their portions of the inheritance themselves, but the fact that they have emigrated (often before they inherit) enables those siblings who remain on the land to establish claims on the property which will most effectively support their households. Furthermore, emigration frequently results in renting or eventually selling the owner's part of the land to one of the other offspring if it is useful to them. Emigration therefore contributes to perpetuation of land use consolidation as well as to actual consolidation of property. This reduces the problem of land fragmentation which has contributed to large-scale emigration in other parts of Europe, such as Italy, where partible inheritance is practiced.

The broad category of 'primary sector' emigrants obscures the type of resources that these people actually have access to. A person classified as working on the land and owning nothing may in fact be a well-to-do *proprietário* who has not yet inherited his or her share of the property, but will in the future. Such a person, as illustrated in this section, is in a very different situation with regard to emigration than the truly landless agricultural laborer. For the young family of *proprietário* background the allocation of opportunities within the family is a decisive force in migration decision-making.

For the large property owners of São Miguel, emigration has not been associated with the distribution of family resources in the same way as for *proprietários*. Emigration *per se* is not an alternative to active use of property. However, emigration has affected the dispersion of assets, the diversification of family resources, by providing contacts abroad and access to dollars at home. One form of investment that is now being made with those dollars is education, and in this sense a pattern of going to school in America may become analogous to that of the emigration pattern among the *proprietários* in the sense of diversifying family resources.

STUDENTS

In recent years more high school educated youth are seeking higher education in America. Student (non-immigrant) visas constitute only about 2% of the total visas granted, but many students go as immigrants if possible. To what extent this nascent trend should be defined as emigration will be addressed in the course of examining how factors of socioeconomic mobility, political climate, and migration associated flows of information and money affect decisions to seek education in America.

For students in São Miguel, obtaining higher education has traditionally necessitated leaving the island after high school to attend a university in mainland Portugal or another part of Europe. Education has therefore involved geographical mobility, but it has never been defined as emigration. Yet education is one of the channels through which young people leave the island without their parents and, as with emigration, they do not always return. Part of the distinction arises from the fact that until twenty years ago it was primarily the wealthy who could afford to send children off for higher education, whereas it was primarily society's lower levels that emigrated to the New World.

Higher education is the basic avenue for social mobility in São Miguel. Even wealthy returning emigrants do not substantially alter their own social standing unless their children obtain higher education. Marriage, too, is a mechanism of moving up socially, but this rarely occurs without educational compatibility. Marriage between different social levels appears to have increased with social mixing in educational institutions. Higher education traditionally has been the domain of the elite and the professionals, the only ones who could afford to send their children to the mainland. Education is thus associated with a special, honored status. Students rarely are employed and are not expected to do any manual labor, even at home in the villages. For the upper levels of society, which have traditionally monopolized higher education and professional occupations, education is associated with stable socioeconomic position. For the people who can only newly afford it, higher education is associated with socioeconomic mobility within the home system.

Consideration of American institutions as viable options for higher education has increased in recent years. This results from a combination of political circumstances in Portugal and characteristics of migration-associated information and monetary flows between São Miguel and America. The other options available are study on the mainland or study at one of the local Azorean colleges. Study on the mainland is still expensive and scholarships, as well as entry places, are difficult to obtain. One drawback of the government established regional colleges is that they do not have equivalent status to universities on the mainland, and are limited in the kind of degrees they can grant.

In the last two decades a much broader cross-section of the Michaelense population has gained access to high school and higher education. The number of high school students increased by 48% in São Miguel between 1970 and 1977, even though the total population declined 10% (DREPA 1977). Judging by the increase in students with college preparation, access to higher education has improved at home but so has the demand.

Incentives for students seeking higher education in America have been associated with conditions in the Portuguese educational system. The 1974 coup in Portugal resulted in disruption of university activities and by 1977 they still had not regained normal functioning. Student protests, combined with instructors leaving the country, created difficulties during the initial period of disruption, and these were compounded by the rapid shifts in governments, and hence policies, which crippled the effective operation of many institutions. Reluctance to send children to the disrupted universities was exacerbated by Michaelense students who took up the leftist cause, crying 'down with the fascists' against their own kin. The newly formed colleges on the islands were not subject to leftist political organizing but were adversely affected by changing government policies, sometimes going for months without sufficient faculty to open.

Cultural attitudes also influence the consideration of educational options. Among the upper levels of Michaelense society family ties have for generations bridged the spatial distance between island and mainland. Europe is seen as the cultural center of their world. Lisbon and Coimbra are the foci of intellectual endeavors, fashion is set by the major European cities, and the traditions of centuries are still alive. America, on the other hand, is sometimes crudely referred to as the 'piss pot' of the world, receiving the waste rather than the best. Some elite who travel there observe that there is 'no art', 'no culture', 'no history', only wooden houses and factories. They also observe, as do the emigrants, that life is rich in material goods and investments seem more secure than at home. In recent years, the criticisms of American cultural paucity have not deterred offspring from going to study there. Twenty years ago it was different, but following the 1974 revolution in Portugal people changed their views about American education, if not about anything else American.

> Mario went to Canada about fifteen years ago, got a degree and then worked for a large company for several years before returning to the island. His father, a well-heeled businessman, had gone to the U.S. to college many years before, which was quite unusual at the time. Mario recalled that when he went to Canada many people said that his father was crazy to send him there instead of to Europe. But now, he says, since 1974, his cousins and other people have been asking him what would be the best university in America to send their own children to.
>
> (Fieldnotes, São Miguel 1978)

It is clear from this example, and the many others that note the same change in attitudes toward American education, that at least on the part of the parents, internal political transformations have led to reevaluation of educational options in mainland Portugal. The political climate, along with cultural history, has played a significant

role in shaping perceptions of desirable options, but
migration feedback has also played its part.

Reevaluation of the American option for higher
education has been facilitated by two main aspects of
migration: flows of information and flows of dollars.
Information has influenced people's perceptions of
opportunities, and the flow of black market dollars from
the hands of affluent visitor-emigrants has increased the
feasibility of going to America to study:

> A well-to-do professional, Sr. G., told me that it is
> very easy now to buy American currency because
> many of the emigrants come back to visit and
> bring dollars which they sell. He said that very
> few people had dollars before 1974, just the
> relatives of emigrants who saved a few, and that he
> had been one of the only ones to collect them at
> that time.   He had been in Boston to get
> specialized training for a year in the 1950's and
> since then had decided it would be a good place
> for his daughter to study. He said that nowadays
> people who think they may send a child to school
> in America start collecting dollars and transferring
> them years in advance. Before 1974 he said the
> more affluent people were only interested in the
> mainland for education, but now "everyone is
> looking to America."
>
>   (Fieldnotes, São Miguel 1978)

Since 1974 many people have been extra-legally
transferring dollars out of São Miguel to banks or
investments in America. Also, because they already had
dollars in America, some people began to think about

educating their children there even though this was not the original intention.

A student who is able to amass the necessary money and is accepted by an educational institution in America can then apply for a visa. Immigrant visas are preferable because the student can work, or be out of school for awhile without having the visa revoked. However, the people who have the money to go to America to study are generally the ones who have the fewest close relatives there. Roundabout means are sometimes employed to get to America, as in the case of a young woman who arranged for her factory-owning grandfather to apply for an immigrant visa at the age of eighty-two, through his brother who was a U.S. citizen, and to take her mother and herself as his dependents. She was the only one who planned to stay. Although someone on a student visa cannot legally stay after the degree is completed, it is believed that given time, money, and the right connections, it is possible to arrange permanent immigrant status.[9] Everyone claims to know someone who has changed their visa status from non-immigrant to permanent immigrant, and students do not always return.

The case of the grandfather applying for the visa to get his granddaughter in points out the extent to which the entire family may be involved in the decision-making process. In addition, the decision made for one member of the family may affect opportunities for the rest. One young woman explained that she was extremely anxious to pass her exams and get a place in the local college because her sister had just been sent to Boston to study, and she knew that her parents, even with professionals' salaries, could not afford to send her as well. In agricultural families education is also a means of obtaining a livelihood

which takes pressure off the land base. The child that is
selected is not necessarily in a senior position; the choice
is more a function of which child first shows greatest
aptitude for academic work at a time when extra funds are
available. If one child is sent to a university on the
mainland, financial considerations may curtail the
prospects for a younger child with equal aptitude.

Decision-making about education thus involves not only
the students but other family members, and different
people in the family are affected by different kinds of
information.   Parents' perceptions are influenced by
political conditions as well as by ideas about upward social
mobility. Students, more than the parents, are influenced
by flows of information about lifestyle and opportunity in
America.   In addition to the formalized media sources,
there are basically two informal channels of information
that reach them.   The first is through emigrant-tourists
who come back to visit the island. The young people in
particular mix with local educated youth in the summer
vacation areas and entertainment spots.   The second
channel is through family and colleagues who have
emigrant kin. This channel of information is facilitated by
increased attendance at high school by children from
varied backgrounds, thus bringing the youth from rural
proprietário families into contact with children of the
elite. A survey of high school students from Ponta Delgada
and other larger towns revealed that about one half were
from families in which one or both parents had
professional level occupations while the other half came
from homes where the parents worked in secondary or
primary production.[10]

The type of information students have about America
depends in part on who transmits it to them. Emigrant-
tourists tend to be better educated and are familiar with

educational and non-factory employment opportunities in America. Students hear things about life in America that are contrary to the stereotype of factory drudgery. They hear of discos and night life, and the wide variety of courses to choose from in the colleges. They learn that they can work to have extra things and that employment other than manual labor and jobs in the factories is available. Emigrant-tourists generally add that America is a good place to study, but not a good place for the elite to work because they are not used to that type of work and community. Students with close kin in America also receive information about the more traditional opportunities for emigrants, such as factory work, but the ones whose relatives are better educated are often encouraged by those relatives to come to America to further their studies.

Homeland value systems influence the way that information about America is used in decision-making. The students from *proprietário* and rural backgrounds are to some degree caught between two contradictory methods of evaluating going to America. In the town high schools they are exposed to the urban-educated values which denigrate America as cultureless and fit only for people who cannot succeed at home. At the same time they have grown up with the example of emigration as the road to success, perhaps even for their own families, and America as the salvation of the island. The emigrants they have the most contact with are family, some of whom are educated, but most of whom only completed the compulsory level. Emigration signifies socioeconomic mobility without education and outside of the home system. By contrast, education represents the prestigious road to mobility which stays more or less within the home system. The view that emerges is one of emigration and

education as incompatible alternatives which involve the
locational choice of America or Portugal. How some of
these elements come to the fore in the process of
decision-making can be seen in the following case:

> Lourdinha was back to spend the summer on the
> island after a year spent studying in Lisbon. Two
> years ago her *proprietário* parents emigrated to
> the U.S., where her uncle had been living for some
> years. At the time she had completed her
> university entrance exams, but did not know the
> results. She went to visit her parents for three
> months and to look into the possibility of staying
> there. Both parents were working in factories and
> she said the work was terrible but they didn't
> seem to mind. She was unimpressed by life in
> America and did not like the lack of manners of
> people in the neighborhood. She visited the
> nearby college, but decided to return to the island
> and await her exam results, rather than apply in
> the U.S. Accepted eventually at the University of
> Lisbon, she went there the following year. During
> the summer she had planned to live with an aunt
> and an uncle in her natal village, but now was
> spending more time with her urban located
> brother and seeing her university colleagues who
> were also from São Miguel.
>
> (Fieldnotes, São Miguel 1978)

For this young woman of *proprietário* background
America was clearly associated with emigration, and
Portugal with education. Opting for education, her choice,
like that of many others in her position, was for the more
prestigious path of Portugal. Some students who have

close emigrant kin with higher education do view America as a viable educational alternative, but in other cases emulation of traditional elite patterns is more desirable given the chance to do so.

> Anna had recently completed a higher degree in the U.S. and has a good job teaching. She was back in São Miguel visiting her family and vacationing as a tourist. After visiting one aunt she came back irate, exclaiming that the woman had nerve to be so critical of Azoreans in America when she had only six years before written her asking how to go about arranging a visa for herself and her daughter's family. That daughter's son has since gone to Lisbon to study and is becoming a lawyer. Now, says Anna, the aunt does not need to go to the U.S. so she criticizes it freely and then praises the great success of her grandson.
>
> (Fieldnotes, São Miguel 1978)

This case illustrates both the clinging to the elite model of success and the way in which perceptions of opportunities can change rapidly with changing circumstances.

The urban educated and elite, in contrast to the *proprietários*, have an easier time distinguishing education in America from emigration to America. Not only do they tend to have fewer close kin ties there, but what they hear about America is largely shaped by their contacts with more highly educated and sophisticated emigrant-tourists and the experiences of other students. In the following case the parents of a student were quick to make the distinction that their daughter who had gone to America was there as a student, not as an emigrant.

Maria's businessman father had arranged, with the assistance of a colleague who has connections in Boston, for her to enter college there. She has no relatives in America except for a distant cousin in Fall River. She has one friend who went to study in Boston the year before and will either live with her or some other Azorean girls in an apartment, or in the dorm. She does not plan to work, but said her friend was working part-time in a restaurant for extra money, and she may have to do the same. She plans to return to the island after completing a course in sociology. When I asked her about the possibility of staying in America she replied that the student visa would not allow this, but added that one of her brother's friends had gone on a student visa and arranged immigrant status after being there three years.

(Fieldnotes, São Miguel 1978)

The above cases illustrate two basic orientations toward education in America which are associated with family background. The rural *proprietários* may have closer kin in America, but those kin have generally chosen economic mobility without educational prestige, while those in the homeland tend to follow, if possible, the traditional elite model that good education is found in Portugal or other parts of Europe. For social mobility at home they need all the prestige they can muster. The urban educated and the elite, on the other hand, already have prestige, and for them the crucial factor is to maintain their position, defining education in America as education, not emigration.

The orientations described here were confirmed by a study on student attitudes toward emigration and

education (White and Pollnac 1979). Over one third of the
sample said that if they were able to study anywhere they
wanted for a degree higher than high school they would
choose America, and usually the U.S.[11] Of those who said
they wanted to study outside of the Azores, more of the
students with white collar and professional backgrounds
said they wanted to return, and fewer of them said they
wanted to emigrate than students from lower level
backgrounds, thus indicating that they separate education
from emigration. On the other hand, the rural-background
students, the ones with a greater likelihood of having close
contacts with emigrants, expressed less of a desire than
their urban counterparts to return to the Azores if they
studied abroad. This fits the model of rural *proprietários*
associating any move to America with emigration.[12]

The main transitional period that has been considered
in this section is that of high school educated youth faced
with decisions about where to go for higher education.
Going to America is one of the options considered. The
student rarely acts alone in making that decision, which
often necessitates mobilizing family resources to obtain a
visa and transfer funds to America.

Structurally, the pattern of leaving the island to obtain
a higher education is similar whether students go to the
mainland or America. The main difference lies in the legal
aspects of arranging visas and funds for going to America.
Culturally, going to America involves a perceptual shift
which distinguishes the choice from that of going to the
mainland and has important implications for future
migration patterns. The perceptual shift is noted in the
upper levels of Michaelense society who have redefined
America as no longer solely the last resort of people unable
to succeed in the homeland, but additionally as a viable
resource for those who stay in the homeland. By using

America as a resource the upper levels of the society are no longer impermeable to the effects of contact with American cultural systems, as its members are actively participating in transactions within those systems.

The main factors which influence decision-making about higher education in America differentially affect students from urban educated or elite backgrounds compared to students from *proprietário* rural backgrounds. For the former particularly, the change in political climate has encouraged positive orientation toward America, and the flows of information from well-educated emigrant-tourists and black market dollars have intensified this orientation.

The status of America with respect to education is being redefined by the upper levels in São Miguel as conditions at home stimulate them to look for different options. The threat of political instability to individual security is not as intensely felt by the smaller property-holders. For them, the rural *proprietários* in particular, the constraints of conditions in Portugal are outweighed or subordinated to their perception that education is a path of upward mobility superior to emigration if a person wants to stay within the home status system. Twenty years ago and earlier their best chance of obtaining higher education was through a patron or emigration. However, at that time education was generally not the reason for emigration, and most people went to America precisely because it offered the possibility of getting ahead without education. For most *proprietários* and *trabalhadores* emigration to America is still an alternative to attempting to get higher education. Very few students from this background decide to go to America for education disassociated from emigration, although some who emigrate have both purposes in mind.

The *proprietários*, by continuing to perceive Portugal as the center of prestigious education, are emulating an elite cultural pattern that has already been transformed.[13] Ironically, this cultural lag perpetuates the institutionalized norm of Europe as the center of culture, whereas the behavior of some upper level society students who chose to study in America contradicts the traditional norm. The contradiction is justified by the upper levels through a redefinition of America which is part of their response to perceived threats to their security and an attempt to maintain their positions in society. America is now seen as having resources, such as educational institutions, that can be utilized to bolster their position at home, and the way to do this has been paved by previous migration.

For the upper level students going to America is defined as 'going to study,' not to emigrate; yet the pattern has the potential for developing into emigration. Some students in America have managed to obtain permanent immigration status even though they arrived on student visas, and others who go on immigrant visas are free to stay. In some respects the pattern does resemble emigration because, unlike Azorean students in Portugal, many students who go to America do work part-time. The fact that they tend to go to institutions near Portuguese-American enclaves also means that many of them do interact in these communities and are becoming aware of the improved opportunities for educated Portuguese-Americans. It is possible that these factors will deter students from returning permanently to São Miguel, making them emigrants, and not just students abroad.

CONCLUSIONS

In São Miguel migration touches the lives of people throughout society: young and old, unskilled workers and the better educated. Migration decision-making has been examined for people of different social levels and at different stages in life in order to present a picture of the variation in migration attractiveness throughout the homeland population. Decision-making has been used to discuss changes in influential factors that are reflected in the patterns of migration, such as the increase in skilled migrants, over the last twenty years. The main findings are summarized in the following sections with respect to who makes the migration decision, what is the timing of that decision, and what constraints and incentives come into play in the decision-making process.

Who Decides

The semantic emphasis on 'the actor' (singular) in decision-making models reifies the tendency to focus on male, single or household head deciders in migration studies. In São Miguel it is rare that the individual makes the migration decision alone; it is almost always a matter which involves other family members. The family aspect of decision-making may even include the participation of family in America. Within the family, women play a decisive role in the decision-making process even if they are not the ones to make the final pronouncement.

Formulation of the decision-making unit as potentially greater than one (as, for example, in Barth's (1967:608) term 'unit of management') is shown in this study to be conceptually clearer for migration research than classifiying the effects of more than one decider as part of the individual context.

Timing of the Decision

In São Miguel the migrants are people at specific transitional points in the life cycle. At those transitional points emigration is one of the culturally sanctioned strategies that many individuals consider.

The data from São Miguel suggests that models which employ the concept of marginality may be less fruitful than an approach which takes into account specific transitional points within life stages. DuToit (1975:13) suggests that emigrants are culturally 'marginal' individuals, a concept that harks back to Park's (1928) discussion of the culturally marginal man in rural to urban migration. If migration is seen as one of several culturally sanctioned options, then migrants are not marginal in the sense of being outside the norm in the home context. In São Miguel the cultural orientation toward America has become integral to mainstream rural culture and is fast becoming part of urban culture. However, migrants are people at specific transitional points in life and it is the attributes of these points which provide insight into migration behavior.

The main transitional points for older people occur when they are widowed, make a significant change in their productivity, or when their family in America have young children. As many migration studies have demonstrated, young families tend to be the most mobile. In São Miguel this mobility is associated with specific transitional points such as marriage or intended marriage, and the period when family size is still expanding or children are still young. For students the transitional point comes when they must decide where to seek higher education. At all of these points people are faced with decisions about opportunities; going to America is one of the options they may consider.

There are specific points at which people appear to be most likely to emigrate, and at these life stages there is variation in the factors which affect their decisions. Further variation is found with respect to the operation of constraints and incentives for individuals of different social levels. Classification of decisive factors as primarily economic or primarily sociocultural is shown to form the poles of a continuum in most facets of migration decision-making (see Table 6.2).

Life Stages

In the elderly and student life stages sociocultural factors dominate in migration decision-making. The elderly are influenced by factors of family unity and consolidation, and students' decisions are strongly affected by aspects of status of education, social mobility, and modernity. These factors do have economic components; higher education is a prerequisite for professional employment, and the strengthening of family support

Table 6.2 A Continuum of Economic and Sociocultural
Factors in Migration Decision-Making, by Life
Stages

	Type of Factor	
Life Stage	Primarily Economic	Primarily Sociocultural
Elderly		
	Financial Support ----------------------	Family Support Systems (child-care and assistance of family members)
	----------------------	Family Consolidation
	Employment Availability -------------	Independence
Young Families		
	Family Income Potential --------------	Family Support Systems
	----------------------	Family Consolidation
	Wage Differentials ---------------------	Independence in Lifestyle
	----------------------	Modernity of Lifestyle
	----------------------	Property Ownership
	Economic Mobility ---------------------	Social Mobility
	----------------------	Education
	Employment Availabilty --------------	Status of Work
	-------------	Modernity of Work
	-------------	Independence in Work
Students		
	Cost of Education and Availability ----------------------	Social Status of Education
	----------------------	Quality of Education
	----------------------	Family Support Systems
	Employment Availability ------------	Social Mobility
	------------	Modernity of Lifestyle

systems affects family income and financial support for the older people as well as their families.

For young families the basic economic factors are essentially clear; their contact with emigrants reinforces the belief that people earn more in America and that jobs are available to everyone. These are strong incentives, but incentives that are modified by a wide range of sociocultural factors. Family income potential is important as an incentive to families with children and little property but it is moderated by considerations of where family support networks are located and values of family unity. Similarly, wage differentials and economic mobility are incentives for migration but are shaped by specific attributes of status, independence, and modernity associated with the work and by values connected with social mobility. Economic and sociocultural factors form a continuum, but the greatest variation is found in the sociocultural factors.

Social Level

Different factors are important at different stages in life and at those stages there is significant variation by social level. Table 6.3, based on data from case studies, summarizes the general importance of factors by social level.14

There is strong uniformity in the role of economic factors as incentives, with the exception that unemployment at home is a factor for the non-technical, high school skilled and that commercial opportunity is an attitudinal incentive for the trades and business people.

Table 6.3 Factors Affecting the Attractiveness of Migration, by Social Category

Factors Constraints (-) and Incentives (+)	Social Category				
	Trabal-hador	Prop-rietário	Skilled Tech.	Skilled H.S.	Prof. H.Educ.
Economic					
Employment Availability--America	+	+	+	+	+
Unemployment--S. Miguel				+	
Economic Mobility in America	+	+	+	+	+
Higher Wages in America	+	+	+	+	+
Commercial Opportunities--America			+		+
Greater Family Income--America	+	+	+		
Sociocultural Work					
Non-Manual Employment--America				+	+
Manual Work in America	+	+	+	-	-
Modern Work in America	+	+	+	+	+
Work for Someone Else--America		-			-
Independent Work in S. Miguel		-	-	-	-
Whole Family Works--America	+	-	-	-	-
Social Status					
Soc. Mobility without Education--America	+	+	+	+	-
Soc. Mobility through Education--S. Miguel	+	-	+	+	
Educational Opportunity--America				+	+
Loss of Social Status--S. Miguel				+	+
Lifestyle					
Modernity of Life--America	+	+	+	+	+
Social Problems--America		-		-	-
Political Uncertainty--S. Miguel					+
Family					
Immediate Family in America	+	+	+	+	
Family Support Systems--S. Miguel	-	-	-	-	-
Family Support Systems--America	+	+	+	+	

The greatest variation is found in the primarily
sociocultural factors relating to work, social status, and life
style. Family appears to be a consistent concern, with the
exception of the higher educated for whom family is less of
an incentive because they are less likely to have kin in
America.

Some factors act as incentives for one social level and
as constraints for another. The predominance of factory
and service type work in America and the necessity for the
whole family to be employed are incentives for
trabalhadores and constraints for people with higher
education. It appears that the greater the degree of
independence in São Miguel, for example owning property
or a business, the less is the propensity to migrate to
America. Independence at home as a constraining factor
is modified by incentives of greater potential for social
mobility in America. Perceptions of social mobility, as
seen in the case of *proprietário* youth and higher
education, are filtered through cultural screens which are
themselves affected by previous migration patterns.
Within social levels, what is a constraint and what is an
incentive are affected by life stage. Young *proprietário*
students are more influenced by ideas of prestigious social
mobility through education in Portugal than are young
proprietário families, who are less concerned about
status differentials between homeland and America and are
more concerned about factors such as independence.

As has been noted for other situations of migration
(e.g. Philpott 1973), expectations in São Miguel are
affected by social level. Within different social levels, the
value systems and circumstances which shape
expectations are also influenced by the experiences of
previous migrants. The *trabalhadores* are unperturbed
about the prospect of working for a 'boss' in America; they

already work for a *patrão* in São Miguel. They want the whole family to work in America, just as the whole family contributes to the subsistence base at home. They are attracted by the potential for social and economic mobility without higher education in America; at home mobility through education is rarely a viable option for them. By contrast, those people who are already at a higher social level are more concerned than *trabalhadores* with maintaining or enhancing their status. Educated *proprietários* are threatened by the knowledge that in America education is not an essential criteria for social mobility. But they may also feel 'stuck' or constrained by the home system that limits their social status even though they are educated. There are some home examples, i.e., the *novos ricos*, that modernity and wealth contribute to greater social equality at the upper levels. Those who strive upward may therefore be attracted by the potential for modern status through wealth in America, even at the cost of traditional respect and deference patterns associated with status at home.

Throughout society life stage and social level affect what information about migration is received and how it is perceived. The young urban educated get information that differs significantly from that which most village youth receive. The former learn about educational, non-factory opportunities and general American life, whereas the latter learn of factory work and Portuguese-American life. People over forty years of age have a storehouse of information about emigration as a salvation in the poverty ridden world of past decades. Younger people rarely make the same association, having grown up in better times.

Interpretations of information vary with social level. *Trabalhadores*, the poorest, tend to glorify America as the land of unlimited opportunity for those who are willing to work. *Proprietários* are more apt to point out the limitations. They benefit from the effect of emigration on access to land, but they suffer from the loss of inexpensive labor as workers emigrate and wages rise. The two sides of their position is expressed in their tendency to praise America among themselves but point out the problems of life there in conversations with *trabalhadores*. The more highly educated, who have also suffered the loss of labor, are critical of America except when opportunities suitable to their own social level are presented.

In general, personal information on the experiences of people in America has the greatest affect on migration decision-making in São Miguel. It is for this reason that examination of primarily sociocultural factors reveals the most about variation in migration behavior. Some models of migration, e.g. Cardona and Simson (1975:24), assume that migrants go where the 'best' economic opportunities are. In São Miguel, emigrants go where they have family ties even if the unemployment rates are high in that destination and the only available work is at the minimum wage and may take weeks to arrange. This emphasizes the utility of an approach that views migrants as maximizing a wide range of sociocultural and economic factors in an attempt to make their lives better in their own terms.

Position in the Family

Another factor that affects the relative attractiveness of migration for individuals is position in the family in terms of sex and order of migration or educational behavior. Because of their work patterns and greater involvement in communications with emigrants, women differ from men in what they hear about America. Factors of family ties, modern lifestyle, and job availability appear to have more importance for women than for men. Thadani and Todaro (1979) note the paucity of data on female migration, stating that it must be distinguished from male and household migration. In São Miguel, a further distinction is necessary: women who have close family in America or who know a lot about opportunities in America and have few themselves at home are likely to be very active in the migration decision-making process within the household thus distinguishing their households from others.

Position of the individual in terms of who else in the family has migrated or gone away for higher education affects opportunities and access to family support systems. A sibling's migration that improves opportunities for a person at home decreases the propensity of that person to migrate. If opportunities are not improved, the migration of a sibling generally increases the likelihood of migration for other siblings.

Analysis of who makes the decision, when it is made, and what are the decisive factors in São Miguel illustrates that migration is a complex, dynamic process occurring in both time and space. To understand the whole process, one must ascertain what specific attributes of individual circumstances and information make migration more attractive to specific types of people. Events and conditions in both the home and adoptive areas interact to affect the home context of migration decisions; people and information flow between both systems continuously, but selectively. Within the broader, more inclusive process of adaptation, migration decision-making is itself affected by the migration process.

CHAPTER 7
CONCLUSION

Historically, emigration from São Miguel has been both permanent and temporary. Both the educated and the workers have emigrated. They have left both to obtain higher socioeconomic status and to maintain status, to work and to seek higher education. The flexibility this has created in cultural orientations is a critical component in the shifting composition of the migrant flow. Motivations for mobility are not based solely on current economic opportunities; they are conditioned by perspectives fostered over two centuries of migration history.

For the individual the migration alternative becomes most attractive at particular stages in life within a complex nexus of constraints and incentives. Emigration is a personal strategy, but a strategy which is chosen within a particular sociocultural context. That context is conditioned by the links between migrants and the homeland, the circulation of people and information, which have profound effects throughout the home society, not just on those most closely tied to the migrants but on virtually everyone. In analyzing the home system as a whole migration can be viewed over time as interacting with other processes such as national development of educational facilities, modernization of basic amenities, and political transformation. The context in which migration takes place is thus mercurial. Conditions of life and opportunities have changed in São Miguel since the 1950's: emigration rates fluctuated, and the characteristics of migrants changed, but people continued to emigrate.

Each case of voluntary migration presents a somewhat different mix of factors and the migration process is constantly changing. In our present understanding of migration phenomena this suggests that particularistic explanations within a framework of broader social processes are more satisfactory than general theories of migration *per se.* The development of a processual approach to the study of migration, focusing on migration flows, elucidates changing interactions at the micro-level, the local context in which individuals make decisions, and the interaction of migration with other processes of regional development and political change at the macro-level. The value of this approach is that it offers a more explicit explanation of the dynamics of patterned migration than does an aggregate approach focusing on overall trends or a static approach which assumes that all else remains equal. This approach, which aims to incorporate a broad view of the home society yet retain the richness of individual behavior, has thus been appropriate for examining questions arising from the Michaelense data on how specific migration patterns have developed and how they tie in with continuity and change in the society as a whole.

MIGRATION PATTERNS IN SÃO MIGUEL

For other situations of migration it has been suggested that an improved job market and higher wages at home would curtail emigration (Lianos 1975). In São Miguel improved wage structures for both skilled and unskilled workers, better social service benefits, job availability, and higher standards of living did not dramatically curb the outflow of people in the 1970's. Extensive family ties in America and increasing familiarity with American culture and opportunities are important factors in shaping continued migration. The expectations about quality of life and work which are fostered through increased familiarity are always ahead of the improvements in conditions at home, despite relatively rapid improvement of living standards since 1960. It is still said of the Azores that they 'have one foot in America and one foot in the middle ages'.

One response to this perceived economic 'backwardness' is a local emphasis on expanding tourist facilities and milking the potential for Azorean-American tourists. The number of visitors to São Miguel increased from 31,760 in 1975 to 85,261 in 1985, an average increase of about 10.4%. The largest increase has been in foreign visitors and according to travel agents in 1978 the majority of foreign visitors are people of Azorean descent.[1] As a result, the interaction between emigrant visitors and better-educated sectors of the home population has expanded. One potential effect of this increased familiarity with America throughout society may be the stimulation of what some local officials fear is a 'brain drain' of even more highly skilled human capital, and further diversification of the migrant stream.

In contrast to many situations of rural-urban migration in other parts of the developing world, migration from São Miguel to North America has become increasingly selective since the mid 1960's. Selectivity, defined in terms of education and income, has increased as indicated by the growing proportion of skilled and better educated workers in the migrant stream and the recent interest in obtaining higher education in America. The factors associated with this increase in selectivity are strongly influenced by the effects of previous and ongoing migration flows.

Azorean officials attributed the outpouring of emigrants in the late 1950's and the 1960's to the lack of opportunity at home and the stress that high population growth put on limited resources. As discussed in Chapter Six, when local planners became alarmed at the loss of laborers from the primary sector, improved access to education was emphasized as a way to decrease emigration (Monjardino 1967). As a result of improved facilities the number of high school (and technical school) educated youth increased sharply in the 1970's without a concurrent increase in job opportunities. Thus, homeland policies inadvertently contributed to the creation of a more highly skilled sector of emigrants, diversifying but not immediately reducing the flow of emigrants as intended. Although total emigration has declined, there has been no dramatic change in Azorean unemployment levels since 1970. Unemployment increased only slightly from 2.8% in 1970 to 3.2% in 1981 (DREPA 1984). This is in part attributed to overall population decline, decline in the active sector, and the increase in numbers of 10 to 14 year olds now attending school and thus not included among the unemployed as they were in 1970. This means that in fact unemployment has increased more than the figures indicated for certain sectors of the population. In 1981, for the Azores as a whole, 39% of the unemployed were between 15 and 19 years old. In São Miguel, where unemployment was 3.7% in 1981, 2.6% were seeking their first job and 1.1% were looking for another job. Of the total unemployed in São Miguel, 56% had education above the primary level but not beyond grade twelve. Thus unemployment is most acute for young people with a moderate education seeking their first jobs and hence may continue to provide a strong stimulus for emigration in this sector of the population.

Migrant selectivity is related to characteristics of the migration stream. Numerous models of migration, drawing on Ravenstein's (1885) classic generalizations about human mobility, stress that migration takes place within well-defined streams, along particular routes, to specific destinations. The process of migration in these streams has been seen as reducing the cost of subsequent migration through the flow of information and sometimes the actual recruitment of migrants at the place of origin. Early migrants overcome 'obstacles', thus decreasing the difficulties encountered by later migrants (Lee 1966:55). The reduced cost of migration over time has sometimes been associated with decreased selectivity of migrants because it becomes easier for people of any background to migrate (Cardona and Simmons 1975). In other cases, as the previous discussion implies, reduced cost may be a factor in increased selectivity. Clearly, in the Azores the cost of migration has been progressively less through time. By 1978 the majority of the home population had some close or distant kin living in America and everyone was familiar with some aspects of American life. The question then becomes what effect this reduced cost has had on who actually migrates.

As depicted in the literature on migration, cost has two components: objective and subjective. The objective aspect of reduced cost is exemplified by the recruitment of migrants or by assistance given to help people in the place of origin to migrate, as in chain migration. The use of information about opportunities or jobs, such as the networks of contact and job channels for the Portuguese in Canada, discussed by Anderson (1974), is also an objective component of cost. Much of the rural to urban migration literature focuses on these mechanisms of adaptation which involve interaction between already settled migrants and new migrants. The subjective component of cost, which has been reduced through previous migration, involves changes in perception of risks through increased knowledge of the destination area and the adaptation of residents in the place of origin to ideational systems, or what has been called anticipatory socialization (Kasdan 1965; Hackenberg 1971).

In São Miguel the American policies giving preference to immigration of immediate relatives mean that the objective cost of migration is reduced as more and more people have family ties in America.[2] Ties with emigrants have facilitated the arrangement of visas, housing and jobs for new migrants. Contacts with kin and neighbors have led to increasing familiarity with American culture, which reduces subjective cost. The *trabalhadores* and *proprietários*, who have the most contact with emigrants, have a detailed but extremely localized knowledge of American goods, lifestyles, and values. This familiarity preadapts people to life in America and reduces the uncertainty of migration. It also provides people with a broader range of factors upon which to base decisions.

For those who decide to migrate, preadaptation may reduce uncertainty but may also increase levels of disappointment as higher goals are envisioned. The flow of information back to the homeland can influence migrants' decisions about destinations (Douglass 1975). In recent years in São Miguel, however, the major impact of information flows has been to influence goals and expectations rather than destinations. Recent immigrants in Fall River repeatedly stated that although they knew about some of the problems of life in America they had not realized that life would be so difficult initially or that they would have to work so hard. Expectations frequently exceeded the reality of immigrant life. As one recent immigrant from São Miguel lamented, "my America was in the Azores." The very fact that present migrants think that they have extensive knowledge about America and that they are familiar and preadapted to some aspects of the culture, may lead them to expect more than previous migrants who arrived with scanty knowledge and great uncertainty.

Familiarity with America provides people with an increasingly broad range of factors upon which to base decisions. In São Miguel greater familiarity has led some people to decide not to emigrate. A clearer picture of the problems associated with work and family life in America may influence some, particularly the landowning *proprietários*, to remain at home rather than emigrate. On the other hand, the cost of migration for the upper levels of the home society, those who have less direct contact through relatives, is reduced as they learn more about opportunities and general characteristics of American society from better-educated emigrant-visitors. The image of America as a life of drudgery, sweatshops and wooden tenements is being replaced with a vision of educational and financial opportunities which may bolster elite status in a changing home society.

In São Miguel the reduced cost of migration both perpetuates and alters the specific content of the migrant stream. Migrant selectivity did increase between 1960 and 1975 according to the data on occupations of migrants, which shows an increase in the percentage of skilled workers during that period. Two additional points about the migrant stream emerge. First, within the increase of more skilled and educated migrants there is a small proportion of young people who are not only somewhat better educated but who come from a significantly higher social class level than that of previous migrants. This appears to be an extension to America of the traditional pattern of seeking higher education abroad. Viewed from an historical perspective, this nascent trend is reminiscent of the days of primogeniture when among the elite opportunities at home were limited for all but the eldest and the younger siblings sought adventure and riches abroad. Second, the factors influencing migrant selectivity have changed and some people now migrate solely to 'try their luck' because they can, a choice sanctioned by the *povo* cultural tradition that everyone who can emigrate does, even though life at home has improved economically since the 1960's. In her study of Mexican internal migration to Cuidad Juarez, Zoomers (1986) points out that migration may become an institutionalized pattern even though the structural 'push' factors of better opportunities in the destination area no longer are important. Migrants to Cuidad Juarez now go because they can, because they have family there, not because the move will necessarily increase their economic well-being. In São Miguel there are also migrants who go because they can, not out of economic necessity. However, unlike the Mexican case, opportunities for them in the destination areas have not declined.

The major change that has occurred is that the home society is less poverty stricken relative to North America. Migration is a choice, but a choice which now involves both a greater range of possibilities in America and a greater range of options at home than it did in the 1960's. The phrase from the 1890's, 'there is nothing for me here,

I might as well leave' is no longer ubiquitous. Migrants may go, some simply because they can, but they are aware that opportunities for further education or acquisition of property at home do exist.

The data from São Miguel on individual decisions about migration indicates the importance of stage in the life cycle and limitations on resources available within the particular family. Some of the factors which influence the decision to migrate have changed since the early 1960's. Decisions of the late 1970's, compared to those of the early 1960's, are made in a home context where there is less intense poverty, more potential for socioeconomic mobility, more general knowledge of destination areas, and where the migration option has been reaffirmed as a cultural tradition.

With regard to youth, the main changes have been that some youth of *proprietário* background are now opting to seek higher education and social advancement in the home system, rejecting emigration possibilities, while some upper class youth are electing to obtain higher education in America, an option that would have been scorned in the 1960's. For young families, who make up the major proportion of migrants, the improved information of recent years means that options are weighed carefully. Those most likely to emigrate in the late 1970's were those with weaker support networks at home or those with very strong family networks in America. This is similar to findings from research on Mexican migration which indicate that migrant networks lower the costs of international migration (Massey and España 1987). However, allocation of family resources is also a critical factor. A brother who is managing the family shop is less likely to emigrate than a brother who is working small dispersed parcels of land and has a large family of his own. Some families who might have emigrated if they could have in the 1960's are no longer interested because they have established themselves in the homeland. This is particularly true of those individuals who have obtained some higher education or business status and would consequently engage in work of a lower status occupational level if they became factory workers in America. More of the elderly appear to be choosing not to emigrate as they become familiar with the problems of isolation facing them in America. How the elderly who no longer have close kin living nearby will be cared for is an issue of fundamental importance facing Michaelense society. In some villages non-kin networks have been activated through Church and neighbors to provide care that was previously in the family domain, but how pervasive this development will become in a home system where the young adult population continues to be depleted through emigration while the elderly proportion is increasing is questionable.

Economic and non-economic factors affecting migration decision-making are both reflected in characteristics of migrant selectivity and the migration stream. This study stresses the role of sociocultural factors which modify and supplement basic economic factors. While Zoomers (1986) found that the importance of economic factors may decrease even if there is little internal development, other studies have suggested that for cases of internal migration economic factors decrease in importance as migration continues and countries develop (Shaw 1975). The data from São Miguel suggest that a similar pattern can emerge in situations of permanent international migration.

In São Miguel non-economic factors are now of greater importance in the decision-making process than they were in previous years. Based on individual accounts about the past in both São Miguel and America, and historical data on flows, it appears that the primacy of basic subsistence needs in migration decision-making of the 1960's has been modified in the late 1970's emphasis on particular socioeconomic attributes of employment, family concerns, and quality of life. One explanation of this shift in emphasis is that as the socioeconomic status of the potential migrants improves they give greater consideration to non-economic factors (Demko 1974). In São Miguel, migration flows combined with internal development have raised the standard of living for those sectors of the population from which the largest proportion of migrants has been drawn. In addition, more emigrants now have higher socioeconomic status than previous migrants as the migration stream has become more diverse. The lowered cost of migration and associated migration feedback effects are variables in both of these developments. The importance of considering sociocultural variables in the decision is thus supported. Economics may be at the base of decisions to migrate, but strictly economic factors tell the investigator little about the specific characteristics of particular categories of people in the migration stream and therefore have limited predictive powers in examining the development of migration patterns in a society as a whole.

MIGRATION AND SOCIAL PROCESS

Formulation of typologies of the effects of migration

has been one approach taken to the question of how migration is part of broader social processes in the home system. Brandes, for example, suggests that migration has either transformational or institutionalized effects in the homeland. Transformational migration is, "...closely linked to profound changes in the economy and social structure of a people...", as has been the case for migration from parts of rural Spain. Institutionalized migration, such as that which occurred in Ireland, is defined as, "...that which is inherent in, and the supporter of, traditional socioeconomic relationships ... a built-in economic safety valve for the perpetuation of the established order" (Brandes 1975:14-15). Migration is variously viewed as a conservative force, an agent of change, a 'safety-valve', or a force that slows internal development. This approach to the utility of migration for the home system gives an overall view of dominant processes, but is inadequate for examining specific dynamics of migration. In São Miguel there is both continuity and change in different dimensions of the system, and for different groups of people within the system. Migration is a process that is part of the modernization and development of a larger national system, but the individual level of analysis must be taken into account to fully comprehend patterns of variation and change in migration. Viewed from the perspective of both individual and societal levels, migration does not result in stability or change, but rather is part of processes of stability and change (Philpott 1973). In some cases migration is a solution to population pressures but the solution itself has effects on the home society which may in turn affect subsequent migration, as was the case with improved educational facilities in São Miguel in the 1960's.

In the last century the process of migration has

influenced the shape of present day Michaelense society
with respect to social ordering and cultural orientations.
Increased socioeconomic mobility and restructured levels
of social status are among the effects of migration noted
for other parts of Europe (Fel and Hofer 1969; Lopreato
1967; Sensi-Tsolani 1977). Migration from São Miguel at
the turn of the century directly contributed to greater
access to land ownership for the peasantry, and more
recent migration has indirectly contributed to the
development of more accessible educational facilities for
the peasantry. These changes have increased the potential
for upward mobility among the rural sectors. Although
migration has in part contributed to the development of
the *novos ricos* class and the expansion of the
proprietário class, migration has not dramatically
changed the fundamental class structuring of social
relations in São Miguel. Migration has contributed to a
gradual loosening of the existing class lines, a process
which was accelerated by the 1974 revolution in Portugal.
Increased class permeability, or loosened class lines,
serves to entrench the existing class structure as those
few who do succeed in moving upward in the system
uphold the ideology of the class system itself. Although
emigration is one of the factors which has increased
permeability, it has enabled some people to shift their
hopes from mobility outside the system to mobility within
the home system and thus become less likely to emigrate.

According to absolute standards, the contrast between
socioeconomic levels in São Miguel has decreased since
the 1950's. In the rural areas increased assets associated
with emigration have improved the standard of living,
while for the upper social levels workers and servants are
not as readily available as they were in the past. These
kinds of changes have reduced but by no means equalized

the contrasts between town and country and rich and poor. Improvement in socioeconomic position by absolute standards can be distinguished from change in relative position in class and status structures (Friedl 1978). In São Miguel the former, but rarely the latter, takes place as a direct result of migration flows. Poverty has become less acute as a result of migration and internal developments while relative status positions have changed little. Flexibility in the home system of São Miguel accommodates increases in wealth for individuals in association with migration without endowing them with significantly higher social status. Features of the social structure, such as horizontality in social ties and gradual incorporation of families at new social levels, have been instrumental in a process combining absolute change with relative continuity in the island's system of social ordering.

In São Miguel the impact of people and communication flows, without long-term return of migrants, is also significant for cultural change. In rural areas of São Miguel interactions with migrants have contributed to a growing familiarity with attributes of modern urban life. The familiar categories (i.e. appliances, entertainment, etc.) are similar to those of urban São Miguel, but the specific characteristics, the type, names, and uses of appliances, are drawn from an American urban model, not the European model familiar to the urban educated of Ponta Delgada. This cultural familiarity constitutes a form of preadaptation to America which is prevalent in the rural areas, as typified by the statement of one older *Senhora* who said "I know what to buy in the supermarket in Fall River when I visit my daughter, but in the *Supermercado* in Ponta Delgada I am lost!"

The cultural familiarity with America has reinforced dual value systems associated with rural and urban populations in São Miguel. Traditionally the distinction between countryside and town includes a cultural separation of peasants, the *povo*, and the elite. Increasingly better rural standards of living have diminished the outward differences, but at the same time new distinctions have developed in cultural orientation. The rural sector now looks beyond the local setting to America, while the urban educated still look to mainland Europe as their cultural center. Cultural familiarity with America has thus reinforced rural/urban distinctions and accentuated class differences between the *povo* and the more educated and elite levels of the home society. The increase in contact with information flows among the elite has not diminished this difference in orientation because at present the elite are highly selective about what aspects of America interest them, i.e., investment and educational opportunities. These interests do not fundamentally change their cultural orientation toward mainland Portugal. Although a village woman may choose a dress design from the German fashion magazine *Burda*, the fabric is frequently from America and her perception of what is stylish is conditioned by her contact with visiting emigrants wearing American styles. On the other hand, the elite woman is acutely aware of European fashions and disdains most American clothing as garrish and lacking style.

The difference in views is not explicitly recognized by the elite and the *povo*. The *povo* are generally oblivious to the fact that the upper levels do not view America in glowing terms. For them, emigration holds the hope of a better life obtained through the traditionally sanctioned pattern of hard work. The *povo* gloss over the problems which the elite emphasize. The latter may in effect be defending their own position of being unable or unwilling to emigrate by pointing out the woes of emigration. Those in the middle levels must choose to opt either for emigration and socioeconomic mobility in the American system, or the more limited and less assured mobility in the home social system, which confers greater prestige in traditional terms, thereby upholding the existing class structure.

Viewed over time, it becomes evident that emigration has been an option for Michaelense people at all social levels at different periods in the past. Recent migration has been predominantly from the lower social levels but not exclusively so. Although the range of diversity is not statistically impressive, it is culturally significant. Historical diversity in the social level of migrants has fostered a flexibility in the way residents of São Miguel view migration at present. This flexibility has been reinforced by the feedback effect of information which now reaches the upper levels of the home society. The combination of the cultural tradition of migrant diversity and the circulation of information over time has been a key factor in the shift in attitudes of upper class youth towards education in America since 1974, enabling them to redefine emigration as the historically sanctioned pattern of going away for education. It is not clear whether such a shift will serve to uphold class distinctions at home by enabling elite students to obtain higher degrees from abroad when it is difficult to do so in Portugal, or whether the mixing of elite youth with other emigrants in America will facilitate the 'Americanization' of São Miguel and work to erode the class hierarchy. Cultural preadaptation, which in the past has supported class distinctions, may now be contributing to changes in migration patterns which will eventually undermine those distinctions. The

rationale for emigration from the upper levels has been
established and could be further utilized in the future,
particularly if it can be used to enhance their status in the
homeland where political changes have made some
attempt to reduce overt status distinctions and economic
control by the elite.

Migration in São Miguel is both a conservative force
and an agent of transformation. Despite the lack of radical
transformation in social ordering, changes in cultural
orientations have critically affected migration patterns of
particular groups at particular times. These effects are
part of the adaptation of the larger system in the course of
a long history of population mobility.

MIGRATION AND THE FUTURE

In some countries of Europe such as Spain and Italy
internal development has slowed the external flow of rural
migrants by diverting them to opportunities in the cities at
home. In the Azores such internal opportunities are not
well developed and in mainland Portugal opportunities are
already overtaxed by a rapid decline in labor migration and
the return of people from the former African colonies. In
the Azores a cycle has been recurring in which the
population expands, development is slow, and rural
residents emigrate in large numbers. It happened at the
turn of the century and again in the 1960's. What does the
future hold for a region where population mobility has
been such an integral part of recent history? Historical
ebbs and flows of migration have clearly changed the home
system and the combination of current migration feedback

through information flows and a cultural tradition of mobility endow migration with a momentum of its own. Migration from São Miguel could be curtailed by changes in immigration policies in North America, but barring this some level of migration is likely to continue in the future.

In 1980 I suggested that emigration from the Azores would most probably continue with a gradual decline, assuming that internal development proceeded at a moderate pace. The most recent figures available do show that Azoreans are still emigrating, but at a rate in 1985 that was less than half of the 1980 rate. In 1985, 1660 people emigrated from the Azores, compared to 4378 in 1980 and 7947 in 1975. The 1982 figures also indicate that the migrant stream has become slightly more skilled, with the greatest increase in the proportion of secondary or skilled labor from 25% in 1970 to 32% in 1982. Because of numerous factors which can affect variations in annual statistics, however, caution must be applied in making generalizations. Nevertheless, an increase in the proportion of skilled workers and even more highly educated individuals in the migrant stream might be expected as the general level of education rises in the home population. In 1981 the primary sector of the active work force in the Azores had declined from 50% in 1970 to 32% in 1981, and both the secondary and tertiary sectors had increased.[3] In addition, the proportion of individuals in the primary sector working for themselves increased from 36% in 1970 to 47% in 1981. As previously discussed this is partly a consequence of previous migration, but a consequence which decreases the likelihood of those individuals migrating in the future unless there are strong incentives based on family ties. The overall decline in emigration suggests that individuals have become more selective in their choice of the migration option. It also reflects a declining population, where the potentially active population, between the ages of 15 and 65 years, declined 13.6% between 1970 and 1981. This decline is associated with the depletion of the most fertile sector of the society through emigration since the 1960's, and the introduction of state initiated family planning programs in the late 1970's. The total population of the District of Ponta Delgada was 158,800 in 1975, but by 1982 it had declined to 138,400. It appears that the historical pattern of rising population followed by a flood of emigration has for the time being been replaced by a more stable population size and a constant trickle of emigrants.

From within the society, the *povo* view migration as a 'salvation' and say that without it life would have been a misery. Emigrants returning to visit do their best to reinforce this belief, yet for the upper levels of society post-1960 migration has eroded traditional social structure, resulting in fewer workers, a shortage of skilled workers, a general decline in willingness to work, higher wages, pressure to shift from intensive cultivation to milk production, and the gradual dispersal of their land base (a process which started with migrants returning from Brazil but has continued in recent years). From their perspective migration has been good for the peasantry but a misfortune for themselves.

The predominance of rural workers in the migrant stream represents lost human capital for the employers in the home system At the same time the emigration of workers has reduced population pressure on limited resources in the homeland, thereby acting as a conservative mechanism. The emigration of skilled workers is an offshoot of previous emigration of rural workers. This flow is a long-term investment for the homeland despite the loss of their training costs.

Emigrants have contributed to development in the destination areas and in doing so have created infrastructures which serve as American extensions of the home system. The more skilled workers and better educated migrants appear to be the ones who are particularly active in developing opportunities for Azoreans in the adoptive communities. They utilize the resources of America to improve their own statuses, cultivate ties with the homeland, and respond to the efforts of homeland government and businesses to create resources in America. The smallest flow, young student-emigrants, is at the moment a short-term investment for the homeland. If these students return they will balance the funds they took out by the professional skills they bring back. In addition, they will add to the development of resources for São Miguel through broadened perspectives on business and commercial opportunities and through connections to America. However, some do not return. Whether or not migrant selectivity for skills and education increases dramatically, it is likely that the future will see more emigration from the urban educated sector of São Miguel. Opportunities are beginning to open up for them in America, increased familiarity with American culture has lowered the cost of migration, and opportunities for them at home are limited by slow internal development and a stratified social structure.

At the turn of the century the emigrants to Brazil were sometimes called *desperdicios*, the lost or disappeared ones, because many of them were never heard from again. Contemporary emigrants frequently say that they will return, when they have made some money or are ready to retire, but the people at home do not expect them to return other than to visit. Migration in São Miguel is not the "emigration to return" of northern Portugal discussed by Brettell (1986); it is migration for good. Yet the ethos of return, the *saudades* or longing for the homeland, noted for northern Portugal, is also present in the Azores. It is not permanent return, but the importance of maintaining ties to the homeland is strongly embodied in the emigrants' world view. The term *desperdicios* is no longer applied to emigrants; emigrants now rarely return for good but they are a vital presence in the culture both through their absence and through their visits to the homeland. Emigration is no longer the great salvation for the people of São Miguel, but it continues, as one strategy among others, a strategy that still holds the promise of hopes and dreams fulfilled.

The future of migration in São Miguel will be shaped by legal and economic developments at both local and national levels. Whatever the outcome it is highly unlikely that migration will cease altogether. If flows of people to America are reduced, the island will still reap the benefits of strong connections with America.   Now and in the future, São Miguel is likely to draw increasingly on that capital in the forms of business enterprises, cultural exchanges, and tourism.

Statements by the Portuguese government in the late 1970's about emigration from the Azores indicate that they are seeking to slow the departure of all types of emigrants. They say they need the manpower; yet emigrants claim there are few opportunities at home. Past attempts to slow emigration misjudged the critical factors in migration and resulted in more trained people joining the migrant flow. Judging from the findings of this study, effective migration policy must fully grasp the variations in small group and individual perceptions throughout the system rather than basing programs solely on aggregate statistics characterizing the dominant migrant flow.

NOTES

CHAPTER ONE.   INTRODUCTION

1.   In comparison to other European countries such as
        Spain, Italy and Greece, relatively little social
        research has been done in Portugal.   The
        dissimilarity between the Azores and many parts of
        the mainland limits the applicability of those studies
        which do exist such as Reigelhaupt's (1967; 1973)
        and Seigel's (1961) work in central Portugal, or
        Cutileiro's (1971) work on a community in southern
        Portugal. The literature which pertains to migration
        in Portugal is of limited utility because of
        sociocultural disparities and the focus on situations
        of primarily seasonal migration to Lisbon or France
        (Brettell 1979; Trindade 1976; Leeds 1979).   For
        recent work on Portuguese migration see Brettell
        (1986) on demography, emigration history and the
        role of women in a parish of northern Portugal;
        Caspari and Giles (1986) on immigrant Portuguese
        women in the U.K. and France; and Chaney (1986)
        on remittances in mainland Portugal.   Studies of
        contemporary problems in the Azores are few
        (Clymer 1977; Pavão 1977; Constancia 1962;
        Rogers 1979; Rodriques 1976), and there is only
        one small publication on emigration (da Costa
        1972).

The literature on the Portuguese in America is less
prolific than for some other ethnic groups but does
include a substantial number of works on historical
immigration which are discussed in Chapter Two.
Contemporary works on New England Portuguese
include Rogers (1974), Adler (1972), Al-Khazraji
(n.d.), Smith (1974, 1975, 1976), and Gilbert
(1976).   Gilbert (1976) and Smith (1974, 1976)
specifically discuss Azorean immigrants.   These
sources provided important background information
on the destination area 'adoptive system', which
supplemented my own research in Azorean-
American communities.   Other works on
contemporary Portuguese immigration to North
America include Anderson (1974, 1977), and
Brettell (1977).   More recent work includes
Avendaño's (1982) very brief overview of the history
of Portuguese immigration to the U.S.; Alpalhão and
Pereira da Rosa's (1980) detailed monograph on the
Portuguese communities of Quebec; and Lamphere
(1986) on Portuguese immigrants in New England.
A volume on modern Portugal by Bruneau, Da Rosa
and Macleod (1984) includes several articles on
emigration such as Brettell and Da Rosa (1984)
comparing receiving areas in North America and
France and Dias (1984) on regional patterns of
immigration to the U.S.

2.   Previous fieldwork was carried out as a research
assistant to M. Estellie Smith.   The project in the
summer of 1972 involved research on Portuguese-
Americans, and a subsequent project in the summer
of 1973 involved research on the Azorean

background of ethnic enclaves in Massachusetts and N.Y. state.

3.   The importance of links to the homeland, particularly for Azoreans who are said to 'carry their islands on their backs', is also noted by Dias (1984:112) in his work on Portuguese immigrants in North America.

4.   The study was funded by a Vilas travel fellowship from the University of Wisconsin in 1976 and a pre-doctoral fellowship from the Social Science Research Council, 1976-79.

5.   The concept of level for ordering differences in societal integration has proven useful in discussions of complex societies, e.g. Schreiber (1976) notes the utility of multilevel analysis for Italian migration data.   In São Miguel the constraints impinging on migration decisions originate at different levels of society.   At the international and national levels there are some clear-cut constraints such as the restrictions on who can legally immigrate to the U.S. or Canada, as well as some less definitive constraints, such as the economic repercussions or speculated repercussions associated with the 1974 revolution in Portugal. At the regional level, in the Azores and São Miguel in particular, the context of present migration is embedded in the history of both the sending region and the specific receiving areas.   Local poverty and population growth in the islands, for example, have provided strong incentives for emigration in the past.   At the community level, individual views of migration are

affected by national and regional constraints and by factors within families and communities such as the specific nature of contact they have with previous migrants. The context of migration decisions for any one individual thus involves factors interwoven from different levels of society.

6.   The bulk of migration literature deals with internal or seasonal movements, as illustrated in the volumes by Kosinski and Prothero (1975) and Richmond and Kubat (1975) on internal migration and Tapinos (1974) on international seasonal migration. The literature on international permanent migration primarily includes anthropological and sociological studies on European migrations, for example, from Italy, Ireland, Sweden, Poland, and Spain to the Americas or Australia (Foerster 1968; Lopreato 1967; Cronin 1970; Kennedy 1973; Runblom and Norman 1976; Thomas and Znaniecki 1918; and Douglass 1974).

7.   Studies of rural to urban adaptation of migrants discuss, for example, how social networks (Kemper 1975), ethnic and regional affiliations (Doughty 1970; Little 1973; Mitchell 1956; Southall (1975), kinship (Lewis 1965; Bruner 1970; Buechler 1975), and values (Butterworth 1970) affect the perpetuation of migrant flows and adjustment patterns in the city. These are only a few examples from the vast literature in this area.

8.   For more extensive reviews of migration literature the reader is referred to Shaw (1975) and Mangalem (1977) for a sociological perspective;

Todaro (1976) for an economist's view; and Weaver and Downing (1976) and Graves and Graves (1974) for an anthropological viewpoint.

9.   An underlying assumption of this discussion is that people have given wants, goals, and values and that they select among possible strategies the most effective means to achieve their goals or most preferred goal (Heath 1976:83).   The idea that people make rational choices is widely used in explanatory models of economic and social behavior (e.g., Blau 1964; Homens 1961; Barth 1966; Paine 1974).   However, the question still arises as to how rationality is evaluated.   Are objective or subjective standards employed?   Heath (1976:83) points out that in many respects, choice is problematical.   In the study of decision-making, rationality is most fruitfully seen from the perspective of the decision-makers' evaluations of what is best in their own terms, which may not even include niceties like rationality, or distinctions of a subjective/objective nature.

CHAPTER TWO.   HISTORICAL PERSPECTIVES ON AZOREAN MIGRATION

1.   The term 'Michaelense' means to be of São Miguel.

2.   Although the Portuguese were the first to settle the islands there is evidence that sailors in previous

centuries knew about them. Carthaginean coins were found, for example, on the tiny island of Corvo (Sykes 1965:19).

3. Speaking of fifteenth century expansion, Payne (1973:200) states that the vigor and self-confidence of the Portuguese was incomparable. Portuguese migration was initially an inherent part of this expansionist mentality. The period of colonization, for example in Brazil, was not conceived of as the development of a "new society", according to Payne, but rather as the extension and projection of the old society which had failed to sustain the momentum of progress achieved in the fifteenth century (Payne 1973:204).

4. Pastel, or woad, was introduced by the Flemish and first cultivated on Fayal. A blue dye was extracted from the leaves which were exported to northern Europe. The wealth enjoyed from this trade was short-lived and cultivation had ceased by the end of the seventeenth century when competition from anil produced in Brazil and the West Indies had become stiff.

5. Smith (1974:87) suggests that the intensity of contacts and the movement back and forth combined to create a passive stance among Azorean immigrants in New England. They did not push to achieve a place in the power structure or fight to be accepted, because they were still integrally tied to the homeland and could choose to return there.

6. Reports from mainland Portugal in 1916 stated that

emigration had resulted in higher wages and a lack of labor that forced small and medium landholders to sell land which formerly landless emigrants then bought. In the period 1877-1907 the number of rural landholdings increased 51% and urban property increased 36% (Caqueja 1976:161-163). The same author concluded that the returnees came back more politically aware and better educated, and formed a force for rural democracy. Twenty years later another author said of returnees from Brazil that they were infected with a 'novo rico' mentality, spending their money on luxuries and travel rather than investing it (Ramires 1976:178).

7. In São Miguel, the *liceu* or high school was established in 1852 in Ponta Delgada and a technical school was started in 1890 (Da Costa 1978:302). Older informants in São Miguel described how until very recently only the rare village child had a chance for high school level education, and then only through the patronage of a wealthy family.

8. Of the emigrants from Ponta Delgada district in 1887 listing occupation, slightly less than half were listed as servants (Martins 1976:122). The data is incomplete, but it suggests that there may have been an increase in the demand for servants, a form of wage labor open to women. The data on occupation may reflect this in that more women would have been listing an occupation and that occupation would have been the category of servant.

9.   This view was presented to me by representatives in
        the Canadian Consulate and is supported in
        Anderson (1974).

CHAPTER THREE.   THE ISLAND OF SÃO MIGUEL:
DIMENSIONS IN THE SOCIOCULTURAL MATRIX OF
MIGRATION

1.   São Miguel and the other eight islands form the
        Autonomous Region of the Azores, with
        representatives to the Regional Assembly elected
        from each *concelho.* The region is in turn part of
        the Portuguese national system, operating with its
        own regional Assembly but represented in the
        National Assembly in Lisbon.   In addition, the
        national government has a representative in the
        Regional government. The gradual implementation
        of greater autonomy for the archipelago is in
        process, but subjugation to the mainland,
        particularly in economic spheres, is an omnipresent
        sore point in local discussions.

2.   This continues to be said despite the overwhelming
        evidence to the contrary that very few emigrants
        return to stay, but it does indicate the high visibility
        of those that do return.

3.   Bus service has improved in the last ten years, with
        more routes and frequent service, but how long it

takes to get to the city depends on whether it is necessary to change bus lines or not.

4. The primary sector category is composed of over 90% agricultural labor, the remainder including cattle raising, fishing, and extractive industries. The secondary sector includes workers in processing industries, electric, gas and water utilities, construction and public works. The tertiary sector is composed of commercial, tourism, transport, communication, banking, public administration and other service activities.

5. The source for these statistics shows rounded figures which for the secondary and tertiary sectors add up to 99% rather than 100%.

6. In 1981 the illiteracy rate for men and women over 14 years old was 22.6% for the Azores and 24.3% for São Miguel.

7. Literacy and educational level in the active work force in 1981 was as follows:
    17.0%- illiterate
    0.6%- read and write only
    48.6%- primary level education
    27.5%- some level of secondary education
    6.3%- education higher than grade 12

8. In São Miguel, where the primary sector is over 90% agricultural, the percent of people working for themselves in the primary has increased since 1970 while the percent working for someone else has decreased. In 1970, 36.4% worked for themselves,

compared to 46.8% in 1981. The percent working for others declined from 52.8% in 1970 to 42.3% in 1981. This is in part associated with the significant decrease in the number of workers in the less specialized professions due to emigration since 1970.

9.   Politically the island is divided into six municipalities, *concelhos*, each of which has a *câmara* or town council to which representatives are elected. The *concelhos* are further sub-divided into fifty parishes, *frequesias*, which have their own community council, the *Junta da Freguesia*, which has an elected president and representatives.

10.   I follow Wolf's (1973:2) use of the term informal structures as "interstitial, supplementary, and parallel" to formal structures.

11.   Fictive kinship is an additional form of 'familial' tie that in São Miguel today is mainly confined to kin.

12.   See Fallers (1964:113-117) for a discussion of the moral and cultural aspect of stratification related to Parson's notion of 'good'.

13.   Cattle production has continued to increase. In 1974, 154,468 tons of milk was purchased for factory processing and in 1985 that had increased 34% to 210,654 tons. Tonnage of beef cattle slaughtered and exported live has more than doubled in the period 1974-85 (Bêdo 1986).

14.   In 1981 the percent of women in the active work force had increased to 17.9% for the Azores as a whole (DREPA 1984).

CHAPTER FOUR. THE EMIGRANTS: 'THEY CAN SEE THE OCEAN AND THEY WANT TO GO'

1.   This viewpoint was reported in a 1973 Report of the District of Ponta Delgada published by the Regional Planning Office (DREPA 1973).

2.   See Appendix for further detail on this survey.

3.   Legal prerequisities include immediate kin in America or skills which qualify the applicant for occupational preference.

4.   Correlations between specific migration figures and historical circumstances should be made with caution. To base correlations on figures from a one or two year period may be misleading, as was pointed out by staff at the U.S. Consulate in Ponta Delgada. Annual variations in numbers of emigrants are associated with the number of interviews granted to applicants for immigrant visas at the U.S. and Canadian consulates. This number can be affected by a variety of factors including how well organized the particular consulate is, changes in personnel, sickness among the staff, the philosophy of the resident consul, and changes in immigration

policy. A change in consul has in the past as much
as doubled the number of applicants interviewed
per month. An example of policy change can be
seen in the 1978 U.S. decree that all outstanding
petitions had to be activated within one year in
order to be valid. People in São Miguel with
petitions their relatives in America had sent
(sometimes as long as ten years ago) had to decide if
they wanted to apply for a visa within the year. The
consulate consequently expected this policy change
to be reflected in higher numbers of emigrants for
1978-79. Such an increase would not therefore
necessarily reflect specific responses to conditions
in the homeland at that time.

5.   If a person in São Miguel is engaged to a citizen or
permanent resident in the U.S. they can arrange a
non-immigrant visa that entitles him/her to
permanent immigrant status if he/she marries
within three months. If he/she does not marry
he/she must return like any other non-immigrant
visitor.

6.   The statistics used in this section are both for the
District of Ponta Delgada, which includes São
Miguel and the smaller island of Santa Maria, and
for the island of São Miguel alone. In some
instances figures for the island alone are not
available. All figures are from the Instituto Nacional
de Estatistica unless otherwise specified.

7.   Another factor in population decline was fertility
regulation, and although this has not been the major
factor in recent population decline in São Miguel it

has increasingly contributed to smaller family sizes. Nurses in São Miguel, for example, have estimated that anywhere from one quarter to one third of the fertile women in urban areas use birth control pills. Other forms of fertility regulation, such as abstinence and condoms, are also in use. There is evidence that some form of birth control was being used as early as the 1930's (Livi Bacci 1971). A second factor affecting population growth is the improvement in maternal-infant health care since the 1950's and a decline in infant mortality which appears to make couples more comfortable limiting the number of children conceived.

8.   In 1982 the rate of emigration was 6.8 per 1000 inhabitants compared to 32.7 per 1000 in 1975 for the District of Ponta Delgada.

9.   The number under ten years old is recorded in the Portuguese statistics, but the numbers for other ages are not broken down. The estimate that the majority of adults are between twenty and forty is based on interviews with emigrants, staff of the U.S. and Canadian consulate, and the medical examiner for visa applications.

10.   Since almost 60% of births take place among women under the age of thirty (I.N.E. 1976), and younger women are a major element in the emigrant flow, it can be assumed that a signifcant fertility potential is being removed from the population through emigration.

11.   There has also been a very small flow of returnees

from former African provinces since the early 1970's, but these *retornados* have only added a few dozen people to the population of São Miguel. This is a very different situation from mainland Portugal where an estimated 700,000 immigrants arrived from Africa in 1974 alone (Chaney 1986:28). In spite of a decreasing rate of emigration the total population of the District of Ponta Delgada continued to decline from 158,800 in 1975 to 138,400 in 1982.

12.   Travel agents offer special rates. In effect, the return rates offered by travel agents, often Azorean run businesses, have encouraged the 'successful' emigrants to return for visits, which serves to demonstrate the benefits of emigration.

13.   Non-immigrant visas are primarily issued for visitors, but they also include small numbers of visas for students and fiancé(e)s of U.S. citizens or permanent residents.

CHAPTER FIVE. THE SCENT OF AMERICA: FLOWS OF INFORMATION, MONEY, AND GOODS

1.   For an excellent discussion of the literature on the economic effects of migration and remittances see Paul Shankman (1976:6-21).

2.   These numbers were estimated from statistics in

Jornal de Fall River, 1 March 1978, page 11.

3.   In the survey described in the Appendix the responses to what people in the households do with money received from emigrants in America were as follows: 44% bought foodstuffs, 31% bought clothes, 21% saved, 5% fixed up the house (e.g. painting), and 8% used the money for other miscellaneous household costs.

CHAPTER SIX.   MIGRATION DECISION-MAKING IN TIME AND SPACE

1.   The terms insider and outsider are used here rather than the anthropological concepts of 'emic' and 'etic' in order to avoid any confusion that might result from the association of emic with analysis of cognitive structures.   The insider's view is approximated, but not structurally analyzed.

2.   Focusing on life-cycle stages in social process is an old theme in the anthropological literature.   Van Gennep (1909) employed the concept of critical life stages in his model of the transitions an individual makes from one category to another in a society and what happens when people cross those thresholds. In a different context, the Wilsons (1945:59-61) used the concept of 'social circulation' to designate the ongoing social process of splitting and reforming of groups which they associated partially

with stages in the life-cycle, such as marriage. Goody (1958) further elaborated the idea of fission and fusion in families into a developmental model of domestic groups. In migration studies the concept of *rite de passage* has been applied to ceremonial aspects of migration (Philpott 1973:154).

3.   In a survey sample of one community, 30% said that life is better at home, 18% said that work is better at home, 15% said that they did not want to leave their family, 28% said that they were too old or afraid, and 18% said it was not easy to emigrate so they never had tried.

4.   The data for this section is drawn primarily from case history materials on people deciding to emigrate. In order to attain a dynamic process of people over time, materials have also been used from a series of open-ended interviews and case histories of a cross-section of the home population which include people who are contemplating emigration, people who have decided against it, people who never considered it an option, and people who emigrated. The use of data on people throughout the society approximates the range of data collected using the concept of 'phases' in decision-making which has been applied to other migration studies (Taylor 1969, and Goldsmith and Beegle 1962). The context of decision-making is limited for any given individual, but looking at the process as a whole, the context is the home system and all of these people are part of that system.

5.   Only adults are considered to be 'migrant deciders'.

Although 25% of all migrants are under ten years old, it is assumed here that they do not make the decision, even if their opinions do form part of the context.

6. Since 1976 all people over 60 years old are eligible for a monthly state compensation of 600 *escudos* (about $15 U.S.) as well as subsidized medical care.

7. A recent article in a Providence newspaper, for example, ran a story on an Azorean-American father who was arrested for keeping his son out of school on the grounds that he didn't need the education and was being adversely affected by the behavior of fellow students who take drugs.

8. The political atmosphere in the homeland may affect investments in land. After the 1974 Portuguese coup, this family started buying property in Canada rather than in São Miguel, considering it a safer investment.

9. For example, in 1972 in Newark, N.J. it was possible, given the right connections to make a rush arrangement for permanent immigrant status for about $10,000. For a person who had time to work on it the arrangements might cost as little as $500.

10 A questionnaire was developed and administered in cooperation with the local college. It was given to a sample of 99 students in São Miguel, 71% of whom were in their second to last year of high school, and 28% of whom were in the year between high school and college entrance (*anopropedeutico*). The rest

were just beginning a course at the local college. Students were asked open-ended questions as to what they thought were good and not so good things about emigration and emigrants. Additional questions included data on where they would most prefer to study, emigrant relatives, and sociocultural background variables such as sex, education, parents' professions, and rural/urban residential origin.

11.   Percent distribution of preferred location for further study.

Location	Percent
U.S.	32
Canada	9
Mainland Portugal	21
Azores	23
Other	14

12.   Relationship (Phi) between selected background variables and desire to emigrate and to return if study done abroad.

	Want to Emigrate	Return if Study Abroad
Sex	.15	.10
Father's Profession	.23*	-.23*
Education	-.21*	-.17*
Urban Residence	.02	.17*

----

*p ≤ .05 based on Chi Square   N = 99

13. Freidl (1967:94) uses the concept of lagging emulation with respect to Greece, suggesting that peasantry in a transitional state strive for prestige by emulating the elite, but this emulation 'lags' in that it imitates mainly those upper class traits which are retained from the preindustrial segment of the contemporary upper classes.

14. Generalizations about constraints and incentives for emigration are based on a sample of 55 case studies consisting of 38.2% *Trabalhadores*, 29.1% *Proprietários*, 9.1% Skilled-Technical, 7.3% Skilled-High School, and 16.3% Professional and Higher-Educated.

CHAPTER 7. CONCLUSION

1. Tourist accommodations have also expanded. The number of hotel beds increased from 1384 in 1975 to 1997 in 1985 in São Miguel and more expansion is planned (Bêdo 1986).

2. One reflection of the increase in family ties is the decrease in transatlantic fictive kin ties. Priests in São Miguel reported that in the 1960's and earlier years it was common for godparents to be in America, ceremonies performed by proxy, but in the late 1970's it is rare. People in the villages explained this decrease by saying that first, local godparents contribute more to the child in gifts and

second, unless you are sure you will emigrate it is better to have your resources where you are living and it is no longer important to have godparents in America to help you emigrate.

3. Active Population of the Azores, by Sector, Excluding Unemployed and Military.

Sector of Activity	Percent by Year	
	1970	1981
Primary	49.8%	31.5%
Secondary	17.2%	25.2%
Tertiary	32.0%	43.3%

(Source: DREPA 1984)

APPENDIX - FIELDWORK

In São Miguel the data was collected from a wide variety of sources, using participant-observation, informal interviewing, structured interviews, questionnaires, and the available demographic and archival data. In the course of collecting the data I visited three of the other eight islands and spent three weeks in Lisbon consulting archival materials. Fieldwork in Fall River primarily involved participant-observation and case history interviewing. Extensive case histories were collected from non-migrants, returned migrants, migrants in America and potential or visiting migrants in São Miguel. For a small number of families, case histories were elicited both from members in America and their relatives in São Miguel.

Information on flows of people and communications between São Miguel and America was gathered through government statistics, village surveys, content analysis of local newspapers, and interviews with local travel agents, the American and Canadian consulates, local medical and social service personnel who deal with emigrants, airline employees, priests, bankers, and shopkeepers and business owners. Additional information came from interacting with emigrants and the families and neighbors they came to see in São Miguel.

Data included the results from one written questionnaire and two surveys conducted in São Miguel. A

287

questionnaire was used in combination with informal interviews to examine attitudes toward migration among a sample of high school age students and formal interviewing was conducted in two villages to collect basic household data and information on migration.

STUDENT QUESTIONNAIRE

The questionnaire for Michaelense students was developed and administered in cooperation with the Instituto Universitário dos Açores   in Ponta Delgada. It was given to a sample of ninety-nine students. In this sample 71% were in their second to last year of high school. Of these students, 32% were enrolled in the local technical school and 68% were attending a college preparatory school in the Ponta Delgada area. A smaller proportion of the sample, 28%, were in the year of study between high school and college *(anopropedeutico)* in which students prepare for and take university qualifying exams. The remaining 1% of the sample were enrolled in the Instituto.

Open-ended questions elicited information on what the students thought about emigrants and emigration. Additional questions included data on the students' desire to emigrate, their plans to obtain higher education, where they most preferred to study, where they most preferred to work, emigrant relatives, and background variables such as sex, education, parents' professions, and rural or urban residential origin. Detailed results of this questionnaire are discussed in White and Pollnac (1979).

The basic content of the questions asked is as follows:

1. Age, sex, school attending, level, scholarship or not, marital status, work or not, place of birth, occupations of father and mother, preferred profession.

2. Are you planning to take a college (university) level degree?

    If yes, where do you plan to study?

3. If you could choose anyplace, where would you most like to study?

    Why would you prefer this place?

4. If you want to study outside of the Azores, would you want to return after finishing your course?

5. If you could choose anyplace, where would you most prefer to work?

6. For the Azores, mainland Portugal, and America, where do you think it is 'very true', 'more or less true', or 'not very true' that a) it is easier to obtain an education, b) the education is better, c) it is easier to arrange work, d) it is easier to obtain the type of work you want to do, e) people work harder, f) people live happier, and g) the quality of life is better?

7. Are you familiar with any places in America where Azoreans live?

    Write the names of places where you think many Azoreans live in America.

8. Have you ever traveled or lived in any of the following places?

    The U.S., Canada, Portugal (mainland), other islands, Brazil, Africa, or other places?

9. Do you have relatives who live in any of these above places?

10.   Are you thinking seriously about emigration to another country?

11.   See if you can think of three characteristics which you think well describe Azorean emigrants in a positive sense. See if you can think of three characteristics which you think well describe Azorean emigrants in a negative sense.

VILLAGE SURVEYS

Two surveys were used as a means of substantiating data collected through informal methods in several areas of São Miguel. Survey A employed a broad range of questions addressed to a sample of household heads or their spouses in a primarily agricultural community. Survey B consisted of a limited number of questions on households and emigration which were asked of a sample of household heads who were fishermen.

Survey A

A random sample of households was taken in Village A using parish records and the chart of random numbers. The sample consisted of 24 households, 17% of the total 145 households in the village. The head of the household or spouse was interviewed for each household. Interviews generally required two or more visits to the house or place of work and were conducted as informally as possible.

Additional data was collected in the form of case histories of the respondents.

The survey elicited information through both structured and open-ended questions. The basic questions and responses are listed in the following sections.

PERSONAL DATA

a   Would you tell me who lives in your house and give me some information about yourself and the other people living with you? (age, do you know how to read, marital status, occupations full and part-time, place of work, occupations of spouse if married, place of work of spouse, number of live children and ages, number of people living in the house and relationships)   N=24   Male=11   Female=13

Table 1. Respondents' Marital Status and Literacy by Age for Total, for Male and for Female Respondents.

Total Respondents

Age	Married	Widowed	Single	Literate	Total #
25-35	5	-	-	5	5(21%)
36-45	4	-	-	4	4(17%)
46-60	4	1	-	2	5(21%)
61+	5	3	2	6	10(21%)
Total	18(75%)	4(17%)	2(8%)	17(71%)	24(100%)

Male Respondents

Age	Married	Widowed	Single	Literate	Total #
25-35	2	-	-	2	2
36-45	1	-	-	1	1
46-60	3	-	-	-	3
61+	5	-	-	3	5
Total	11 (100%)			6 (55%)	11(100%)

Female Respondents

Age	Married	Widowed	Single	Literate	Total #
25-35	3	-	-	3	3
36-45	3	-	-	3	3
46-60	1	1	-	2	2
61+	-	3	2	3	5
Total	7 (54%)	4 (31%)	2 (15%)	11 (85%)	13 (100%)

Table 2.   Total Respondents' Number of Live Children and Household Size, by Age.

Age	# Live Children			# in Household			
	0	1-3	4-6	1	2	3-5	6+
25-35	1	3	1	-	1	3	1
36-45	-	2	2	-	-	1	3
46-60	-	3	2	-	-	5	-
61+	3	5	2	3	6	1	-
Total	4 (17%)	13 (54%)	7 (29%)	3 (13%)	7 (29%)	10 (42%)	4 (17%)

Table 3. Place of Work and Occupational Category for the Head of Household by Age.

Age	Place of Work Village	Town	Both	Occupational Category Proprie-tário	Trabal-haldor	Skilled	Profes-sional
25-35	2	2	1	-	4	1	-
36-45	3	-	1	2	2	-	-
46-60	5	-	-	-	5	-	-
61+	10	-	-	5	4	-	1
Total	20(84%)	2(8%)	2(8%)	7(29%)	15(63%)	1(4%)	1(4%)

Table 4. Respondents' Place of Birth by Age.

Age	Home Village	Neighboring Village	Other Island
25-35	2	3	-
36-45	4	-	-
46-60	5	-	-
61+	9	-	1
Total	20 (84%)	3 (12%)	1(4%)

b. Who are the godparents (baptismal) of your children, and are they relatives or people from outside of your family?

18 = members of the family (86%)
3 = non-family godparents (14%) N=21

Do any of your children have godparents who now live in America?

$$17 = no \quad (81\%)$$
$$4 = yes \quad (19\%)$$

CONTACT WITH EMIGRANTS

a   Have any of your relatives lived, or now live, outside of the Azores?

$$0 = no$$
$$24 = yes \quad (100\%) \qquad N=24$$

b.   Have any of your relatives lived in any of the following places?   (U.S., Canada, Continental Portugal, Bermuda, Brazil, and Others) For each, how long? Have they returned to visit or to stay? Do they correspond with? Do they send money sometimes?   What relationship are they to you?

$$N=24$$

Relatives in the U.S. at present

$$3 = no \quad (14\%)$$
$$18 = yes \quad (86\%)$$
$$8 = \text{close relative who could}$$
$$\text{qualify the respondent for fifth}$$
$$\text{preference visa } (38\%)$$
$$10 = \text{more distant relative, i.e., cousins,}$$

Correspond regularly

    8 = yes
    10 = rarely or not at all

Relatives in <u>Canada</u> at present

    11 = no (48%)
    13 = yes (52%)
        6 = could apply for visa
            with immediate family preference
            points (26%)
        6 = more distant relatives(26%)

Correspond regularly

    8 = yes
    5 = rarely or not at all

Immediate family in <u>both the U.S. and Canada</u> at
present

    23 = no (96%)
     1 = yes (4%)

Relatives in <u>Bermuda</u> at present

    16 = no (57%)
     8 = yes (33%)

Correspond regularly

    8 = yes

Relatives in <u>Brazil</u> at present

  22 = no (92%)
   2 = yes (8%)

Correspond regularly

   2 = no

Relatives in <u>Continental Portugal</u> at present

  20 = no (83%)
   4 = yes (17% All went there initially to
      study)

Correspond regularly

   4 = yes

c. Do you have any relatives who live outside of the Azores who participate or send things for the *festas* here in S. Miguel?

   9 = no(39%)
  14 = yes(61%)   N=23

What do they do if yes?

  14 = send money for the family and
      the Church

d. Do you know other people, like former neighbors, godchildren, or associates, who live outside of the

Azores who correspond with your family or send things to you sometimes?

8 = no (33%)
16 = yes (67%)   N=24

What is their relationship to you?

10 = godchildren or godparents
6 = former neighbors or villagers

e.   Who in your family writes letters to relatives abroad?

15 = wife or daughter(62%)
4 = husband and wife both write(17%)
5 = rarely keep in touch(21%)   N=24

f.   When you receive dollars from America in your family what kinds of uses do you put them to?

9 = to buy clothes and food for the household (57%)
3 = keep as savings (19%)
2 = to buy food for special occasions (12%)
2 = to pay off cash debts (12%)   N=16

g.   Do you ever have occasion to send money out of the Azores?

14 = no (94%)
6 = yes (6%)Sent by *procuradors* to the owners of property who now live in America   N=16

h.   Does your family ever send things to people outside
      of the Azores?

         14 = no (87%)
          3 = yes, presents *(lembranças)* (13%)

i.   With respect to the things and money people send
      back from America, do you think they have changed
      the standard of living here?

         14 = yes (70%)
          3 = no (15%)
          3 = don't know (15%)   N=20

      If yes, in what ways?

         12 = helped out (86%) ('made life
              easier','better clothes,')
          2 = don't know (14%)

j.   Do you ever make telephone calls to America?

         23 = no (96%)
          1 = yes (4%)   N=24

      Do you ever receive telephone calls from America?

         21 = no (88%)
          3 = yes (12%)   N=24

TRAVEL

a   Have you ever traveled outside of S. Miguel?

     13 = no (54%)
     11 = yes (46%)   N=24

If yes, where?

     7 = other islands
     7 = America
     2 = Continental Portugal
     1 = Africa (in the army)
     1 = Europe

b.   How frequently do you go to the city?

     3 = once a week or more often (13%)
     9 = once a month (37%)
    10 = once every six months (42%)
     2 = once a year or less (8%)   N=24

EMIGRATION

a   Do you think that everyone for whom it is possible
        to emigrate, does emigrate?

     1 = no (4%)
    18 = yes (75%)
     5 = don't know (21%)   N=24

b.   Why do people leave for America these days?

        9 = to get more money (52%)
        2 = to join their family (12%)
        2 = for a better life (12%)
        2 = better life and money (12%)
        2 = better work for women(12%)   N=17

c.   Are the reasons different now than they used to be, and if so, in what ways are they different?

        5 = people go nowadays because it is
            more expensive to live here than
            it used to be(29%)
        3 = people who go now don't need
            to go for financial reasons (18%)
        9 = don't know (53%)   N=17

d.   Have you ever thought seriously about emigrating?

      18 = no(75%)   N=24

        Why not?
           8 = have a good life here
           3 = don't want to leave family
           3 = too old by the time
               it was considered
           2 = never tried but don't
               think a visa obtainable
           2 = never thought about it at all

      6 = yes (25%)

Why didn't you emigrate?
- 2 = emigrated and returned
- 2 = waiting for a visa, or a permit, or trying to arrange the passage fare
- 1 = denied visa
- 1 = family member sick and can't leave

If you could go, for how long would you want to stay in America?
- 1 = forever
- 4 = for some years and maybe return
- 1 = for only one or two years

Are you thinking of emigrating within the next year?
- 4 = no
- 2 = yes

e. Do you think that people who emigrate now are different from the type of people who went before?

- 12 = no (57%)
- 7 = yes (33%)
- 2 = don't know (10%)   N=21

If yes, in what ways?
- 3 = they live better here before they go, not so poor

          2 = it is easier to arrange to leave and
                they have an easier time when
                they get to America
          1 = they don't return
          1 = they are greedier

     Since when has this changed?
          4 = over ten years ago
          2 = in the last five years

PROPERTY-HOUSES

a   How did you arrange the house where you live?

          19 = bought it (79%)
           5 = rent it (21%)   N=24

b.   Who did it belong to before?

          13 = parents or in-laws in the
                village (65%)
           2 = former neighbors who sold the
                house when they got too old to
                manage alone (10%)

     or,
     Who is the house rented from?

           3 = non-relatives in America (15%)
           1 = relative in America (5%)
           1 = relative in village   (5%)   N=20

c. How many other houses do you own?

    5 = one other (22%)
    18 = none (78%)   N=23

d. Nowadays do you think that owning your own house is

    16 = more difficult than in the past (73%)
     2 = easier than in the past (9%)
     4 = about the same as in the past (18%)
                                        N=22

Why?

    6 = more expensive now (27%)
    6 = emigrants won't sell houses
        when they leave (27%)
    2 = there is more money available
        nowadays (9%)
    8 = not sure why or hasn't
        changed much (37%)   N=22

Since when has it changed if you think it has?

    12 = since 10-15 years ago (67%)
     4 = since 2-5 years ago (22%)
     2 = not sure (11%)   N=18

e. Nowadays do you think that renting a house here is

    18 = more difficult than before (86%)
     1 = easier than in the past (5%)
     2 = about the same as in the past (9%) N=21

Why?

> 10 = emigrants have left houses
>   shut up and won't rent them (48%)
> 5 = no one wants to rent (24%)
> 2 = renters don't respect the rights of owners
>   (9%)
> 4 = not sure (19%)   N=21

f.   Has your house been fixed up in the last five years?

> 7 = yes (29%)
> 17= no (71%)   N=24

How did you arrange the money to do this?

> 1 = borrowed from former employer
>   now in America
> 2 = borrowed locally
> 2 = saved
> 2 = money earned from working in
>   America

g.   Do you have any of the following in your house?
      (mostly observed)

> 22 = bottled gas stove (92%)
> 21 = electricity (88%)
> 21 = wash tank with water tap outside house
>   (88%)
> 19 = inside water tap (79%)
> 7 = inside bathroom (29%)
> 7 = hot water (29%)
> 4 = telephone (17%)

             7 = refrigerator (29%)
             1 = freezer (4%)
             1 = washing machine (4%)
            13 = sewing machine (54%)
            20 = traditional bread oven (83%)   N=24

MEDIA

a   Do you read a newspaper at least once a week?

             3 = yes
            21 = no   N=24

b.   Do you have a television in your house?

            10 = yes (42%)
            14 = no (58%)   N=24

c.   Do you watch television sometimes?

            17 = yes (71%)
             7 = no (29%)   N=24

     If yes, where do you usually watch it?

            10 = in own house
             4 = in a neighbor's house
             3 = in a relatives's house   N=17

     How frequently?

             9 = every day

   6 = now and again (two or three
         times a week)
   2 = once a week or less   N=17

d.   Do you have a radio in the house that you listen to?

      22 = yes (92%)
       2 = no (8%)   N=24

PROPERTY-LAND

a   Do you cultivate some land?

      23 = yes (96%)
       1 = no (4%)   N=24

b.   Are the fields you own or rent adjoining?

       1 = yes (4%)
      23 = no (96%)   N=24

c.   How much cultivable land do you own? do you rent?
      How much pasture do you own? do you rent?
      How much other land do you own?   do you rent?

Cultivable Land or Pasture Owned Area in *alqueires* (one third of one acre approximately)	Number of Owners	Occupational Category of Owner			
		Proprie-tário	Profes-sional	Skilled	Trabal-hador
50+	2 (8%)	2	-	-	-
20-49	4 (17%)	3	1	-	-
10-19	5 (21%)	2	.-	-	3
5- 9	5 (21%)	-	-	-	5
1- 4	6 (25%)	-	-	1	5
0	2 (8%)	-	-	-	2

N=24

Type of Land Tenancy per household

    9 = private ownership only (38%)
    12 = own some land and rent some (50%)
    2 = rent only (8%)
    1 = share crop (4%)   N=24

d.   Do you have a cultivated kitchen garden?

    19 = yes (79%)
    5 = no (21%)   N=24

e.   Nowadays do you think that to obtain land it is

    11 = more difficult than in the past (50%)
    3 = easier than in the past (14%)
    8 = about the same as in the past (36%) N=22

Why?

7 = it is more expensive now (50%)
3 = emigrants don't want to sell it (22%)
2 = people are afraid to buy or sell
     because of the unstable government (14%)
2 = people have more money now (14%) N=14

Since when has it changed if you think it has?

10 = since 10-15 years ago (71%)
4 = since 2-5 years ago (29%)   N=14

PROPERTY-OTHER

a   Do you own any of the following animals? How
        many?

21 = own chickens (88%)
10 = own 1-5 pigs (42%)
 1 = own over 5 pigs (4%)
 2 = own burro (8%)
 2 = own horse (8%)
 1 = own more than one horse (4%)
 1 = own more than 20 milk cows (4%)
 2 = own pigeons (8%)   N=24

b.   Do you own any of the following things?

4 = motorbikes (17%)
4 = small truck (17%)

2 = car (8%)
3 = large grape press (12%)   N=24

HELP IN WORK

a   Do you have any people regularly working for you?

14 = no (58%)
10 = yes (42%)*   N=24

*The survey was done during the harvest period and some of these respondents regularly employed workers at this time of year but not during other months.

b.   When you need extra help with your work how do you arrange it?

11 = hire someone (52%)
7 = family helps   (34%)
3 = neighbors help (14%)   N=21

Survey B

The second survey was conducted with a sample of 19 heads of households in a fishing community, Village B. A series of questions on emigration were given in addition to a longer survey being conducted by students from the

Instituto Universitario dos Açores under the direction of Sr. Francisco Carmo. Selected results of the longer survey are written up in Pollnac and Carmo (1979).

In addition to personal data (including travel experience) and general household information, information was elicited on aspects of emigration through the following questions:

1. If it was possible to choose any country or place to live where would you choose?
   For how long would you want to stay there?
2. Are you thinking about emigrating within the next year?
3. If you were to go to the U.S. or Canada what do you imagine would be different from life in S. Miguel?
   What do you imagine might be more or less the same?
4. Do you think that the people who now leave the Azores are different from the types of people who emigrated in the past?
   If yes, in what ways?
5. Do you think that the people who emigrate nowadays are going to find a different kind of life in America than people found when they went in the past?
   In what ways? Since when?
6. Can you think of some characteristics or ways of being which you think well describe the Azorean emigrants?
   Describe three good things, and three not so good things.

BIBLIOGRAPHY

Abu-Lughod, Janet
    1975   "Comments: The End of the Age of Innocence
           in Migration Theory", pp. 201-206. In B.
           DuToit and H. Safa (eds.), Migration and
           Urbanization. The Hague: Mouton.

Adler, James P.
    1972   Ethnic Minorities in Cambridge: The
           Portuguese. Vol. 1 (unabridged). Prepared for
           the Cambridge Planning and Development
           Department. Cambridge: The City of
           Cambridge Printing Department.

Al-Khazraji, Majid G. and Emilie M. Al-Khazraji
    n.d.   Immigration and Beyond: The Portuguese
           Community of New Bedford, Mass. Action
           Research Project. New Bedford, Mass.:
           Onboard, Inc., Migrants Inc.

Alpalhão, Antonio and Victor M. P. Da Rosa
    1980   A Minority in a Changing Society: The
           Portuguese Communities of Quebec. Ottawa:
           University of Ottawa Press.

Amaral, Pat
    1978   They Ploughed the Seas: Profiles of Azorean
           Master Mariners. St. Petersburg, Fl.: Valkyrie
           Press Inc.

Anderson, Grace M.
    1974   Networks of Contact: The Portuguese and
           Toronto. Waterloo: Wilfrid Laurier University
           Publishers.

Andromedas, John N.
    1968   "The Enduring Urban Ties of a Modern Greek
           Folk Subculture", pp. 269-278. In J. G.
           Peristiany (ed.), Contributions to
           Mediterranean Sociology. Paris: Mouton &
           Co.

Archivo dos Açores
    1878   "Edital", Archivos dos Açores, Vol. I,
           pp. 381-383.

    _____.

    1890   "População das Ilhas dos Açores em 1796",
           Archivo dos Açores, Vol. XI, pp. 145-151.

Arensberg, Conrad and Solon Kimball
    1968   Family and Community in Ireland. Cambridge,
           Mass.: Harvard Univ. Press.

Avendaño, Fausto
    1982   "Portuguese Immigration into the United
           States", pp. 155-172. In Dennis Cuddy (ed.),
           Contemporary American Immigration. Boston:
           Twayne Publishers.

Azorean Times
    1979   "Portugueses no Hawaii." Azorean Times, Fall
           River, Mass., Oct. 10, p. 7.

————————.

1980a "Galo!" Azorean Times, Fall River, Mass., April
1, p. 17.

————————.

1980b "Emigrantes Mandaram em 1979 cerca de
755 mil contos para os Açores." Azorean
Times, Fall River, Mass., April 15, p. 1.

Bannick, Christian John
1971 Portuguese Immigration to the United States:
Its Distribution and Status, (A.B. thesis,
Stanford University, 1916). Reprinted 1971
from the 1917 edition. San Francisco: R. and
E. Research Associates.

Baric, Lorraine
1967 "Traditional Groups and New Economic
Opportunities in Yugoslavia", pp. 253-277. In
Raymond Firth (ed.), Themes in Economic
Anthropology. New York: Tavistock
Publications.

Barrett, Richard A.
1974 Benabarre: The Modernization of a Spanish
Village. New York: Holt, Rinehart and
Winston, Inc.

Barrow, Christine
1977 "Migration from a Barbados Village: Effects on
Family Life", New Community 4:4:381-391.

Barth, Fredrik
    1966   Models of Social Organization, Occasional
            Paper of the Royal Anthropological Institute,
            #23. London: Royal Anthropological Institute.

_____.
    1967   "On the Study of Social Change". American
            Anthropologist 69(6)661-669.

Baucic, Ivo
    1974   "Yugoslavia As a Country of Emigration", pp.
            254-265. In Georges Tapinos (ed.),
            International Migration. Proceedings
            of a Seminar on Demographic Research in
            Relation to International Migration, held in
            Buenos Aires, Argentina, 1974. (CICRED).

Bêdo, Carlos
    1986   "Balanço do Desenvolvimento Economico ao
            Fim de Dez Anos do Autonomia" in Análise
            Demográfica. São Miguel: Departamento
            Regional de Estudos e Planeamento.

Bee, Robert L.
    1974   Patterns and Processes. New York: The Free
            Press.

Benedict, Burton
    1966   "Sociological Characteristics of Small
            Territories and their Implications for
            Economic Development", pp. 23-35. In M.
            Banton (ed.), The Social Anthropology of
            Complex Societies. New York: Tavistock
            Publications.

Benjamin, S. G. W.
    1878   The Atlantic Islands as Resorts of Health and
            Pleasure. New York: Harper and Bros., Pub.

Bennett, John W.
    1969   Northern Plainsmen: Adaptive Strategy and
            Agrarian Life. Chicago: Aldine Pub. Co.

——————.
    1976   The Ecological Transition: Cultural
            Anthropology and Human Adaptation. New
            York: Pergamon Press Inc.

Bishop, John
    1976   A Life Cycle Theory of Migration: Whether to
            Migrate as a Function of Change. Institute for
            Research on Poverty, Paper # 322. Madison,
            Wisconsin: University of Wisconsin-Madison.

Blau, Peter M.
    1964   Exchange and Power in Social Life. New York:
            J. Wiley.

Böhnung, W. R.
    1975   "Some Thoughts on Emigration from the
            Mediterranean Basin." International Labour
            Review 14: 251-277.

Boid, Capt.
    1834   A Description of the Azores, or Western
            Islands. London: Bull and Charton, Holles St.

Boissevain, Jeremy
    1974   Friends of Friends: Networks, Manipulators,
            and Coalitions. Oxford: Basil Blackwell.

Boxer, C. R.
      1969   The Portuguese Seaborne Empire:
             1415-1825. New York: A. A. Knopf.

Bradfield, Stillman
      1973   "Selectivity in Rural-Urban Migration: The
             Case of Huaylas, Peru", pp. 351-372. In Aidan
             Southall (ed.), Urban Anthropology. New York:
             Oxford University Press.

Brandes, Stanley H.
      1975   Migration, Kinship, and Community. New
             York: Academic Press.

Brettell, Caroline B.
      1977   "Ethnicity and Entrepreneurs: Portuguese
             Immigrants in a Canadian City", pp. 169-180.
             In G. Hicks and P. Leis (eds.), Ethnic
             Encounters: Identities and Contexts.
             North Scituate, Mass.: Duxberry Press.

      _____.
      1979   "Emigration and its Implications for the
             Revolution in North Portugal", pp. 281-298.
             In Lawrence S. Graham and Harry M. Makler
             (eds.), Contemporary Portugal: The
             Revolution and Its Antecedents. Austin: Univ.
             of Texas Press.

      _____.
      1986   Men Who Migrate, Women Who Wait:
             Population and History in a Portuguese Parish.
             Princeton, N. J.: Princeton University Press.

Brettell, Caroline B. and Victor M. P. Da Rosa
   1984   "Immigration and The Portuguese Family: A
          Comparison Between Two Receiving
          Societies", pp. 83-110. In Thomas C. Bruneau,
          Victor M. P. Da Rosa and Alex Macleod (eds.),
          Portugal in Development: Emigration,
          Industrialization and The European
          Community. Toronto: University of Toronto
          Press.

Bruner, Edward M.
   1970   "Medan: The Role of Kinship in an Indonesian
          City", pp. 122-134. In William Mangin (ed.),
          Peasants in Cities. Boston: Houghton Mifflin
          Co.

Buechler, Hans C.
   1970   "The Ritual Dimension of Rural-Urban
          Networks: The Fiesta System in the Northern
          Highlands of Bolivia", pp. 62-71. In
          William Mangin (ed.), Peasants in Cities.
          Boston: Houghton Mifflin Co.

Butterworth, Douglas S.
   1970   "A Study of the Urbanization Process among
          Mixtec Migrants from Tilantongo in Mexico
          City", pp. 98-113. In William Mangin (ed.),
          Peasants in Cities. Boston: Houghton Mifflin
          Co.

Caldwell, J. C.
   1976   "Toward a Restatement of Demographic
          Transition Theory", Population and
          Development Review 2:321-366.

Caqueja, Bento
  1976 "Consequencias da Emigração", pp. 161-165.
        In J. Serrão (ed.), Testemunhos sobre a
        Emigração Portuguesa. Lisboa:
        Livros Horizonte.

Cardona, Ramiro and Alan Simmons
  1975 "Toward a Model of Migration in Latin
        America", pp. 19-48. In B. DuToit and H. Safa
        (eds.), Migration and Urbanization. The
        Hague: Mouton.

Cardoza, Manoel da Silveira
  1976 The Portuguese in America 590 B.C.- 1974: A
        Chronology and Fact Book. Dobbs Ferry, New
        York: Oceana Pub. Inc.

Caspari, Andrea and Wenona Giles
  1986 "Immigration Policy and The Employment of
        Portuguese Migrant Women in the UK and
        France: A Comparative Analysis", pp. 152-177.
        In Rita Janis Simon and Caroline B. Brettell
        (eds.), International Migration: The Female
        Experience. N. J.: Rowman and Allanhead.

Cerase, Francesco P.
  1974 "Expectations and Reality: A Case Study of
        Return Migration from the United States to
        Southern Italy." International Migration
        Review 8(2):245-262.

Chaney, Rick
1986   Regional Emigrants and Remittances in
        Developing Countries: The Portuguese
        Experience. New York: Praeger.

Chapman, Murray and R. Mansell Prothero
1985   "Themes on Circulation in the Third World",
        pp. 1-26. In R. M. Prothero and M. Chapman
        (eds.), Circulation in Third World Countries.
        London: Routledge and Kegan Paul.

Clymer, Bruce
1977   "Traditional Diagnosis and Curing in the
        Azores." (Mimeo.) Paper presented at the
        joint colloquium of Anthropology and
        Portuguese-Brazilian Studies, Feb. 24, 1977.

Constançia, João de Medeiros
1962   Quadro Fisico da Ilha de São Miguel. Coimbra:
        Universidade de Coimbra, Faculdade de Letras.

_____.
1963-4 Evolucão da Paisagem Humanizada da Ilha de
        São Miguel. Coimbra: Coimbra Editora.

Connell, John, B. Dasgupta, R. Laishley, and M. Lipton
1976   Migration from Rural Areas: The Evidence
        from Village Studies. Delhi: Oxford Univ.
        Press.

Correa, Marquez de Jacome
1924   Leituras sobre a Historia do Valle das Furnas.
        Ihla de S. Miguel: Oficina de Artes Braficas.

————————.
1926   Historia da Descoberta das Ilhas. Coimbra:
        Imprensa da Universidade.

Cronin, Constance
1970   The Sting of Change: Sicilians in Sicily and
        Australia. Chicago: Univ. of Chicago Press.

Cutileiro, José
1971   A Portuguese Rural Society. Oxford:
        Clarendon Press.

Da Costa, Carreira
1972   Para a Historia da Emigração do Distrito de
        Ponta Delgada. Ponta Delgada, Açores.

————————.
1978   Esboço Historico dos Açores. Braga: Livraria
        Editora Pax, Ltd.

Davis, John
1977   People of the Mediterranean. London:
        Routledge and Kegan Paul.

Demko, Donald
1974   "Cognition of Southern Ontario Cities in a
        Potential Migration Context." Economic
        Geography 50:20-33.

De Jong, Gordon F. and Robert W. Gardner (eds.),
1981   Migration Decision Making: Multidisciplinary
        Approaches to Microlevel Studies in
        Developed and Developing Countries.
        New York: Pergamon Press.

Dias, Eduardo Mayone
1984   "Portuguese Immigration to the East Coast of
        the United States and California: Contrasting
        Patterns", pp. 111-119. In Thomas C.
        Bruneau, Victor M. P. Da Rosa and Alex
        Macleod (eds.), Portugal in Development:
        Emigration Industrialization and the European
        Community. Toronto: University of Toronto
        Press.

Doughty, Paul L.
1970   "Behind the Back of the City: 'Provincial' Life
        in Lima, Peru", pp. 30-46. In William Mangin
        (ed.), Peasants in Cities. Boston: Houghton
        Mifflin Co.

Douglass, William A.
1970   "Peasant Emigrants: Reactors or Actors?", pp.
        21-35. In Robert F. Spencer (ed.), Migration
        and Anthropology. American Ethnological
        Society. Seattle: Univ. of Washington Press.

_____.

1974   Amerikanuak. Reno: University of Nevada
        Press.

_____.

1975   Echalar and Murelaga: Opportunity and Rural
        Exodus in Two Spanish Basque Villages.
        London: C. Hurst and Co.

_____.

1984   Emigration in A South Italian Town: An
        Anthropological History. New Jersey: Rutgers
        University Press.

DREPA
  1973   A Situação Regional: O Distrito da Ponta
         Delgada. Ponta Delgada: Departamento
         Regional de Estudos e Planeamento.

_____.
  1976   O Distrito de Ponta Delgada. Ponta Delgada:
         Departamento Regional de Estudos e
         Planeamento.

_____.
  1977   Diagnostico da Situação Socio-Economica
         Açores. Ponta Delgada: Departamento
         Regional de Estudos e Planeamento.

_____.
  1984   Análise Demográphica, 1970-1981. Ponta
         Delgada: Departamento Regional de Estudos e
         Planeamento.

Duncan, T. Bentley
  1972   Atlantic Islands: Madeira, the Azores and the
         Cape Verdes in Seventeenth-Century
         Commerce and Navigation. Chicago:
         Univ. of Chicago Press.

DuToit, Brian M.
  1975   "A Decision-Making Model for the Study of
         Migration", pp. 49-76. In B. DuToit and H.
         Safa (eds.), Migration and Urbanization. The
         Hague: Mouton.

Eisenstadt, S. N.
  1966   "Communication Processes among Immigrants
         in Israel", pp. 576-587. In Alfred G. Smith
         (ed.), Communication and Culture.
         New York: Holt, Rinehart and Winston.

Epstein, A. L.
    1969   "Gossip, Norms, and Social Network", pp.
            117-127. In J. C. Mitchell (ed.), Social
            Network in Urban Situations. Manchester:
            Manchester Univ. Press.

Fallers, Lloyd A.
    1964   "Social Stratification and Economic
            Processes", pp. 113-130. In M. Herskovits
            and M. Harwitz (eds.), Economic Transition
            in Africa. Northwestern African Studies #12.
            Evanston, Ill.: Northwestern Univ. Press.

Fel, Edit and Tamas Hofer
    1969   Proper Peasants: Traditional Life in a
            Hungarian Village. Viking Foundation
            Publications in Anthropology, Sol Tax
            (eds.), # 46. Chicago: Aldine Pub. Co.

Ferreira, Eduardo Sousa
    1976   Origins e Formas da Emigração. Lisboa:
            Iniciativas Editoriais.

Foerster, Robert F.
    1968   The Italian Emigration of Our Times. (Reprint
            of 1919 edition). New York: Russell and
            Russell.

Forman, Sylvia H.
    1976   "Migration: A Problem in Conceptualization",
            pp. 25-35. In D. Guillet and D. Uzzell (eds.),
            New Approaches to the Study of Migration.
            Rice University Studies Vol. 62(3).

Foster, George M.
    1967   Tzintzuntzan: Mexican Peasants in a Changing
            World. Boston: Little Brown.

Fox, Robin
    1962   "The Vanishing Grael." New Society
            1(2):17-19.

Friedl, Ernestine
    1967   "Lagging Emulation in Post-Peasant Society: A
            Greek Case", pp. 93-106. In J. G. Peristiany
            (ed.), Contributions to Mediterranean
            Sociology. The Hague: Mouton.

    _____.

    1978   "Kinship, Class and Selective Migration", pp.
            363-387. In J. G. Peristany (ed.),
            Mediterranean Family Structures.
            Cambridge: Cambridge Univ. Press.

Frucht, R.
    1968   "Emigration Remittances and Social Change."
            Anthropologica 10(2):193-208.

Furtado, Arruda
    1884   Materiaes para o Estudo Anthropologica dos
            Povos Açorianos: Observações sobre o Povo
            Michaelense. Ponta Delgada, São Miguel.

Gilbert, Dorothy A.
    1976   Recent Portuguese Immigrants to Fall River,
            Massachusetts: An Analysis of Relative
            Economic Success. Ph.D. Thesis,
            Columbia University, New York, New York.

Gilsenan, Michael
    1977   "Against Patron-Client Relations", pp.
            167-183. In Ernest Gellneer and John
            Waterbury (eds.), Patrons and Clients in
            Mediterranean Societies. London: Duckworth
            and Co. in association with the Center for
            Mediterranean Studies, A. U. F. S.

Gluckman, M.
    1955   The Judicial Process Among the Barotse.
            Manchester: Manchester Univ. Press.

Goldsmith, Harold and J. Allan Beegle
    1962   The Initial Phase of Voluntary Migration.
            Rural Sociology Studies, #1. E. Lansing,
            Michigan: Agricultural Experiment
            Station, Department of Sociology and
            Anthropology, Michigan State University.

Goldstein, Sidney
    1964   "The Extent of Repeated Migration: An
            Analysis Based on the Danish Population
            Register." Journal of the American
            Statistical Association 59:1121-1132.

Gonzalez, Nancie L.
    1969   Black Carib Household Structure: A Study of
            Migration and Modernization. American
            Ethnological Society, #48. Seattle:
            Washington Univ. Press.

—————.

1975 "Types of Migratory Patterns to a Small
       Dominican City and to New York", pp.
       209-223. In B. DuToit and H. Safa (eds.),
       Migration and Urbanization. The Hague:
       Mouton.

Goody, Jack R. (ed.),
    1958 The Developmental Cycle in Domestic Groups.
          Cambridge: Cambridge Univ. Press.

Graves, Theodore D.
    1966 "Alternative Models for The Study of Urban
          Migration." Human Organization 25:295-307.

Graves, Theodore and Nancy Graves
    1974 "Adaptive Strategies in Urban Migration."
          Annual Review of Anthropology 3:117-152.

Guill, James H.
    1972 A History of the Azores Islands. Menlo Park,
          California.

Gygox, Katherina Elisabeth
    1969-70 "Contribuições para a Geografia de Ponta
             Delgada, Angra do Heroismo e Horta, Açores."
             Boletim do Instituto Historico   27-28:17-230.

Hackenberg, Robert A.
    1971 "Secondary Development and Anticipatory
          Urbanization in Davao, Mindanao." Pacific
          Viewpoint 12:1:1-20.

Halpern, Joel M.
1975 "Some Perspectives on Balkan Migration Patterns (With Particular Reference to Yugoslavia)", pp. 77-115. In B. DuToit and H. Safa (eds.), Migration and Urbanization. The Hague: Mouton.

Hannan, Damian
1970 Rural Exodus: A Study of the Forces Influencing the Large-Scale Migration of Irish Rural Youth. London: Geoffrey Chapman Ltd.

Harris, Richard S. and Eric G. Moore
1980 "An Historical Approach to Mobility Research." Professional Geographer 32:1:22-29.

Heath, Anthony
1976 Rational Choice and Social Exchange. Cambridge: Cambridge Univ. Press.

Hebbe, Jean Gustave
1888 "Descripção das Ilhas dos Açores." Archivo dos Açores Vol. X, pp. 515-537 (originally published in Stockholm, 1802).

Herculano, Alexandre
1976 "A Emigração para o Brasil", pp. 93-99. In J. Serrão (ed.), Testemunhos sobre a Emigração Portuguesa. Lisboa: Livros Horizonte.

Homens, George
1961 The Human Group. New York: Harcourt and Brace.

Howard, Alan and Sutti Ortiz
    1971   "Decision Making and the Study of Social
            Process." Acta Sociologica 14:4:213-226.

Hsu, Francis L. K.
    1959   "Structure, Function, Content, and Process."
            American Anthropologist 61(4(1)):790-805.

Hudson, Ray and Jim Lewis
    1985   Uneven Development in Southern Europe:
            Studies of Accumulation, Class, Migration and
            the State. London: Methuen.

Hugo, Graeme J.
    1979   "Community Ties, Norms, and Social
            Networks in Migration Decision-Making and
            Behavior: A Review with Special Reference to
            the Third World." Abstracted in Summary
            Report of the Tenth Summer Seminar in
            Population, p. 14. Honolulu: East-West
            Center.

Instituto Nacional de Estatística (I.N.E.)
    1950   Estatística Anuário. Lisboa: Imprensa
            Nacional.

_____.
    1960   Estatística Anuário. Lisboa: Imprensa
            Nacional

_____.
    1970   Estatística Anuário. Lisboa: Imprensa
            Nacional

—————.
1970-75 Boletim Anual. Secretariado Nacional da
Emigração. Lisboa: Mirandela and C.

—————.
1973 A População do Distrito de Ponta Delgada
(1864-1970). Lisboa: Papelaria Fernandes
S.A.R.L.

—————.
1976a Estatística Anuário. Lisboa: Imprensa
Nacional.

—————.
1976b Boletim Trimestral de Estatística, Distrito de
Ponta Delgada. # 4. Lisboa: I.N.E.

—————.
1977 Estatística Anuário. Lisboa: Imprensa
Nacional.

—————.
1982 Boletim Anual. Secretaria de Estado
Emigração. Lisboa: Mirandela and C.

—————.
1986 A Emigração Portuguesa Dados Estatísticos
Retrospectivos 1966-1986. Secretaria de
Estado Emigração. Lisboa.

Isbell, Billie Jean
1974 "The Influence of Migrants Upon Traditional
Social and Political Concepts: A Peruvian Case
Study", pp. 237-259. In Wayne A. Cornelius
and Felicity M. Trueblood (eds.), Latin
American Urban Research, Vol. 4. Beverly
Hills: Sage Publications.

Jornal de Fall River
      1978   "Emigrantes." Jornal de Fall River, Fall River,
             Mass. March 1, p. 11.

Karpat, Kemal H.
      1976   The Gecekondu: Rural Migration and
             Urbanization. Cambridge: Cambridge
             University Press.

Kasdan, Leonard
      1965   "Family Structure, Migration and the
             Entrepreneur." Comparative Studies in
             Society and History 7:345-357.

Kemper, Robert V.
      1975   "Social City", pp. 225-244. In B. DuToit and
             H. Safa (eds.), Migration and Urbanization.
             The Hague: Mouton.

      _____.

      1977   Migration and Adaptation: Tzintzuntzun
             Peasants in Mexico City. Sage Library of Social
             Research, Vol. 43. Beverly Hills: Sage
             Publications.

Kennedy, Robert E. Jr.
      1973   The Irish: Emigration, Marriage, and Fertility.
             Berkeley: Univ. of California Press.

Kenny, Michael
      1962   A Spanish Tapestry: Town and Country in
             Castile. Bloomington: Indiana Univ. Press.

Klassean, Leo H. and Paul Drewe
    1973   Migration Policy in Europe: A Comparative
          Study. Westmead, England: D.C. Heath Ltd.

Kosinski, Leszek and R. M. Prothero (eds.)
    1975   People on the Move: Studies on Internal
          Migration. London: Methuen and Co.

Kritz, Mary M., and Charles B. Keely
    1981   "Introduction", pp. xii-xxi. In Mary M. Kritz,
          Charles B. Keely and Silvano M. Tomasi (eds.),
          Global Trends in Migration: Theory and
          Research on International Population
          Movements. Staten Island, N. Y.: Center for
          Migration Studies.

Kritz, Mary M., Charles B. Keely and Silvano M. Tomasi
          (eds.)
    1981   Global Trends in Migration: Theory and
          Research on International Population
          Movements. Staten Island, N. Y.:
          Center for Migration Studies.

Kroeber, Alfred
    1948   Anthropology. New York: Harcourt.

Lamphere, Louise
    1986   "Working Mothers and Family Strategies:
          Portuguese and Columbian Women in a New
          England Community", pp. 266-283. In Rita
          Janis Simon and Caroline B. Brettell (eds.),
          International Migration: The Female
          Experience. N. J.: Rowman and Allanhead.

Lang, H. R.
    1892 "Portuguese Element in New England."
          Journal of American Folk-Lore 5:9-17.

Lee, E. S.
    1966 "A Theory on Migration." Demography
          3(1):47-57.

Lee, Sun-Hee
    1985 Why People Intend to Move: Individual and
          Community-Level Factors of Out-Migration in
          The Philippines. Boulder, Colorado: Westview
          Press.

Leeds, Anthony
    1965 "Brazilian Careers and Social Structure." In
          Dwight Heath and Richard Adams (eds.),
          Contemporary Cultures and Societies of Latin
          America. New York: Random House.

_____.
    1976 "Women in The Migratory Process: A
          Reductionist Outlook." Anthropological
          Quarterly 49:69-76.

_____.
    1979 "Portuguese Political Economy and Migration."
          Current Anthropology 20(2):402-403.

Leslie, Gerald and Arthur Richardson
    1961 "Life-Cycle, Career Patterns and the Decision
          to Move." American Sociological Review
          26:894-902.

Leite, Furtado
    1940   "Economia Açoreana", pp. 444-449. In
            Primeiro Congresso Açoreana: 8 a 15 Maio de
            1938. Lisboa: Casa dos Açores.

Lewis, J. R.
    1986   "International Labour Migration and Uneven
            Regional Development in Labour Exporting
            Countries." Tijdschrift voor Economische en
            Sociale Geografie, 77(1):27-41.

Lewis, Oscar
    1965   "Further Observations on the Folk-Urban
            Continuum and Urbanization with Special
            Reference to Mexico City", pp. 491-503. In
            Philip Hauser and Leo Schnore (eds.), The
            Study of Urbanization. New York: John Wiley
            and Sons.

Lianos, Theodore P.
    1975   "Flows of Greek Out-Migration and Return
            Migration." International Migration
            13(3):119-133.

Little, Kenneth
    1973   "Urbanization and Regional Associations:
            Their Paradoxical Function", pp. 407-423. In
            Aidan Southall (ed.), Urban Anthropology.
            New York: Oxford Univ. Press.

Livermore, H. V.
    1966   A New History of Portugal. Cambridge:
            Cambridge Univ. Press.

Livi Bacci, Massimo
    1971   A Century of Portuguese Fertility. Princeton,
            N.J.: Princeton Univ. Press.

Lomnitz, Larissa
    1976   "An Ecological Model for Migration Studies,"
            pp.131-146. In D. Guillet and D. Uzzell (eds.),
            New Approaches to the Study of Migration.
            Rice University Studies Vol. 62(3).

Long, Larry H.
    1977   "Review Symposia." Demography
            14(4):557-562.

Lopreato, Joseph
    1961   "Social Stratification and Mobility in a South
            Italian Town." American Sociological Review
            26:585-596.

    _____.

    1967   Peasants No More. Scranton, Pa.: Chandler
            Pub. Co.

MacDonald, John S. and Leatrice D. MacDonald
    1964   "Chain Migration, Ethnic Neighborhood
            Formation, and Social Networks." Milbank
            Memorial Fund Quarterly 42:82-97.

Mangalem, J. J. and Harry K. Schwartzweller
    1970   "Some Theoretical Guidelines Toward a
            Sociology of Migration." Internal Migration
            Review 4(2):5-21.

    _____.

    1977   "Review Symposia." Demography
            14(4):562-569.

Mangin, William (ed.),
1970   Peasants in Cities. Boston: Houghton Mifflin.

Manners, Robert A.
1965   "Remittances and the Unit of Analysis in
        Anthropological Research." Southwestern
        Journal of Anthropology 21(3):179-195.

Martins, Hermínio
1971   "Portugal." In M. Archer and S. Giner (eds.),
        Contemporary Europe: Class, Status and
        Power. London: Weidenfeld and Nicolson.

Martins, Oliveira
1976   "Esta Nossa Criação de Gado Humano Para
        Exportação", pp. 109-145. In J. Serrão (ed.),
        Testemunhos sobre a Emigração Portuguesa:
        Antologia. Lisboa: Livros Horizonte.

Massey, Douglas S. and Felipe García España
1987   "The Social Process of International
        Migration." Science 237:733-738.

Medeiros, Maria de Deus
1977   Mimeographed manuscript. Inspeção Socias,
        Ponta Delgada.

Mendonça Dias, Urbano de
1940   "Baldios de Logradouro Comum e de
        Particulares na Ilha de São Miguel", pp.
        418-427. In Primeiro Congresso Açoreano:
        8 a 15 Maio de 1938. Lisboa: Casa dos Açores.

Mitchell, J. C.
    1956 The Kalela Dance. Rhodes-Livingston Papers,
          #27.

Momsen, J. D.
    1986 "Migration and Rural Development in the
          Caribbean." Tijdschrift voor Economische en
          Sociale Geografie 77(1):59-67.

Monjardino, Alvaro
    1967 "Problemas de Educação numa Região Insular."
          Instituto Historia da Ilha Terceira, Boletim
          25/26:165-184.

Monteiro, Domingos
    1944 Paisagem Social Portuguesa. Porto: Editora
          Educação Nacional.

Moustaka, Calliope
    1967 "Attitudes Towards Migration", pp. 207-214.
          In J. G. Peristiany (ed.), Contributions to
          Mediterranean Sociology. The Hague:
          Mouton.

Os Açores
    1978 "Serviços do Emprego". Os Açores, Ponta
          Delgada, Abril 3,p.1.

Paine, Robert
    1974 Second Thoughts About Barth's Models.
          Occasional Paper of The Royal Anthropological
          Institute, # 32. London: Royal
          Anthropological Institute.

Pap, Leo
    1949   Portuguese-American Speech. New York:
            King's Crown Press.

    _____.
    1981   The Portuguese-Americans. Boston: Twayne
            Publishers.

Parenti, G.
    1967   "The Role of Emigrants' Remittances", pp.
            220-224. Proceedings of World Population
            Conference, 1965, Vol. IV. United Nations,
            Department of Economic and Social Affairs.

Park, R. E.
    1928   "Human Migration and the Marginal Man."
            American Journal of Sociology May: 881-893.

Parreira, Miguel Abreu de Castro
    1969   "Imigração Portuguesa na America do Norte:
            Considerações Historico-Sociaise Linguisticas."
            Boletim do Instituto Historico da Ilha Terceira
            29/30 (1971-1975).

Parry, John H.
    1968   "New England and the Portuguese World:
            Source Materials", pp. 151-154. In Raymond
            Sayers (ed.), Portugal and Brazil in Transition.
            Minneapolis: Univ. of Minnesota Press.

Pavão, J. Almeida
    1977   Aspectos Populares Micaelenses no
            Povoamento e na Linguagem. Ponta Delgada:
            Edição do Instituto.

Payne, Stanley G.
    1973   A History of Spain and Portugal. Vols. I and II.
           Madison, Wisconsin: Univ. of Wisconsin Press.

Perez-Diaz, Victor M.
    1971   Emigracion y Cambio Social. Barcelona:
           Ediciones Ariel.

Philpott, Stuart B.
    1973   West Indian Migration: The Monteserrat Case.
           London School of Economics Monographs on
           Social Anthropology #47. London: The
           Athlone Press.

Piore, Michael J.
    1979   Birds of Passage: Migrant Labor and Industrial
           Societies. New York: Cambridge University
           Press.

Pitt-Rivers, Julian
    1960   "Social Class in a French Village."
           Anthropological Quarterly 33(1):1-13.

Plotnicov, Leonard
    1976   "Migration Studies: Some Observations about
           Theory", pp. 177-181. In D. Guillet and D.
           Uzzell (eds.), New Approaches to the Study of
           Migration. Rice University Studies, Vol. 62(3).

Pollnac, Richard B. and Francisco Carmo
    1979   "Attitudes toward Cooperation among
           Small-Scale Fishermen and Farmers in the
           Azores." Anthropological Quarterly
           53(1):12-19.

Prothero, R. Mansell and Murray Chapman (eds.),
    1985   Circulation in Third World Countries. London:
            Routledge and Kegan Paul.

Pryor, Robin J.
    1981   "Integrating International and Internal
            Migration Theories", pp. 110-129. In Mary M.
            Kritz, Charles B. Keely and Silvano M. Tomasi,
            (eds.), Global Trends in Migration: Theory
            and Research on International Population
            Movements. Staten Island, N. Y.: Center for
            Migration Studies.

Ramires, Baptista
    1976   "Saldo Negative da Emigração", pp. 175-179.
            In J. Serrão (ed.), Testemunhos sobre a
            Emigração Portuguesa. Lisboa: Livros
            Horizonte.

Ravenstein, E. G.
    1885   "The Laws of Migration." Journal of the Royal
            Statistical Society 48:167-235.

Read, Margaret
    1942   "Migrant Labour in Africa and its Effects on
            Tribal Life." International Labour Review
            45:605-631.

Redfield, Robert
    1955   The Little Community. Chicago: Univ. of
            Chicago Press.

Reigelhaupt, Joyce F.
    1967   "Saloio Women: An Analysis of Informal and
           Formal Political Economic Roles of Portuguese
           Peasant Women." Anthropological Quarterly
           40(3):109-126.

    _____.

    1973   "Festas and Padres: The Organization of
           Religious Action in a Portuguese Parish."
           American Anthropologist 75:835-852.

Richmond, Anthony H. and Daniel Kubat (eds.),
    1975   Internal Migration: The New World and the
           Third World. Beverly Hills, Ca.: Sage Pub.

Ross, M. H. and T. S. Weisner
    1977   "The Rural-Urban Migrant Network in Kenya:
           Some General Implications". American
           Ethnologist 4:359-75.

Rodrigues, A. Cortes
    1976   Os Açores. 2nd Edition. Lisboa: Livraria
           Bertrand.

Rogers, Francis M.
    1974   Americans of Portuguese Descent. Sage
           Research Papers in the Social Sciences Vol.
           2, Series 90-013 (Studies in Religion and
           Ethnicity). Beverly Hills: Sage Publications.

    _____.

    1979   Atlantic Islanders of the Azores and Madeiras.
           North Quincy, Mass.: Christopher Pub. House.

Runblom, Harald and Hans Norman (eds.),
1976   From Sweden to America: A History of
        the Migration. Minneapolis: Univ. of
        Minn. Press.

Schreiber, Janet M.
1976   "To Eat the Bread of Others: The Decision to
        Migrate in a Province of Southern Italy", pp.
        73-90 In D. Guillet and D. Uzzell (eds.), New
        Approaches to the Study of Migration, Rice
        University Studies Vol. 62(3).

Sensi-Tsolani, Paola
1977   "Class and Status in a Southern Italian
        Emigrant Village." (Mimeo.) Paper presented
        at the American Anthropological Assoc.
        Meetings, Houston, Tx., Nov., 1977.

Serpa, Caetano Valadão
1978   A Gente dos Açores: Emigração e
        Religiosidade Seculos XVI-XX. Lisboa: Prelo
        Editora.

Serrão, Joel
1977   A Emigração Portuguesa. Lisboa: Livros
        Horizonte.

Serviços de Emigração
n.d.   "Dados Estatisticos sobre Emigração de
        Região Açores." Serviços de Emigração,
        Delegação de Ponta Delgada. (Mimeo.)
        S. Miguel.

Shack, W. A.
    1973   "Urban Ethnicity and The Cultural Process of
            Urbanization in Ethiopia", pp. 251-285. In
            Aidan Southall (ed.), Urban Anthropology.
            New York: Oxford Univ. Press.

Shanin, Teodor
    1971   "Introduction", pp. 11-19. In T. Shanin (ed.),
            Peasants and Peasant Societies. Baltimore:
            Penguin Books.

Shankman, Paul
    1976   Migration and Underdevelopment: The Case
            of Western Samoa. Boulder, Co.: Westview
            Press.

Shaw, R. Paul
    1975   Migration Theory and Fact: A Review and
            Bibliography of Current Literature.
            Philadelphia: Regional Science
            Research Institute.

Siegel, Bernard J.
    1961   "Conflict, Parochialism and Social
            Differentiation in Portuguese Society." Journal
            of Conflict Resolution Vol.5(1):35-42.

Silverman, Sydel
    1970   "Stratification in Italian Communities", pp.
            211-229. In L. Plotnicov and A. Tuden (eds.),
            Essays in Comparative Social Stratification.
            Pittsburgh: Univ. of Pittsburgh Press.

Smith, M. Estellie
　　1974　"Portuguese Enclaves", pp. 81-91. In T. K.
　　　　　Fitzgerald (ed.), Social and Cultural Identity.
　　　　　SAS Proceedings #8. Atlanta: Univ. of Georgia
　　　　　Press.

_____.
　　1975　"Closing Up and Leaving Room: The Villages
　　　　　Emigrants Leave Behind." (Mimeo.) Paper
　　　　　Presented at the Northeastern Anthropology
　　　　　Association Meetings, 1975.

_____.
　　1976　"Networks and Migration Resettlement:
　　　　　Cherchez la Femme." Anthropological
　　　　　Quarterly 49:20-27.

Soares, Celestino
　　1939　California and the Portuguese. Lisbon: SPN
　　　　　Books.

Southall, Aidan
　　1961　"Introductory Summary", pp. 1-66. In A.
　　　　　Southall (ed.), Social Change in Modern Africa.
　　　　　London: Oxford Univ. Press.

_____.
　　1973　Urban Anthropology (ed.). New York: Oxford
　　　　　Univ. Press.

_____.
　　1975　"Forms of Ethnic Linkage Between Town and
　　　　　Country", pp. 273-283. In B. DuToit and H.
　　　　　Safa (eds.), Migration and Urbanization. The
　　　　　Hague: Mouton.

Sykes, E.
　1965　The Azores and the Early Exploration of the
　　　　Atlantic. London: Markham House.

Taft, Donald R.
　1971　Two Portuguese Communities in New England
　　　　(Reprinted from 1923 Ph.D. Dissertation,
　　　　Columbia Univ.). New York: Arno Press and
　　　　The New York Times.

Tapinos, Georges (ed.),
　1974　International Migration. Proceedings of a
　　　　Seminar on Demographic Research in Relation
　　　　to International Migration, Buenos Aires,
　　　　Argentina, March, 1974, under the Auspices
　　　　of the Committee for International
　　　　Coordination of National Research in
　　　　Demography (CICRED).

Tavares, Belmira E.
　1973　Portuguese Pioneers in the United States. Fall
　　　　River, Mass.: Smith Printing Co., Inc.

Taylor, R. C.
　1969　"Migration and Motivation: A Study of
　　　　Determinants and Types", pp. 99-133. In J. A.
　　　　Jackson (ed.), Migration. Cambridge:
　　　　Cambridge Univ. Press.

Thadani, Veena N. and Michael P. Todaro
　1979　Female Migration in Developing Countries: A
　　　　Framework for Analysis. Center for Policy
　　　　Studies Working Papers, # 47. New York: The
　　　　Population Council.

Thomas, Brinley
  1954   Migration and Economic Growth: A Study of
         Great Britain and the Atlantic Economy.
         Cambridge: Cambridge Univ. Press.

Thomas, William I. and Florian Znaniecki
  1918   The Polish Peasant in Europe and America.
         Chicago: Univ. of Chicago Press.

Tilly, Charles and O. Harold Brown
  1969   "On Uprooting, Kinship, and the Auspices of
         Migration." International Journal of
         Comparative Sociology 7:139-164.

Todaro, Michael P.
  1976   Migration and Economic Development: A
         Review of Theory, Evidence, Methodology and
         Research Priorities. Occasional Paper # 18,
         Institute for Development Studies. Nairobi:
         University of Nairobi.

Trindade, Maria Beatriz Rocha
  1976   "Comunidades Migrantes em Situação Dipolar."
         Analise Social XII (48): 983-997.

Trindade, Maria José Lagos
  1976   "Portuguese Emigration from the Azores to the
         United States during the Nineteenth Century",
         pp. 237-295. In Studies in Honor of the
         Bicentennial of American Independence.
         Lisbon: Luso-American Educational
         Commission and the Calouste Gulbenkian
         Foundation.

Um Grupo de Estudantes Açoreanos Alunos do
Instituto Superior de Economia de Lisboa
   1977   Açores: Do 25 de Abril ate aos Nossos Dias.
          Lisboa: Cooperativa Arma Critica.

U.S. Commission on Civil Rights
   1980   The Tarnished Golden Door: Civil Rights
          Issues in Immigration. Washington, D.C.: U.S.
          Government Printing Office.

Uzzell, Douglas
   1976   "Ethnography of Migration Breaking out of the
          Bipolar Myth." (Mimeo.) Program of
          Development Studies, Paper # 70. Houston:
          William March Rice University.

Van Gennep, A.
   1909   Les Rites de Passage. Paris: Libraire Critique
          Emily Nourry.

Van Velsen, J.
   1960   "Labour Migration as a Positive Factor in The
          Continuity of Tribal Society." Economic
          Development and Culture Change 8:265-278.

Watson, James L.
   1975   Emigration and the Chinese Lineage: The
          Mans in Hong Kong and London. Berkeley:
          Univ. of California Press.

Weaver, Thomas and Theodore E. Downing (eds.),
   1976   Mexican Migration. Bureau of Ethnic
          Research, Dept. of Anthropology. Tuscon, Az.:
          Univ. of Arizona.

Weinberg, Daniella
    1972   "Cutting the Pie in the Swiss Alps."
           Anthropological Quarterly 45(3):125-131.

White, Frances A. and Richard B. Pollnac
    1979   "Sociocultural Aspects of Attitudes toward
           Emigration in the Azores." (Mimeo.)
           Anthropology Working Paper, # 33.
           Kingston: University of Rhode Island

White, Stephen E.
    1980   "A Philosophical Dichotomy in Migration
           Research." Professional Geographer
           32(1):6-13.

Wilson, Godfrey
    1941   An Essay on the Economies of Detribalization
           in Northern Rhodesia, Part I.
           Rhodes-Livingstone Papers, # 5.
           Livingstone: Rhodes-Livingstone Institute.

Wilson, Godfrey and Monica Wilson
    1945   The Analysis of Social Change. Cambridge:
           The University Press.

Wolf, Eric R.
    1970   "The Inheritance of Land among Bavarian and
           Tyrolese Peasants." Anthropologica
           12(1):99-114.

————————.
    1973   "Kinship, Friendship, and Patron-Client
           Relations in Complex Societies", pp. 1-22. In
           M. Banton (ed.), The Social Anthropology of
           Complex Societies. New York: Tavistock Pub.

Wright, C.
    1976   "The History of Mexican Migration." In T.
            Weaver and T. Downing (eds.), Mexican
            Migration. Bureau of Ethnic Research, Dept.
            of Anthropology. Tuscon, Az.: Univ. of
            Arizona.

Young, Nancy (ed.),
    1974   Portuguese in Hawaii. Ethnic Research and
            Resource Publication # 11. Honolulu: Hawaii
            Foundation for History and Humanities.

Zaltman, Gerald and Robert Duncan
    1977   Strategies for Planned Change. New York:
            John Wiley and Sons.

Zelinsky, W.
    1971   "The Hypothesis of the Mobility Transition",
            Geographical Review 61:219-249.

Zoomers, E. B.
    1986   "From Structural Push to Chain
            Migration-Notes on Persistence of Migration
            to Cuidad Juarez, Mexico." Tijdschrift voor
            Economische en Sociale Geografie,
            77(1):59-67.

INDEX